Challenges of International Law in the Asian Region

Vitit Muntarbhorn

Challenges of International Law in the Asian Region

An Introduction

Springer

Vitit Muntarbhorn
Faculty of Law
Chulalongkorn University
Bangkok, Thailand

ISBN 978-981-16-2046-1 ISBN 978-981-16-2047-8 (eBook)
https://doi.org/10.1007/978-981-16-2047-8

This Springer imprint is published by the registered company Springer Nature Singapore Pte Ltd.
The registered company address is: 152 Beach Road, #21-01/04 Gateway East, Singapore 189721, Singapore

Preface

The idea for this book can be traced back to a paper I presented at a conference organized by the Asian Society of International Law in Beijing in August 2011. The paper was titled: 'International Law and Asia: A New Era ... Miracle or Mirage?' (That paper is reproduced in Appendix A at the back of this book.)

For a long time since then, I have been looking forward to delve more deeply into some key challenges of International Law and their interface with the Asian region. In this volume, I thus address a number of issues as part of that nexus, for example, whether there are some identifiable roots of International Law in the region and whether/where one can find some space for providing inputs for evolving International Law. This is accompanied by a survey of the important relationship between sovereignty, responsibility and Asian situations.

The study is also a search for contributions from Asian countries to the development of International Law, particularly through various themes singled out in the subsequent chapters, for instance, territorial and maritime matters, human rights, international trade and commerce, and regionalism. The role of the UN is later discussed. The study then covers the emerging techno-phenomenon in the shape of digitalization and Artificial Intelligence in the final part. Of course, in identifying positive contributions, it should not shy away from identifying key challenges and discrepancies involving the Asian region. In regard to fundamental issues, such as peace, human rights, democracy and sustainable development, there is an underlying orientation from this author as the preferred way for and from the region: Asian countries should abide by International Law and elevate its yardsticks rather than lower those standards and/or undermine them.

What might be the expectations from this humble volume? The book is intended primarily for students of International Law/international relations and the general public who might be interested in the relationship between International Law and the Asian region, especially through the lens of various challenges of interest to me. It provides relevant cases and materials, excerpted, to accompany the discussions, in a simple and hopefully informative way. It is but an initial introduction to key issues and does not aim or claim to be an evolved treatise on each of them. It is a mix between the descriptive and the analytical through my own perspective.

Intentionally, I began the first draft of this study at Keble College, Oxford, on 1 August 2019, as I was fortunate to be there as part of the college's celebrations. The final chapter was first drafted on 12 April—Easter Sunday 2020, in the midst of the COVID-19 pandemic, and the whole text was revised at the end of 2020 and the beginning of 2021 after receiving comments from various readers. I would like to convey my warmest thanks to the following friends and colleagues who helped to provide support and some of the information cited and/or to read/advise on the draft of the book: Judge Abdul Koroma, Judge Raul Pangalangan, Ambassador Thani Thongphakdi, Ambassador Manasvi Srisodapol, Ambassador Sek Wannamethee, Ambassador Sunanta Kangvalkulkij, Prof.Monica Pinto, Prof. Michael O'Flaherty, Prof. Manfred Novak, Prof. Alex Bellamy, Director General Azevedo through WTO staff (Graham Cook, John Adank, Robert Koopman and Masahiro Hayafuji who were very kind to me) and Dean Asst. Prof. Dr. Pareena Srivanit of the Faculty of Law, Chulalongkorn University, Bangkok.

My special thanks to the Chulalongkorn University ex-students ("author's team") who kindly helped with the boxes, maps and tables: Art Paisit Pusittrakul, Praew Thanjira, Kong Pichaya and Poom Sitikorn. Many thanks also to the Academic Support staff of the Faculty of Law: Prapai, Nueng and Yui; UN librarians in Geneva; and the Law Faculty Chulalongkorn University librarians, Anne and Mookda. All views expressed are my personal views, and the mistakes are mine alone.

This book is dedicated to my Private International Law teacher and tutor, Prof. Sir Peter North, and my Public International Law teacher and tutor, Prof. Ian Brownlie. It is also a homage to my Jurisprudence teacher and tutor, Prof. Jim Harris; my EU teachers, Prof. Michel Waelbroeck and Prof. Jean Victor Louis; my history teachers, Ralph Blumenau and Trevor Birchell; and in remembrance of my friend, Prof. Phijaisakdi Horayangkura. I am most grateful to my parents, Prof. Dr. Smarn and Khun Niramol Muntarbhorn, for supporting my studies at school and university which provided me with the knowledge and drive to write this book.

This book is the second in a series in honour of the Faculty of Law, Chulalongkorn University, and the royalties will be given to educational purposes. (The first tome was titled 'The Core Human Rights Treaties and Thailand' published in 2016). It is also in celebration of the forthcoming significant Anniversary of the Faculty. My heartfelt greetings and congratulations to all academic members of the Faculty, and all the students, ex-students and administrative staff—for the great community which you have built and are building!

Bangkok, Thailand
September 2020 AD (BE 2563)

Vitit Muntarbhorn
Professor Emeritus

Contents

Abbreviations

AA	Agreement on Agriculture
AALCC	Asian-African Legal Consultative Committee
AALCO	Asian-African Legal Consultative Organization
ACD	Asia Cooperation Dialogue
ACIA	ASEAN Comprehensive Investment Agreement
ACTIP	ASEAN Convention Against Trafficking in Persons, Especially Women and Children
ACWC	ASEAN Commission on the Rights of Women and Children
AD	Anno Domini
ADA	Anti-Dumping Agreement
ADB(I)	Asian Development Bank (Institute)
AEC	ASEAN Economic Community
AFAS	ASEAN Framework Agreement on Services
AHRD	ASEAN Human Rights Declaration
AI	Artificial Intelligence
AICHR	ASEAN Intergovernmental Commission on Human Rights
AJIL	American Journal of International Law
Am. Soc'y Int'l L. Proc.	American Society of International Law Proceedings
AMS	Aggregate Measure of Support
APEC	Asia-Pacific Economic Cooperation
APLPJ	Asia and Pacific Law and Policy Journal
Arab Law Q.	Arab Law Quarterly
ARF	ASEAN Regional Forum
Art.	Article
AS	Artificial System
ASCM	Agreement on Subsidies and Countervailing Measures
ASEAN	Association of Southeast Asian Nations
ASEM	Asia–Europe Meeting

Asian JIL	Asian Journal of International Law
Asian Surv.	Asian Survey
Asian yearb. int. law	Asian Yearbook of International Law
ASIL	Asian Society of International Law
ASLP	Archipelagic Sea Lanes Passage
ATC	Agreement on Textiles and Clothing
ATIGA	ASEAN Agreement on Trade in Goods
AYBIL	Australian Yearbook of International Law
AYPVC	ASEAN Young Professionals Volunteer Corps
AYVP	ASEAN Youth Volunteer Programme
BC	Before Christ
BE	Buddhist Era (543 years before AD)
BIMSTEC	Bay of Bengal Initiative for Multi-Sectoral Technical and Economic Cooperation
BIT	Bilateral Investment Treaty
BLR	Bureau of Labour Relations
BOP	Balance of Payment
BRI	Belt and Road Initiative
Bull. World Health Organ.	Bulletin of World Health Organization
BYIL	British Yearbook of International Law
CACO	Central Asian Cooperation Organization
CANWFZ	Central Asian Nuclear-Weapon-Free Zone
CAR	Central African Republic
CAREC	Central Asian Regional Economic Cooperation
CAT	Convention against Torture and Other Cruel, Inhuman and Degrading Treatment
CCW	Convention on Certain Conventional Weapons
CEACR	Committee of Experts on the Application of Conventions and Recommendations
CED	Convention for the Protection of All Persons from Enforced Disappearance
CEDAW	Convention on the Elimination of All Forms of Discrimination against Women
CERD	Convention on the Elimination of All Forms of Racial Discrimination
CGD	Centre for Global Development
Chic. J. Int. Law	Chicago Journal of International Law
China Perspect.	China Perspectives
Chinese JIL	Chinese Journal of International Law
CIS	Commonwealth of Independent States
Clim.Law	Climate Law
CMW	Convention on the Protection of the Rights of All Migrant Workers and of their Families
Colum. J. Transnat'l L.	Columbia Journal of Transnational Law
Contemp. Southeast Asia	Contemporary Southeast Asia

CPPNM	Convention on Physical Protection of Nuclear Material
CPTPP	Comprehensive and Progressive Agreement for Trans-Pacific Partnership
CRC	Convention on the Rights of the Child
CRPD	Convention on the Rights of Persons with Disabilities
CS	Continental Shelf
CSO	Civil Society Organizations
CUP	Cambridge University Press
CVA	Customs Valuation Agreement
Denv. J. Int'l L. & Pol'y	Denver Journal of International Law and Policy
DILA	Foundation for the Development of International Law in Asia
DPR	Dewan Perwakilan Rakyat /Indonesian Parliament/House of Representatives
DPRK	Democratic People's Republic of Korea
DRC	Democratic Republic of the Congo
DS(B)	Dispute Settlement (Body)
Duke L. J.	Duke Law Journal
EAEU	Eurasian Economic Union (also known as EEU)
EAS	East Asia Summit
EC	European Community/Communities
ECO	Economic Cooperation Organization
Ed.(s)	Editor(s)
EEC	Eurasian Economic Commission (Council)
EEU	Eurasian Economic Union (also known as EAEU)
EEZ	Exclusive Economic Zone
EJIL	European Journal of International Law
Emory Int'l L. Rev.	Emory International Law Review
ERIA	Economic Research Institute for ASEAN and East Asia
ESCAP	(United Nations) Economic and Social Commission for Asia and the Pacific
ESCWA	(United Nations) Economic and Social Commission for West Asia
Et seq.	Et sequitur
Etc.	Et cetera
EU	European Union
FFMM	(Independent International) Fact-Finding Mission on Myanmar
FGS	Federal Government of Somalia
FIDH	Federation Internationale des Droits de l'homme
FMSs	Federal Member States

FN	Footnote
FTA	Free Trade Area
GATS	General Agreement on Trade in Services
GATT	General Agreement on Tariffs and Trade
GCC	Gulf Cooperation Council
GDP	Gross Domestic Product
Glob. Trade Cust. J.	Global Trade and Customs Journal
GPA	Government Procurement Agreement
GVCs	Global Value Chains
Health Systems and Reform	Health Systems and Reform Journal
HI	Humanitarian Intervention
HIV/AIDS	Human Immunodeficiency Virus /Acquired Immunodeficiency Syndrome
HoDs	Heads of Delegations
IAEA	International Atomic Energy Agency
IBSA	International Blind Sports Federation
ICC	International Criminal Court
ICCPR	International Covenant on Civil and Political Rights
ICESCR	International Covenant on Economic, Social and Cultural Rights
ICG	International Crisis Group
ICJ	International Court of Justice
ICRC	International Committee of the Red Cross
ICSID	International Centre for Settlement of Investment Disputes
ICT	Information and Communications Technology
IFRI	Institut Francais des Relations Internationales (French Institute of International Relations)
IHL	International Humanitarian Law
IIAs	International Investment Agreements
IIIM	International, Impartial and Independent Mechanism
IIMM	Independent Investigative Mechanism for Myanmar
IJIL	Indian Journal of International Law
IJMMU	International Journal of Multicultural and Multireligious Understanding
ILC	International Law Commission
ILM	International Legal Materials
IMF	International Monetary Fund
Int. Aff.	International Affairs (Journal)
Int. J. Dev. Issues	International Journal of Development Issues
Int. J. Hum. Rights	International Journal of Human Rights
Int. Rev. Law	International Review of Law

Int. Organ.	International Organization (Journal)
Int'l J. Legal Info.	International Journal of Legal Information
IP	Intellectual Property
IRRC	International Review of the Red Cross
ISDS	Investor-State Dispute Settlement
ITLOS	International Tribunal for the Law of the Sea
J. Comp. Legis & Int'l Law	Journal of Comparative Legislation and International Law
J. Crim. Law Criminol.	Journal of Criminal Law and Criminology
J. East Asian Stud.	Journal of East Asian Studies
J. Hist. Ideas	Journal of the History of Ideas
J. Int'l Aff.	Journal of International Affairs
J. Middle Eastern and Islamic	Journal of Middle Eastern and Islamic Studies (in Asia)
J. East Asia Int. Law	Journal of East Asia and International Law
J. Hist. Int'l Law	Journal of the History of International Law
J. L. & Relig.	Journal of Law and Religion
J. Transnat'l L. & Pol'y	Journal of Transnational Law and Policy
JCLS	Journal of Civil Law Studies
KYIL	Korean Yearbook of International Law
Lao PDR	Lao People's Democratic Republic (Laos)
LAS	League of Arab States
LDCs	Least Developed Countries
Leiden J. Int. Law	Leiden Journal of International Law
LLDCs	Landlocked Developing Countries
LOS	(United Nations Convention on the) Law of the Sea
LSE	London School of Economics
Mal LR	Malaya Law Review
MDGs	Millennium Development Goals
Melb. J. Int'l L.	Melbourne Journal of International Law
MFN	Most-Favoured Nation Status
MINUSMA	(United Nations) Multidimensional Integrated Stabilization Mission in Mali
MNCs	Multinational Corporations
MOU	Memorandum of Understanding
MSME	Micro, Small and Medium Scale Enterprises
N.C. J. Int'l L. & Com. Reg.	North Carolina Journal of International Law and Commercial Regulation
NAFTA	North American Free Trade Area
Nav. Law Rev.	Naval Law Review
NGO	Non-Governmental Organization
NIEO	New International Economic Order
Nm	Nautical miles
NNWS	Non-Nuclear Weapon State

Nordisk Tidsskrift Int'l Ret	Nordisk Tidsskrift for International Law Journal
NWS	Nuclear Weapon State
OBOR	One Belt One Road
Ocean Dev. Int. Law	Ocean Development and International Law
Ocean Yearb.	Ocean Yearbook
OHCHR	Office of UN High Commissioner for Human Rights
OSS	One-Stop Shop
OUP	Oxford University Press
PCA	Permanent Court of Arbitration
Penn. St. J. L. & Int'l Aff.	Penn State Journal of Law and International Affairs
PIF	Pacific Islands Forum
PRC	People's Republic of China
R2P	Responsibility to Protect
RB	Renmin B
RBPs	Responsible Business Practices
RCEP	Regional Comprehensive Economic Partnership
Res.	Resolution
ROC	Republic of China
ROK	Republic of Korea
RTA	Regional Trade Agreements
RTGNU	Revitalized Transitional Government of National Unity
SA	Safeguards Agreement
SAARC	South Asian Association for Regional Cooperation
SCC	Supreme Court Cases
SCO	Shanghai Cooperation Organization
SDGs	Sustainable Development Goals
SDP	Sustainable Development Provision
SDT	Special and Differential Treatment
SEANWFZ	Southeast Asian Nuclear-Weapon-Free Zone
Sess.	Session
SGS	Societe Generale de Surveillance
SJEAA	Stanford Journal of East Asian Affairs
SLAPP	Strategic Litigation against Public Participation
South. Calif. Interdiscip. Law J.	Southern California Interdisciplinary Law Journal
SPS	(Agreement on) Sanitary and Phytosanitary Measures
Stan J. Int'l L.	Stanford Journal of International Law Studies (in Asia)
Supp.	Supplement
SYBIL	Singapore Yearbook of International Law

TAC	Treaty of Amity and Cooperation
TBT	Technical Barriers to Trade (Agreement)
TFA	Trade Facilitation Agreement
TPPC	Trans-Pacific Partnership Cooperation
TPR(M)	Trade Policy Review (Mechanism)
TRIMs	Trade-Related Investment Measures (Agreement)
TRIPS	(Agreement on) Trade-Related Aspects of Intellectual Property Rights
TS	Territorial Sea
U. S. F. Mar. L. J.	University of San Francisco Maritime Law Journal
UCDavis L'Rev	UC Davis Law Review
UCP	Uniform Customs and Practices (for Documentary Credit)
UN ESCAP	United Nations Economic and Social Commission for Asia and the Pacific
UN ESCWA	United Nations Economic and Social Commission for West Asia
UN GA (OR)	United Nations General Assembly (Official Reports)
UN	United Nations
UNCITRAL	United Nations Commission on International Trade Law
UNCLOS	United Nations Convention on the Law of the Sea
UNCTAD	United Nations Conference on Trade and Development
UNDP	United Nations Development Programme
UNEP	United Nations Environment Programme
UNHCR	United Nations High Commissioner for Refugees
UNIDIR	United Nations Institute for Disarmament Research
UNSC	United Nations Security Council
UNU	United Nations University
UNV	United Nations Volunteers
UOI	Union of India
UPS	United Parcel Services
US	United States
USD	US Dollar
Val. U. L. Rev.	Valparaiso University Law Review
Vol.	Volume
WIPO	World Intellectual Property Organization
WTO	World Trade Organization

List of Boxes

List of Maps

List of Tables

Chapter 1
Discourses and Sources

Should I write "I"? An initial quandary in drafting this book was whether to use the "I" in this Chapter to personalize the approach conveyed. This study was born of my personal experience in studying International Law during my early days and growing gradually with it as a coincidental teacher, writer and learner in my country and the Asian region that surrounds it—and the world beyond.

What might be the expectations from this humble volume? The book is intended primarily for students (especially of International Law and international relations) and the general public who might be interested in the relationship between International Law and the Asian region, especially through the lens of various key challenges of interest to me. It provides relevant cases and materials, excerpted, to accompany the discussions, in a simple and hopefully informative way. It is but an initial introduction to key issues and does not aim or claim to be an evolved treatise on each of them. It is a mix between the descriptive and the analytical through my own perspective.

Peroration?

I decided to use the "I" in this Chapter, at least as a discourse between myself and the subject at hand. With humility, I prefer to see it as an educational conversation rather than a personal peroration. All those years ago, International Law was taught in a rather classical sense beginning with "sources" but in a formal manner, starting with the Statute of the International Court of Justice (ICJ) and then broaching the challenges faced primarily faced by States and to some extent, the United Nations (UN). International Law was premised very much on inter-State relations.[1]

[1] As one well-known Asian scholar has intimated—R. P. Anand, *Studies in International Law and History: An Asian Perspective* (Leiden/Boston: Nijhoff, 2004), p. XI.: 'International Law is understood to be a law applicable among all the States in equal measure in their relations with each other.'

V. Muntarbhorn, *Challenges of International Law in the Asian Region*,
https://doi.org/10.1007/978-981-16-2047-8_1

Moreover, in my student days, there were few references to human rights, and where they appeared, they were mainly in the context of the European human rights system. Not much was said on the lessons from the various regions of the world beyond Europe. In this study, therefore, I would like to interlink more closely between various key issues and the region with which I am now most familiar. The discourses in this book (between myself and the vast amount of literature and analysts/protagonists/catalysts (agonists!)) are thus shaped by the following considerations:

> First, I should add what this book is about and is not about. It has to address and is certainly aware of the narrow view of the emergence of International Law as a European construct emanating only from the time of the Treaty of Westphalia 1648.[2]

Those are also the roots of the Eurocentric approach to International Law, begetting or interlinked with colonization and its interface with (or superimposition on) different parts of the world, grounded on the belief that International Law was more of a "European discourse".[3] Thus there is a need to reevaluate that position in a more plural setting.

Yet, even when the Eurocentric approach of such law has to be questioned, it is also true that in the Asian region, liberal strands of International Law are often less valued or less present in State practice, precisely because a number of Asian settings—in olden times as well as now—are not democratic nor pluralistic, despite their emergence as new States.[4]

More to the point: in essence, this study does not claim that there is a monolithic or single "Asian approach" to International Law, if that phrase is premised on an (imputed) homogeneous position from this continent. In fact and indeed, that geography is too vast and heterogeneous to expect and prospect a common position on the many dimensions of International Law. At times, Asian countries do converge very much as a continental block; for example, many Asian Governments like to invoke the principle of non-interference in the internal affairs of a State. At times,

---

[2]Sterling E. Edmunds, The Lawless Law of Nations: An Exposition of the Prevailing Arbitrary International Law System in relation to its Influence upon Civil Liberty, disclosing it as the Last Bulwark of Absolutism against the Political Emancipation of Man (Washington, D.C: J. Byrne and Company, 1925), p. 28:

> All modern authorities on the Law of Nations affirm that no such body of law did or could exist prior to the Peace of Westphalia, in 1648, which ended the Thirty Years' War, ushered in the modern European States system by confirming the independence and sovereignty of nearly four hundred distinct absolute political entities. There were nations before that time, to be sure, but the Law of Nations, as had been pointed out, is not a law of Nations but a law of Sovereign States; and not until the large group of autocrats arose was there any other comparable community to be found on earth's surface.

[3]C. H. Alexandrowicz, *An Introduction to the History of the Law of Nations in the East Indies (16th, 17th, 18th Centuries)* (Oxford: Clarendon, 1967), p. 68.

[4]Jean d'Aspremont, 'International Law in Asia: The Limits to Western Constitutionalist and Liberal Doctrines', *Asian yearb.int.law*, 13(2001), pp. 27–49; 27.

there is great diversity of positions between different countries (e.g. on the issue of agriculture in the context of world trade rules and regulations).

There is also variability between the different corners of the region. West Asia, Central Asia, South Asia, Southeast Asia and East Asia do not come together on all fronts (e.g. on the issue of sexual orientation and gender identity), while on some fronts, they may have a common position or almost common position (e.g. their membership of the UN, albeit difficult at times). There should also be a distinction between individual countries and various regional (or subregional) organizations to which they belong, and their nexus with International Law. Thus, the phrase I have employed in this study—"Asian region"—is quite intentional and it obviates the unitary implication of the word "Asia".

Second, the discourse here does not propose a strict finite configuration for "what is Asia?". One commentator addresses the issue with an ironic smile as follows:

> Asia, as a concept, stands for little more than not being Europe. Indeed, until the discovery of the New World, the Orient was Europe's first and primary Other against which it defined itself. We see the indeterminacy of Asia in this Symposium as well. For some, Asia refers primarily to (what we call today) South Asia, which is represented metonymically by India. For others, the primary referent is East Asia, which in turn is represented metonymically by China…
>
> In sum, the short answer to the question, "Where is Asia?" is "not in Europe". The definition of Asia is essentially negative and geographically indeterminate.[5]

Add to that the many different religions and cultures in the Asian region which militate against a sense of unity rather than uniqueness.[6] A lot of the literature on "Asia" is about East Asia, implying also Southeast Asia. As a balancing act and replete with flexibility, this study would like to encompass also other parts of Asia, such as West Asia, Central Asia and South Asia.[7]

There is an overlap with the Arab region; this is inevitable, since the Middle East will be covered in some of the discussions here (e.g. Palestine) and is a key test case for International Law. Generally, the study does not extend to the Pacific region, apart from where there are cases/disputes between the countries of the Asian region with countries of the latter, while on the other front, the study may at times refer to Turkey and Russia as countries of the Asian region, since their geographies, steeped in their close ties with the histories, politics, polities and cultures of this continent, have an umbilical affinity with the region.

A tentative answer to the geographic scope of the region covered is thus from West Asia to East Asia (while not forgetting Central, South and North/Northeast Asia). In practical terms, it encompasses the Middle East, including the Palestine and Syrian issues; the Gulf States and nearby (such as Saudi Arabia, Bahrain, Qatar,

---

[5]Teemu Ruskola, 'Where is Asia – When is Asia – Theorising Comparative Law and International Law', *UCDavis L'Rev*, 44(2011), pp. 879–96; 882–3.

[6]Christian Tomuschat, 'Asia and International Law – Common Ground and Regional Diversity', *Asian JIL*, I(2011), pp. 217–31; 218. See also: Stephan Barisitz, *Central Asia and the Silk Road: Economic Rise and Decline over Several Millennia* (Cham/Switzerland: Springer, 2017).

[7]Rima Tkatova, 'Central Asian States and International Law: Between Post-Soviet Culture and Eurasian Civilization', *Chinese JIL*, 9(2010)1, pp. 201–20.

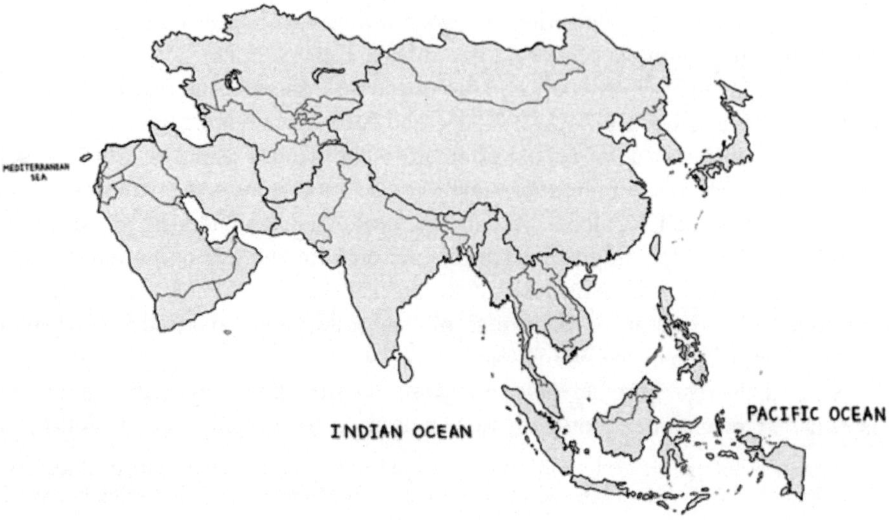

Map 1.1 Silhouette of the Asian region. *Source* map drawn by author's team

United Arab Emirates, Yemen, Oman); the Central Asian group such as Kazakhstan, Uzbekistan, Kyrgyzstan, Turkmenistan and Tajikistan; Iran and its neighbours (such as Afghanistan); the South Asian group (India, Pakistan, Bangladesh, Sri Lanka, Nepal, Maldives, Bhutan); Southeast Asia (namely the Association of Southeast Asian Nations—ASEAN—group of countries and Timor Leste); and Northeast Asia (particularly China, Mongolia, North Korea (Democratic People's Republic of Korea), South Korea (Republic of Korea), and Japan. In other words, from the rim of the Mediterranean on the western side of Asia to the rim of the Pacific on the eastern side of Asia, with the Indian Ocean in-between and to the south (Map 1.1).

Third, there is possibly the perception of International Law as a State instrument and this has to be debated. While it is true that International Law is invoked, on occasions, by various countries and their partners to leverage, if not pressurize, for their own ends, some elements of International Law are fortunately a check and balance against such instrumentalization and open the door to counteraction. The various Chapters of this study are about amplifying those checks and balances. For instance, while some States are favourable towards a broad notion of State sovereignty which is inherently often also a self-justification for the expansive powers of the Executive branch at the national level, globally there has been in recent years a counterargument that such sovereignty is not absolute and is subject to other rules of International Law. Nor is the State sovereignty there to enhance or protect the privileges of the pillars of the State. Rather, its presence is to impose a responsibility on the State and its pillars to behave well towards its population, failing which international accountability might arise (as in the case of the responsibility to protect discussed below).

Fourth, the study endeavours to move beyond the State-centric and vertical approach of International Law. In classical thinking and teaching, much was said of the subjects of International Law (International Legal Persons with Rights at the international level)—primarily States and to some extent, international organizations, particularly the UN. Now is the time for an equally pertinent test of the various dimensions facing the region and their relationship with other constituents, especially communities, peoples and persons—the crux of humanity, who were traditionally viewed as objects of International Law (not as International Legal Persons and thus with no rights or lesser rights).[8] There have arisen also a range of non-State actors, including the business sector and non-government armed groups which are testing International Law to the limit. Poignantly, the human face of International Law is at stake.

With the advent of Automation, Artificial Intelligence (AI) and Algorithms ("the 3 A's"), the future will have to address the issue of inanimate actors and their relationship with animate entities such as human beings, voiced in the final Chapter of this study. In the meantime, humanity's interface with nature—particularly environmental degradation—surely and intuitively foreshadows all too readily our potential demise through natural and other disasters undermining our modus vivendi—unless humanity is audacious and resolute in adopting sustainable measures based on a global/local partnership in that testy cohabitation. As a regional and international mega-jolt, the COVID-19 virus was raging rapaciously when the final Chapter of this study was first being drafted and in that Chapter, there is reflection on its implications for International Law and the Asian region—and vice versa. And the final Chapter also raises the issue of another inanimate actor—the UN and potential reforms as a bridge with peace, human rights, democracy and sustainable development/environment.

Importantly, the search for the roots of International Law, their interplay with the region, and their development today must be matched with a more human-centred and horizontal approach, drawing from the plurality of actors and stakeholders. A simple example of the discourse which will be further elaborated upon in a later Chapter is this: while some Governments would advocate that there is an Asian approach to human rights, this is essentially based upon a governmental approach to human rights (in fact, only some and not all Governments from the Asian region!). Civil society organizations (CSOs) or non-governmental organizations (NGOs) have shown time and time again that their approach, more anchored in the human condition, is not necessarily the same as the governmental position on human rights. There should thus be recognition of diversity in that world of universality. Hence, approaches rather than approach from the Asian region.

[8]Eric C. Ip, *The Power of International Personality in Regional Integration*, United Nations University (UNU) Comparative Regional Integration Studies (CRIS) Working Papers W 2010/4 (Brugge: UNU, 2010).

Mosaic

The classical orientation to identifying the sources of International Law begins with Article 38(1) of the Statute of the International Court of Justice (ICJ):

> The Court, whose function is to decide in accordance with international law such disputes as are submitted to it, shall apply:
>
> a. international conventions, whether general or particular, establishing rules expressly recognized by the contesting states;
> b. international custom, as evidence of a general practice accepted as law;
> c. the general principles of law recognized by civilized nations;
> d. subject to the provisions of Article 59, judicial decisions and the teachings of the most highly qualified publicists of the various nations, as subsidiary means for the determination of rules of law…..[9]

The four sources—treaties, international customs, principles and judicial decisions and teachings of academics (the latter two being subsidiary means)—are generally seen as a starting point and are not exhaustive. A recurrent issue is what/where is the place of State practice in the identification of sources? Moreover, there is the growing presence of the possibly normative force of UN resolutions as part of the spectrum of sources of International Law.[10]

On analysis, there is an intriguing reference in the ICJ Statute above to "civilized nations". This was preceded by Article 22 of the Covenant of the League of Nations which had mentioned the setting up of various mandates to cover territories once held by the losing side as lands held in "sacred trust of civilization".[11]

A Freudian riposte to those words might add: what of the unmentioned condescending antithesis—"uncivilized nations"?

That terminology is redolent with historical sensitivities. The so-called civilizing mission of the powers that came into being with the emergence of European States and statehood at the Treaty of Westphalia (1648) in the seventeenth century increasingly acted as a cloak for territorial aggrandizement by colonial powers, particularly towards the twentieth century. As noted by one commentator concerning the spread of capitulation treaties imposed by European States:

> Capitulations were agreements that tended to grant European countries non-reciprocal privileges (among other things), Europeans could not be expelled from a country without the consent of their consul; had the right to practice worship and build churches, enjoyed freedom of trade and commerce, and were excepted from certain import and export duties; could not be the object of reprisals, especially in case of insolvency; and were not subjected to the

[9] Statute of the International Court of Justice: https://www.icj-cij.org/en/statute accessed 23 June 2020.

[10] Marko Divac Oberg, 'The Legal Effects of Resolutions of the UN Security Council and General Assembly in the Jurisprudence of the ICJ', *EJIL*, 16(2005)5, pp. 879–906.

[11] Alexandrowicz, *supra* note 3, p. 70.

> territorial courts in the event of disputes between Europeans, but to the jurisdiction of the consul of the defendant or the victim.[12]

This was interlinked with unequal treaties imposed on many countries in the Asian region; treaties favouring European powers and entrenching their privileges vis a vis the local population became the norm which would only be rescinded with the demise of colonization. These were intermixed with the arrival of religious personnel, commerce, diplomatic links and extraterritorial jurisdiction giving consular privileges and protection to the nationals of the those powers.[13]

The International Law of that era was thus seen by those who had to fight the colonization process as heavily prejudiced in favour of the colonizers. Hence, the imbalance weighed heavily in favour of European powers of colonial times.[14]

This was particularly the case with rules on territorial acquisition which favoured colonizers, an issue dealt with by a later Chapter of this book. Even with the demise of colonization and after the advent of the UN in the second half of the twentieth century, there remained and remains many unanswered territorial issues which cause problems for newly emergent States in the post colonial world.

Yet, while the above picture represents an important dimension of International Law, viewed very much from the Westphalian and colonial lens, it is incomplete. There are various puzzles. The Asian region, even in olden times, had discourses between different entities with rules interlinking between them, which could be seen as seeds of International Law, even though they might not have belonged to the European club. Some of those rules (such as in the field of warfare) are illustrated below. Those rules were also obscured by the colonial seepage and subjection of those entities here or in other regions to this yoke:

> The international system is frequently called the "Westphalian system"...It is well known that the European nations that dominated the world through their commercial fleets and navies during the eighteenth and nineteenth centuries did not, during that epoch, recognize the governmental entities that existed in Asia as States at the same level of legal parity.
>
> After 1840, China was reduced by those powers to the status of semi-colonial country.'[15]

---

[12]Antonio Cassesse, 'States: Rise and Decline of the Primary Subjects of the International Community', in Bardo Fassbender and Anne Peters (eds.), *The Oxford Handbook of the History of International Law* (Oxford: Oxford University Press (OUP), 2012), pp. 50–69; 53.

[13]Anand, *supra* note 1, citing *Oppenheim's International Law, Vol.1, Peace* (etd. by Sir Robert Jennings and Sir Arthur Watts, 9th ed. (London: Longman, 1997, pp. 87–88), p. XI.

[14]Ibid., p. XI: per Oppenheim:

> The Old Christian States of Western Europe constituted the ongoing international community within which International Law grew up gradually with custom and treaty...In former times European States were not always regarded as being governed by the same rules of international conduct (in their relationship with Non-European States) as prevailed between European States.

[15]Tomuschat, *supra* note 6, p. 219.

Conversely, it could be said that such perspective failed to recognize the fact that the world of the East also had legal regulations which impacted upon the international relations of the time and which may have regarded Europeans as uncivilized.

One could interject that the sense of superiority emerging from Europe was tendentious in that strategically, it was more advantageous to regard others, including the East, with a degree of condescension and this paved the way to conquering the latter.[16] On the other hand, there is the caveat that new States, whether from the East or elsewhere, have been ready to invoke International Law rather than to reject it, precisely because even in its imperfections, there are still some rules which provide a degree of assurance for safeguarding their rights and interests.[17]

Intriguingly, there is the added discourse that at times in history, there have been examples from the Asian region where one country adopted a civilizing approach towards other countries in the region, exemplified by the rise of Japan in the nineteenth century.[18] The drive to be part of the so-called civilized world is explained partly by its declaration of war with China in 1894.[19] Nor did it want European powers to intervene in its civilizing endeavour.[20] Ejection of Britain's extra-territorial presence in Japan was a sign of the rise of the latter as a "civilized" nation.[21] In the meantime, China was seen by some quarters as "semi-civilized".[22]

If a broader kaleidoscope of International Law is projected, especially predating colonization, the Asian region (and other regions of the world) sowed seeds a long time ago for the development of elements of International Law, positing various preferred practices which provide a raison d'etre for the law(s) of today. This was/is particularly the case in regard to rules concerning the protection of humans in times of war or armed conflict; their roots predated colonization and provide an age-old anchor with a more human-centred and horizontal validation of the International Law of today.

What are some of elements drawn from the Asian region which help to globalize and humanize International Law geared towards protecting people on the ground,

---

[16]Ibid.

[17]Anand, *supra* note 1, p. XIII.

[18]Ibid., p. 47.

[19]Ibid., p. 51: 'The Japanese leaders were convinced of the sacred mission of the progressive civilization and, therefore, even the way of waging war itself had to be civilized. The Meiji State, in order to prove that it had become a "civilized nation" and was capable of becoming a member of the family of nations, tried to observe the "civilized" International Law.

This was epitomized by the declaration of war by the country against China in 1894 consistently with the law of nations. Sakuyi Takahashi, *Cases of International Law during the China Japan War* (Cambridge, 1899, p. 2).'.

[20]Ibid., p. 52.

[21]Ibid., p. 55.

[22]Ibid., p. 61: 'On another front, discussing the "international status of non-Christian nations" (Wheaton, *Elements of International Law*, 6th ed, 1929, p. 30), Wheaton questioned China's international status which, he opined, was "semi-civilized". China had also not adopted the rules of war prescribed by the rules of civilized States. In sharp contrast to China, Wheaton praised Japan which had adhered to international conventions, including the 1866 Convention and the Hague Convention (on the laws of war).'.

in their interface with those in power, personified later by the State itself, and their at-times pugilistic ways?

There is a multicoloured mosaic of influences.

For example, while it is tempting to start with Indian and Chinese traditions in their influence on the Asian region, a less traditional approach might start with the Mongolian influence emanating from Genghis Khan who conquered more than half of the known world towards Europe itself in his heyday. While somewhat equivocal as part of the "ruler" and "ruled" relationship, one seed planted by that Mongolian experience (empire!) was to heed and respect freedom of religion as part of not only winning the war but also winning the peace (albeit with conditions attached).

> In 1204, Genghis Khan created the Mongol Empire. It quickly grew into the world's largest, with Genghis learning that one of the major sources of conflict and violence among diverse peoples is religion. Among his subjects were millions of Muslims, Buddhists, Taoists, Christians and animists, and they not only fought each other but among themselves. To stop the bloodshed, Genghis used a powerful two-pronged approach. He gave everyone the right to choose their religion while bringing every organized religion firmly under the rule of law. He offered freedom of religion, in other words, but no separation of church and state. To enforce his power over religions, he lured officials with exemptions from taxes as well as state duties like military service. He also offered financial support, freedom of belief and practice, and respect so long as they obeyed him. If they showed the slightest sign of defiance? Death. Genghis saw that in matters of religion there was no need to persuade, bargain or compromise. The reward was wealth and freedom; the punishment, death.[23]

Of course, one should not doubt the plethora of cruelties committed along the way and in the march of history in all parts of the world by the many "conquerors" and rulers.

From another angle, centuries ago, Islam also laid the seeds for various humane practices in times of war, although as above, subject to some differentiation between believers and non-believers with theocentric underpinnings:

> Stop, O People, that I may give you ten rules for your guidance in the battlefield. Do not commit treachery or deviate from the right path. You must not mutilate dead bodies. Neither kill a child, nor a woman, nor an aged man. Bring no harm to the trees, nor burn them with fire, especially those which are fruitful. Slay not any of the enemy's flock, save for your own food, You are likely to pass by people who have devoted their lives to monastic service; leave them alone.[24]

Muslim leadership used freedom of religion as a means of ruling the Empire. This was witnessed by the practices of Sultan Mahmud of Ghazni and his group (in the vicinity of today's Afghanistan). They 'respected the institutions of embassies, communities, and laws of peace and war. They had a written code of law, applied by their judges called Kazis, which regulated relations between States and subjects inter se. Their notions of sovereignty and kingship had been inherited from their

[23] Jack Weatherford, 'Genghis Khan: Hero of Religious Freedom?' https://www.ozy.com/opinion/genghis-khan-hero-of-religious-freedom/72553 accessed 1 August 2019.

[24] Muhammad Munir, 'Suicide Attacks and Islamic Law', *IRRC*, 90(2008)869, pp. 71–89; 86.

predecessors, the Hindu empires like the Guptas and the Mauryan, and the Sultanate of Delhi.'[25]

On another front, Islamic doctrine advocated the need to distinguish between civilians and military targets in conflicts, protecting the former, while forbidding certain practices such as deception or perfidy in war.[26]

There was also a blending of religion, local rules/customs and geography, as seen in the case of Central Asia:

> Speaking about the sources of International Law in the Central Asian States, one can mention the Koran, which had considerable influence in Central Asia on customs and bilateral agreements. The Koran permitted the existence of such notions as "djihad" and "gazarat" (the war of faith), but at the same time, the necessity of the principle of good neighbourliness with other nations and aspiration of peace and justice. The main source of feudal law in Central Asia was for centuries the oral custom – Adat. The credibility of this customary law derived from the sanctity of the ancient traditions and respect for ancestors. The norms of the Shariah were also common to Central Asian law. However, if the Adat played an important role in the life of Kazakhs and Kyrgyzs, Turkmans and Tajiks were more dependent on Islam and the combination of legal, ethical and religious norms of Islam, proclaiming eternal and unfailing divine advice.[27]

Through another cultural gateway, there is considerable literature on the Indian influence in this field which dates back thousands of years; the rules from various exponents such as Manu and Kautilya included fair treatment of vulnerable groups, the call against war, the injunction to protect civilians and the prohibition of use of various weapons of war:

> Arthasastra (of Kautilya) requires that necessary aid should be granted primarily to "pilgrim,.....ascetics, diseased, those suffering from hunger, thirst and long journey, foreigners". Arthasastra, III. 74–75.20[28]

There were exhortations such as: 'Give up the battle, as war is not worth of approval under any circumstances' (Mahabharata, V.57, 1–9).[29]

In the law or Code of Manu, there is the following stricture prohibiting the killing of:

> one who was on the ground, nor naked, nor unarmed, nor the one who is not fighting but just watching, nor the one who is fighting head-to-head with someone else...nor the wounded, or heavily wounded.[30]

---

[25] Diane A. Desierto, 'Postcolonial International Law Discourse on Regional Developments in South and Southeast Asia', *Int'l J. Legal Info.*, 36 (2008)3, pp. 387–95; 395.

[26] Jacob Turner, 'Towards a Synthesis between Islamic and Western Ius in Bello', *J. Transnat'l L.& Pol'y*, 21(2011)3, pp. 165–204; 193.

[27] Rima Tkatova, *supra* note 7, p. 208.

[28] Olga V. Butkevich, 'History of Ancient International Law: Challenges and Prospects', *J. Hist. Int'l Law* (2003), pp. 189–236; 199.

[29] Ibid., p. 207.

[30] Ibid.

And on limitations on arms:

> In battle, the enemy should not be attacked with treacherous weapons, nor saw-edged, nor poisoned, nor red-hot ones.[31]

Manu was like a "doctrine" setting down many rules based on ethics[32]: As for the Code:

> The Hindu Code of Manu also made formal efforts to prescribe rules of warfare and informal attempts to regulate armed conflict. These are reflected in the Rajput Code of medieval India following the Gupta period of Buddhism. The governing rules of interstate conduct and diplomacy, peace and war, were based on the concept of Dharma.
>
> Manu Smriti is the major codification of the laws governing personal and national life - a comprehensive set of civil and criminal code.
>
> ....Dharma in Sanskrit means both religion and duty, which is of primary importance for understanding the Hindu law of ancient India.[33]

The Code of Manu, a second century BC document, laid down various rules of warfare, including these strictures:

> 91: Nor should anyone (mounted) slay an enemy down on the ground, a eunuch, a suppliant, one with loosened hair, one seated, one who says 'I am thy prisoner'.
>
> 92: Nor one asleep, one without armour, one naked, one without weapons, one not fighting, a looker-on, one engaged with another;
>
> 93: Nor one who has his arms broken, a distressed man, one badly hit, one afraid, one who has fled; remembering virtue, one should not slay them.[34]

As for the rules, they ranged from prohibition of use of various weapons to decent treatment of conquered persons, influenced by Hinduism.[35] So the region already had many rules concerning conduct which embodied a sense of humanity—a good bell weather for any claim to civilization.[36]

There were rules for interstate conduct,[37] enriched by the conglomeration of kingdoms on the Indian subcontinent.[38]

---

[31] Ibid.

[32] Alakh Niranjan Singh and Prabhakar Singh, 'What can International Law learn from Indian Mythology. Hinduism and History', *J. East Asia Int. Law* (Spring 2009), pp. 239–71; 249.

[33] Ibid., p. 250.

[34] H. W. Mouton, 'History of the Laws and Customs of War up to the Middle Ages' (1959) Revue international de la Croix Rouge—(English) Supplement 182; H. W. Mouton, 'History of the Laws and Customs of War up to the Middle Ages' (1959) Revue international de la Croix Rouge—(English Supplement) 198, as cited by Vitit Muntarbhorn, 'The 1899 Hague Peace Conference and the Development of the Laws of War: Asia's Contribution to the Quest for Humanitarianism', in Tim L. H. McCormack, Michael J. Tilbury, and Gillian D. Triggs *(eds.), A Century of War and Peace* (Leiden: Kluwer, 2001), pp. 111–137; 112.

[35] Alakh Niranjan Singh, *supra* note 32, p. 261.

[36] R. P. Anand, 'Development of International Law and South Asia: An Historical Approach', *IJIL*, 47 (2007)4, pp. 535–93; 536.

[37] Ibid., p. 538.

[38] Ibid., p. 539.

As for the issue of weapons:

> It was widely accepted that poisoned weapons or weapons causing unnecessary injury were prohibited; magical methods, which were undeclared must be avoided; devastating the country, poisoning wells etc. was clearly prohibited; all non-combatants, or combatants in difficulties, or at a disadvantage, must be spared; and those who laid down their arms or surrendered were to allowed to live'.[39] The rules were expounded by such compilations as Manu's Manav Dharmasastra and Kautilya's Arthasastra. There were key practices advocated through poetry and history.[40]

In addition, per Kautilya, 'humanitarian treatment of conquered soldiers and citizens…humanitarian policy towards a defeated people was practical, pointing out that if a king massacres those whom he has defeated, he frightens all the kingdoms that surround him…more land and loyal subjects can be gained if the defeated are treated magnanimously.'[41]

The Indian classical work, Mahabharata, prohibited using of destructive weapons, while according to Agni Puraa: 'Prisoners of War should not be enslaved; if soldiers were taken prisoners, they were to be released at the cessation of hostilities.'[42]

In addition, there was this important innovator in the person of Emperor Ashoka in the third century BC who turned to non-violence.[43] There was a law to this effect:

> The Edicts of Indian King Ashoka (264–231 BC) instructed to minimize whenever possible the conduct of war, the killing of people and cattle, prohibition to kill ministers of church, those wounded and disabled.[44] There was thus a lesson to be consecrated by modern International Humanitarian Law (IHL) rules.[45]

Indeed, non-violence later personified by Mahatma Gandhi himself had roots in the Hindu concept of Ahimsa or non-injury.[46]

To the Far East, in ancient China, a similar call appeared as follows:

> He who attacks will not be successful. According to Tao, all this is called an excess wish and vain behavior…he who conducts a war in a humane way will win…The military art says: "I dare not to start first, I must wait…Good people seek agreement, vile ones look for exaction" (Tai-te Ching { { 24, 29, 30, 31, 67, 68, 79, 80).[47]

---

[39] Ibid., p. 540.

[40] Manoj Kumar Sinha, 'Hinduism and International Law', *IRRC*, 87(2005)858, pp. 285–294; 288: 'In early days, the practice was to declare war, and the Ramayana and Mahabharata epic poems both stressed the need to do so in the case of a righteous war. The practice of stopping hostilities at sunset and returning to their respective camps to tend more easily to the days' casualties also dates from very ancient time.'

[41] Ibid., pp. 292–93.

[42] Ibid., p. 292.

[43] Ibid., p. 289.

[44] Butkevich, *supra* note 28, p. 208.

[45] Sinha,*supra* note 40, p. 291.

[46] Ibid., p. 294.

[47] Butkevich, *supra* note 28, p. 205.

In Sun Tzu's The Art of War, the following is advocated as a customary rule in the Law of War:

> To capture the enemy's army is better than to destroy it. To take intact a battalion, a company or a five-man squad is better than to destroy them.[48]

Another key area where the seeds were planted long ago was in regard privileges and immunities for ambassadors. In Indian history, for example, in the epic poetry, 'The Ramayana describes and interesting discussion between Ravana and his brother Vibhishana about the inviolability of an ambassador…His brother Vibhishana reminded him that if he did kill the ambassador, he would be acting against Raj Dharma (the duty of kings).'[49]

Those influences are, of course, illustrative and non-exhaustive. Aptly, this conversation brings me to the potential aims of this study.

First, this book looks at a number of issues interlinking International Law and the Asian region, e.g. the relationship between sovereignty, responsibility and Asian situations. Second, it is a humble search for contributions from Asian countries to the development of International Law, particularly through the lens of various themes singled out in the subsequent Chapters, for instance, territorial and maritime matters, human rights, international trade and commerce, and regionalism. It then casts a glance at future agendas, such as UN reforms and the potential omnipresence of Artificial Intelligence and its implications for International Law. Of course, in identifying positive contributions, the study should not shy away from identifying also key challenges and discrepancies from this region. Third, in this endeavour, the study does not claim that there is a single approach from the Asian region in its nexus with International Law. Rather, it identifies that on some fronts, many Asian countries converge on a position in regard to International Law, while on other fronts, there is a disparity of approaches from the Asian region. Nor does it overlook the viewpoint from non-State sources, such as civil society, on key areas such as human rights, which adds to the plurality of approaches from the Asian region. The perspective is thus variegated and non-monolithic. However, in regard to key issues, such as peace, human rights, democracy and sustainable development, there is an underlying orientation from this author as the preferred way for and from the Asian region: Asian countries should abide by International Law and elevate its yardsticks rather than lower those standards and/or undermine them.

Forum

At this juncture, a pertinent question is this: where can one feel the pulse of the Asian region in its interaction with and possible contribution to International Law?

---

[48] Ibid., p. 207.

[49] Sinha, *supra* note 40, p. 292.

The invitation is to look back to the nineteenth century when an international system started to emerge, such as through treaty-making, and a small number of Asian countries began to participate in the international arena. The limited number from this region was obvious from the fact that most of today's Asian States were not yet born or were merely colonies under the various Powers of the day.

The first treaty with an international scope covering potentially the globe was the treaty emanating from a conference in Paris which in 1865 established the International Telegraph Union[50]—later to become the International Telecommunications Union. Asian countries were not present at the formulation of that treaty unless the Russian Empire (later Russia) and the Ottoman Empire (later Turkey) were counted as Asian; these two countries were part of the original founders of that organization.

The first forum for the participation of a notable number of States, including some Asian States, was the Hague Peace Conference which took place in 1899, followed by another in 1907. Twenty-six States participated at the first Hague Conference, including these Asian States: Persia (now Iran), China, Japan and Siam (now Thailand).[51] In the broader Asian sense, Russia and Turkey counted as States from this region. On the initiative of the Tsar of Russia, with the help of the Netherlands, the first Hague Conference was convened with three issues in mind: arms limitations/disarmament, laws of war and peace, and international dispute settlement.[52](Map 1.2).

There is an underlying conundrum: why were those Asian states invited? My response may be as follows: 'It is worth remembering that the Hague Conference was organized by a State power, primarily for other State powers. There was no room, at the time, for non-State actors, as warfare was seen very much as the prerogative of States and in the eyes of the international community warfare involved international wars, rather than non-international armed conflicts. The latter has become the main preoccupation at the turn of the new millennium. Intriguingly, apart from Mexico, no Latin-American States were invited to the 1899 Conference.

If Powers such as China and Japan were invited, why was a small country such as Siam also invited? Siam was certainly not a power but was seen by many as a buffer State between the various colonial Powers which were vying for influence and territory in the Southeast Asian region. Siam may have been invited precisely because it was a buffer State which had never been colonized and which held the balance of power in the region. Further reasons may have been that Siam was accredited to the court of the Tsar in St Petersburg, and there were close personal links between the Russian royal family and the Siamese royal family. A commentator has, however, cautioned against too much historical speculation or ex post facto rationalization.'[53]

---

[50]https://www.itu.int/en/history/Pages/ITUBorn1865.aspx accessed 19 August 2020.

[51]Muntarbhorn, *supra* note 34, p. 113.

[52]Geoffrey Best, 'Peace Conferences and a Century of Total War, The 1899 Hague Conference and What Came After', *Int. Aff.*, 75(1999)3, pp. 619–34; Nobuo Hayashi, *The Role and Importance of the Hague Conferences: A Historical Perspective* (Geneva: UN Institute for Disarmament Research (UNIDIR), 2017).

[53]Muntarbhorn, *supra* note 34, p. 113.

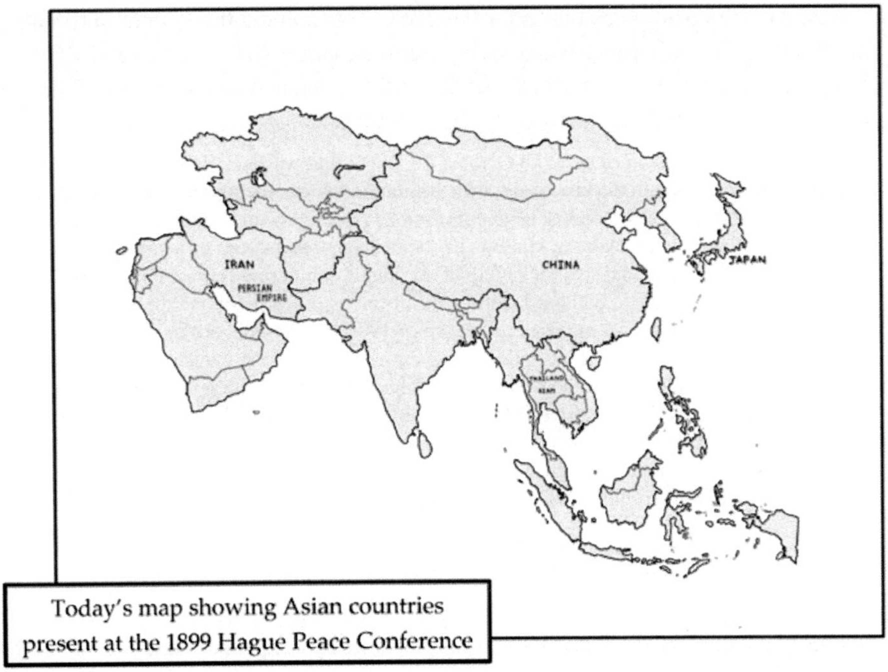

Map 1.2 Asian States present at the 1899 Hague Peace Conference. *Source* map drawn by author's team

At the Hague Peace Conference 1899, the first issue—arms limitations/disarmament—was unresolved, but the other two issues led to more constructive results. A series of Conventions and Declarations on the conduct of war, and on dispute settlement, were adopted, and there was agreement on these instruments:

- I. Convention for the pacific settlement of international disputes;
- II. Convention for the adaptation to maritime warfare of the principles of the 1864 Geneva Convention;
- III. Convention with respect to the laws and customs of war on land;
- IV. Declaration concerning the prohibition of the use of bullets which can easily expand or change their form inside the human body such as bullets with a hard covering which does not completely cover the core, or containing indentations;
- V. Declaration concerning the prohibition of the discharge of projectiles and explosives from balloons or by other new analogous methods; and
- VI. Declaration concerning the prohibition of the use of projectiles with the sole object to spread asphyxiating poisonous gases.[54]

This opened the door to the establishment of the Permanent Court of Arbitration for international dispute settlement, then and now in the Hague. It is still active today as seen later in this book in its role on settling maritime disputes, especially one of today's Asian hotspots—the Spratlys.

[54]Hayashi, *supra* note 52, p. 2.

However, the irony was that after the 1899 Conference, there were outbreaks of war: the Hispano-American War and the Russo-Japanese War, before the 1907 Peace Conference took place, with Russia particularly weakened in the process. The 1907 Hague Peace Conference had broader participation:

> This conference sat from June 15 to October 18, 1907, and was attended by the representatives of 44 states. Again the proposal for the limitation of armaments was not accepted. The conference did, however, adopt several conventions relating to such matters as the employment of force for the recovery of contract debts; the rights and duties of neutral powers and persons in war on land and sea; the laying of automatic submarine contact mines; the status of enemy merchant ships; bombardment by naval forces in wartime; and the establishment of an international prize court. The conference of 1907 renewed the declaration prohibiting the discharge of projectiles from balloons but did not reaffirm the declarations prohibiting asphyxiating gas and expanding bullets. The final acts of the conference were the unanimous acceptance by the delegates of the principle of compulsory arbitration and the stating of a number of *voeux* (resolutions), the first of which was the recommendation that another conference be summoned in eight years, thus establishing the concept that the best way to handle international problems was through a series of successive conferences.[55]

There were 44 signatories, including the Asian countries present at the first Hague Convention. Interestingly, the number of Asian signatories did not increase—precisely because of the limited number of Asian countries in existence as independent countries and the fact that the decolonization process had not yet started.

Not long after, there followed the First World War: Germany, Austria-Hungary, Bulgaria and the Ottomans against Great Britain, France, Italy, Romania, Japan and the US (the Allied Powers).[56]

Siam also declared war and joined the Allied Powers.

The end of World War I was followed by the setting up of the League of Nations where those few Asian countries which had been at the Hague Peace Conferences also became members. The International Labour Organization was also established and this paved the way for many treaties on the labour issue which would be catalytic for all countries. This period saw the demise of the German, Austro-Hungarian and Ottoman Empires, and a Mandates system emerged to look after the various colonies of the former German Empire. Japan, in particular, was spreading its power in China and this led to the setting up of a puppet regime in Manchuria. The 1937 period also witnessed the Second Sino-Japanese war which lasted till 1945. Those Asian countries present in the League had to contend with the issue of warfare which did not cease to take place, and the League later met its demise with the Italian invasion of Abyssinia (Ethiopia) by Italy, followed by German aggrandizement under Hitler with a subsequent alliance with Japan and Italy. This converged fatally with the Second World War 1939–1945.

---

[55] https://www.britannica.com/event/Hague-Conventions accessed 13 July 2020.

[56] World War I began in 1914 after the assassination of Archduke Franz Ferdinand and lasted until 1918. During the conflict, Germany, Austria-Hungary, Bulgaria and the Ottoman Empire (the Central Powers) fought against Great Britain, France, Russia, Italy, Romania, Japan and the United States (the Allied Powers). https://www.history.com/topics/world-war-i/world-war-i-history#:~:text=World%20War%20I%20began%20in,States%20(the%20Allied%20Powers accessed 14 July 2020.

Nevertheless, there were some interesting issues addressed by the League during the time of its operationalization which involved the participation of Asian countries, in particular the issue of human trafficking and drugs trafficking, including the opium trade. Some Conventions emerged during the time of the League to counter the slave trade and other aspects of human trafficking.[57] There was also international conferencing on the issue of the drugs trade and various treaties on the regulation of the opium trade were agreed upon.[58]

The setting up of the UN with the UN Charter was limited to a small number of States which were on the side of the Allies which had won the war. Only a few Asian countries were participants at the San Francisco Conference followed by the signing of the UN Charter, thus becoming the original members. Out of the original 50 signatories, 8 Asian countries belonged to the group: China, India, Iran, Iraq, Lebanon, Philippine Republic, Saudi Arabia and Syria.[59] In the extended sense of Asian geography, Turkey and the Union of Soviet Socialist Republics (later Russia) were also members.

Since then, many more Asian countries have joined the UN and their varied contributions, such as on territorial and maritime issues, human rights, and international trade and commerce, are the subject of the later Chapters of this book.

Turning the leaf to another aspect of Asian participation in International Law making and evolution, since the 1950s, a key forum can be identified as a kind of government lawyers' focal point for the Asian region on International Law. The Asian-African Legal Consultative Organization (AALCO) is the closest that the region has to a regional forum specifically dealing with International Law and its work is complementary to the UN's own International Law Commission (ILC).[60] It is an intergovernmental organization and is comprised of government related lawyers (such as from the Foreign Ministry) from the two regions. Its secretariat is based in India. It is an eminently suitable forum for identifying the contribution from the Asian (and African) region to the development of International Law, precisely because it works in parallel with the ILC. While often it takes up issues under the remit of the ILC, at times it goes further and this is the case of its work on evolving various refugee-related principles as an issue of common concern to the countries, as seen below. The organization was originally known as the Asian-African Legal Consultative Committee (AALCC), founded in 1956.

The original founders were Burma (now Myanmar), Ceylon (now Sri Lanka), India, Indonesia, Iraq, Japan and Syria (then United Arab Republic), and the Committee was to serve as an advisory body of legal experts for States with this mandate: Article 3:

---

[57] 1921 International Convention for the Suppression of the Traffic in Women and Children and 1926 Convention to suppress the slave trade and slavery. https://ec.europa.eu/anti-trafficking/legislation-and-case-law-international-legislation-united-nations/1921-international-convention_en; https://www.encyclopedia.com/history/legal-and-political-magazines/league-nations-convention-suppress-slave-trade-and-slavery accessed 19 August 2020.

[58] International Opium Convention 1915 and a revised Convention in 1925.

[59] https://research.un.org/en/unmembers/founders accessed 19 August 2020.

[60] http://www.aalco.int/ accessed 18 August 2020.

(a) Examination of questions that are under consideration by the International Law Commission, and to arrange for the views of the Committee to be placed before the said Commission.

(b) Consideration of legal problems that may be referred to the Committee by any of the participating countries and to make such recommendations to Governments as may be thought fit.

(c) exchange of views and information on legal matters of common concern and.

(d) to communicate with the consent of the Government of the participating countries the points of view of the Committee on international legal problems referred to it, to the UN, other institutions and international organizations.[61]

The first session was in Delhi, followed by the 2nd in Cairo 3rd in Colombo, 4th in Tokyo, 5th in Rangoon, 6th in Cairo and 7th in Baghdad.[62]

At the first session, the following issues of International Law were raised, illustrating some of the public and private International Law interests at the time:

- Diplomatic immunities (referred by India and Japan)
- Extradition (referred by Burma and India)
- High seas, seabed and subsoil (referred by Ceylon and India)
- Status of aliens including responsibility of States regarding treatment of foreign nationals (referred by Japan)
- Restriction on immunity of States in commercial transactions (referred by India)
- Territorial sea (referred by Ceylon)
- Dual citizenship (referred by Burma)
- Ionospheric sovereignty (referred by India)
- Divorce laws (referred by Ceylon)
- Free legal aid (referred by Ceylon)[63]

These interests were continued in the next few years.[64]

At the 6th session, the issue of refugees started to be discussed.[65] Interestingly, there was the sensitive question of refugee rights, including the proposed innovative right to return and the right to compensation for refugees which were raised for deliberation.

The Report of the 7th session noted:

The Committee decided to postpone consideration of the question as to whether any provision should be made for ensuring the implementation of the right to return and the right to compensation which have been provided for in the articles on the rights of refugees.The Committee could not for lack of time, give detailed consideration to the provisions of the UN Refugee Convention of 1951, and accordingly it decided to postpone its recommendation

[61] AALCC, Report of 2nd session, Cairo 1958 (New Delhi: AALCC Secretariat, 1958), p. 1.

[62] AALCC, Report of 7th session, Baghdad 1965 (New Delhi: AALCC Secretariat, 1965).

[63] AALCC, Report of 2nd session, *supra* note 61, pp. 1–3.

[64] AALCC, Report of 3rd session, Colombo 1960 (New Delhi: AALCC Secretariat, 1960).

[65] AALCC, Report of 7th session, *supra* note 62.

> on the question whether a State should endeavour to afford to the refugee treatment in conformity with the principles contained in that Convention.[66]

However, there started to emerge a draft of Principles on Status and Treatment of Refugees, discussed further below, in 1966, and the 11th session in Accra adopted the Addendum to the Principles concerning Treatment of Refugees.[67] The Principles also stipulated the right of return and right to compensation.[68] The 12th meeting was in Colombo.[69]

As an example of the early years of its work, at its 13th meeting, a report of the AALCC noted:

> The subjects on which the Committee has been able to make its final reports (recommendations) so far include "Diplomatic Immunities and Privileges", "State Immunity in respect of Commercial Transactions", "Extradition", "Status and Treatment of Aliens", "Dual or Multiple Nationality", "Legality of Nuclear Tests", "Arbitral Procedure", "Recognition and Enforcement of Foreign Judgments in Matrimonial Matters", "Reciprocal Enforcement of Foreign Judgments, Service of Process and Recording of Evidence, both in Civil and Criminal Cases", "Free Legal Aid", "Relief against Double Taxation", "the 1966 Judgment of the International Court of Justice in South West Africa Cases" and the Law of Treaties. The Committee had also finalized its recommendations on the subject of "Rights of Refugees" at its eighth session held in Bangkok (1966), but at the request of one of its Member Governments it had decided to reconsider its recommendations in the light of new developments in the field of international refugee law. The subject was accordingly given further consideration by the Committee at its tenth and eleventh sessions. The subjects on which the Committee has made considerable progress are "the Law of International Rivers", "International Sale of Goods and related topics" and "the Law of the Sea with particular reference to peaceful uses of the sea-bed and ocean floor lying beyond the limits of national jurisdiction". At its eleventh session the Committee decided to include the "Law of the Sea and Sea-bed" as a priority item on the agenda … its twelfth and subsequent sessions having regard to the recent developments in the field and the proposal for convening of a United Nations Conference of Plenipotentiaries to consider various aspects of this subject. Having regard to the great importance of the problems concerning the Law of the Sea to the countries of the Asian African region, it was also decided to invite all such countries to participate in the discussions on the subject at the twelfth as also at the thirteenth session. The main object underlying this Committee's taking up the Law of the Sea is to provide a forum for mutual consultation and discussions among the Governments of Asian and African States and to assist them in making concerted and systematic preparations for the forthcoming U.N. Conference. Some of the other topics which are pending consideration of the Committee include "Diplomatic Protection and State Responsibility", "State Succession", "Commercial Arbitration" and "International Shipping Legislation".[70]

---

[66] Ibid., p. 26. See further for early developments of its work: 8th session in Bangkok, 9th session in Delhi: AALCC, Report of 9th Session (New Delhi: AALCC Secretariat, 1967); 10th session in Karachi: Report of the Tenth Session, Karachi 1969 (New Delhi: AALCC Secretariat, 1969); 11th session in Accra which adopted the Addendum to the Principles concerning Treatment of Refugees: Report of the 11th Session, Accra 1970 (New Delhi: AALCC Secretariat, 1970).

[67] Report of the 11th Session 1970, ibid.

[68] Ibid.: references in the 1970 report: re refugees' right of return and right to compensation: pp. 26, 115, 129.

[69] AALCC, Report of the 12th Session, Colombo 1971 (New Delhi: AALCC Secretariat, 1971).

[70] AALCC, Report of the 13th Session, Lagos 1972 (New Delhi: AALCC Secretariat, 1972), pp. 5–6.

Looking back, S. Ogata, the former UN High Commissioner for Refugees (UNHCR), aptly described the work of the organization as a cooperative forum with a specialist regional value added.[71] This was interlinked with the Bangkok Principles, discussed below, in particular.

The organization changed its name to Asian African Legal Consultative Organization (AALCO) in 2001,[72] its mandate being adjusted a little earlier.

Its mandate per adjustment in 1987 is as follows:

Article 4:

(a) To examine questions that are under consideration by the ILC and to arrange for the views of the Committee to be placed before the Commission; to consider the reports of the Commission and to make recommendations thereon to the Governments of the participating States;

(b) To communicate with the consent of the governments of the participating States, the points of view of the Committee on international legal problems referred to UN, other institutions and international organizations;

(c) To consider legal problems that may be referred to the Committee by the participating States and to make such recommendations to Governments as may be thought fit;

(d) To exchange views and information on matters of common concern having legal implications and to make recommendations thereon, if deemed necessary and

(e) To undertake, with the consent of or at the request of the participating States, such other activities as may be deemed appropriate for the fulfilment of the functions and purposes of the Committee.[73]

The evolution of this organization is witnessed through a number of changes. First, it has broader membership than when it was originally established. Thus it has mutated from "Committee" to "Organization" with outreach throughout Asia and Africa. Second, the topics which it takes up are not necessarily the same as the UN's ILC. In some respects, it can be more progressive that the ILC or the current position of International Law (as seen in the case of the Refugee Principles below). Third, it has branched out from the normative aspect of International Law to education and dissemination of such law, as seen later in the samples from its recent training programme.

---

[71] Sadako Ogata, 'Protecting the Human Rights of Refugees and Displaced Persons: The Tasks Ahead', AALCC, *Essays on International Law, 40th Anniversary Commemorative Volume* (New Delhi: AALCC Secretariat, 1997), pp. 23–42; 34.

[72] *Yearbook of the AALCO*, Vol. 1(2003), p. 2.

(The members from the Asian region have increased and are as follows:

In 1956 (Original Members) United Arab Republic (Syria and Egypt), India, Indonesia, Iraq, Japan, Myanmar, Sri Lanka. Then came: Pakistan, Thailand, Jordan, Iran, Republic of Korea, Kuwait, Malaysia, Singapore, Syria, Nepal, Bangladesh, Democratic People's Republic of Korea, Saudi Arabia, Turkey, Oman, Qatar, United Arab Emirates, Republic of Yemen, Mongolia, People's Republic of China, State of Palestine, Kingdom of Bahrain, Lebanon, Brunei Darussalam, and Socialist Republic of Vietnam.).

[73] AALCC, Report of 23rd, 24th and 25th sessions held in Tokyo (1983), Kathmandu (1985) and Arusha (1986) (New Delhi: AALCC Secretariat, 1988), p. 182.

Perhaps the most constructive contribution it has made to date has been to formulate various principles concerning refugees which not only help to fill in the gap whereby few Asian countries are parties to the 1951 International Refugee Convention and its 1967 Protocol but also expand the reach beyond those treaties with new principles from the Asian and African regions. These principles are known as the "Bangkok Principles": Principles on Status and Treatment of Refugees.

After a period of gestation, the "Bangkok Principles" were finally adopted in 2001 by the AALCO.[74]

The principles follow the 1951 International Refugee Convention's definition of "refugee" as someone fleeing the country of origin for a well founded fear of persecution and expands its scope as below, while reiterating the principle of non-refoulement—no push back of persons seeking refuge to areas of danger, particularly the country of origin. The innovations include firstly, the wider range of grounds for refugee status, namely: 8 grounds as compared with 7 grounds under the Refugee Convention: race, colour, religion, nationality, ethnic origin, gender, political opinion or membership of a particular social group. Gender is explicitly included by the Principles. This is innovative as gender differs from "sex" in that the latter refers to the biological link with the person while gender is a social construct which can be broader. Indeed, a person's gender is not necessarily based upon the biological attribution at birth and can be shaped by how a person self identifies in the person's relations with society at large. Moreover, it extends the definition of "refugee" to cover persons fleeing armed conflicts and this converges with the yardsticks of international humanitarian law[75] as well as regional treaties, particularly the Organization of African Unity's Convention on the status of refugees.[76]

The principles thus provide value added beyond the Refugee Convention as follows:

- Coverage of protection for war/armed conflict cases and other violent situations;
- Extension of non-refoulement to non-rejection at the frontier;
- Right to return to the country of origin;
- Availability and assurance of provisional asylum, i.e. temporary refuge or protection;
- Standard of treatment for refugees not less favourable than that accorded to aliens;
- Explicit reference to protection of women and children;
- Non-penalization of returnees in the case of voluntary repatriation;
- The call to address root causes in addition to international cooperation;
- Possible right of compensation for refugees versus the country of origin;

[74] http://www.aalco.int/refugees-2004.pdf accessed 20 August 2020; AALCO, Status and Treatment of Refugees (New Delhi: AALCO Secretariat, 2004).

[75] This is particularly linked with the Red Cross related Geneva Conventions of 1949 and their 1977 Protocols which mention refugees in the context of armed conflicts.

[76] See further: https://www.unhcr.org/about-us/background/45dc1a682/oau-convention-governing-specific-aspects-refugee-problems-africa-adopted.html.

– International solidarity and burden-sharing.[77]

More recent directions of the AALCO point to its interest in providing an analysis of international customary law, with its formation of an informal expert group and a rapporteur on the issue.[78] This should be valuable, and it has to address the fact that some key Asian countries are more willing to abide by treaties to which they consent rather than what they might see as the uncertain parameters of custom arising without their consent. This ambivalence invites discourse based on situations and cases from the field and is much evident in the Chapter on Plights and Human Rights.

This set of Draft Conclusions 6(7) (Form of Practice) on the emergence of international custom is informative:

> (1) Only State conduct in relation to an international question (can) be counted as practice;
>
> (2) Verbal acts taken in connection with a particular commitment or matter count as practice and as evidence of opinion juris and should be given greater weight, while verbal acts expressed in a general and abstract way may count as evidence of opinion juris and should be given less weight or none at all;
>
> (3) Inaction may constitute practice if the situation demands reaction from the concerned State, which is clearly conscious of this situation and has taken a conscious decision not to act.[79]

A key concern is how to deal with persistent objection to a situation which may prevent a custom from arising and or a custom from binding a State. This interrelates with the resolutions of the UN General Assembly (GA) and other organs. The draft above adds:

> Draft conclusions should contain a provision on the persistent objector rule to the effect that a State that objected to a new rule of customary international law at the beginning of its formation and has persisted in its objection ever since is not bound by the rule for as long as it persists in its objection and so long as that rule has not attained the status of *iuscogens*[80]....
>
> (There is a) need for clear rule on how to use such resolution as evidence in the identification of customary international law so as to put States on notice regarding the point so that they can act accordingly during the voting process at the relevant organizations, in order to ensure better quality in and better respect for the exercise of sovereignty and reduce to a minimum the irony involved in using resolutions of a political nature as constituent material for legally binding rules under customary International Law.[81]

---

[77]Derived from AALCO, 'Final Text of the AALCO's 1966 Bangkok Principles on Status and Treatment of Refugees' as adopted on 24 June 2001 at the AALCO'S 40th session, New Delhi.

[78]http://www.aalco.int/TheFormation%26evidenceofCustomaryInternationalLaw accessed 20 August 2020.

[79]Report by Sufian Jusoh, Chairman of AALCO's Informal Expert Group on Customary International Law, 2015. pp. 3–4.

http://www.aalco.int/54thsession/AALCOIEG%20Chairman's%20Statement%20and%20Special%20Rapporteur's%20Report%2020150324.pdf accessed 20 August 2020. See a parallel development: Sienho Yee, Report on the International Law Commission (ILC) Project on "Identification of Customary International Law", *Chinese JIL*, 14(2015)2, pp. 375–98.

[80]Namely, peremptory norm of International Law such as the prohibition of torture.

[81]Jusoh, *supra* note 79, p. 5.

The issue of international custom and the relationship with States, particularly in the UNGA, in the case where the majority of States agree with the emergence of an international rule vis-a-vis a number of States in the minority which reject such rule, was weighed in the Texaco Overseas Petroleum Co. v. Libyan Arab Republic[82] ("Texaco arbitration") case on the issue of expropriation.[83]

The implication from the Texaco case suggests that if a customary international rule is to emerge, it should be founded upon majority opinion derived from States and also drawn from all the various groups (including developed countries and the Superpowers), bearing in mind "opinion juris"—binding legal force. This favours not only a majoritarian rationale but also pluralism in terms of the concerned groups represented.

Another useful activity by the organization is training of officials on International Law. This has been expanding and is a constructive way of building bridges between lawyers from different parts of the geography. For example, a series of training programme have been organized with China for lawyers of the region. The 2019 session dealt with current issues such as dispute resolution mechanism under the UN Convention on the Law of the Sea; strengthening Security Council accountability for sanctions; the role of international responsibility; the state of play of World Trade Organization (WTO) dispute settlement and option for reform; reforming investor-state dispute settlement; the regulation of the use of force under International Law in a changing world; and China's own Belt and Road Initiative.[84] Another such programme was organized in 2019 with Japanese support for the session, covering key topics such as law of the sea, the WTO, international arbitration, treaty making and national implementation of International Law.[85] Another possible area for expansion is cooperation with Arab countries on International Law matters, including education and training on key issues. Several of these key issues are dealt with in the subsequent Chapters of this book. Given the importance of the organization as a source of reflections on International Law from the Asian region, it is important to enable it to strengthen its work in a pluralistic setting in a balanced manner, avoiding politicization.

[82]Texaco Overseas Petroleum Company v. The Government of the Libyan Arab Republic, *ILM*, 17(1978), p. 1 et seq.

[83]Gregory J. Kerwin, 'The Role of United Nations General Assembly Resolutions in determining principles of International Law in United States courts', *Duke L.J.*, 2(1983), pp. 876–99; 883. https://scholarship.law.duke.edu/cgi/viewcontent.cgi?article=2852&context=dlj accessed 20 August 2020.

[84]See further: http://china-aalco.mfa.gov.cn/news/W020190726590397494541.pdf.

[85]See further: http://www.aalco.int/aalcojapantraining2019.

Diffusion

Perspectives from the Asian region are more evident today due to a variety of factors, including more associations and meetings between academics and analysts; more periodicals and publications from the region; and more spaces for examining the contributions of Asian countries and the region to the development of International Law. The spreading scholarship helps to disseminate views and analyses from the Asian region in a perspective of diversity, with possible confluences depending on which issues. This "diffusion" adds to the Asian flavour which provides a palate of varied tastes under the international regime.

Looking back to the nineteenth century, as seen earlier, there were few voices from the Asian region in the international arena. As already noted, for example, at the Hague Peace Conference in 1899, four out of 26 countries were from the Asian region (China, Persia/Iran, Japan and Siam/Thailand), while in 1907, the same four were there out of just over forty participants.[86] Those four countries also participated at the signing of the League Covenant in 1919,[87] with the lingering question whether they were civilized enough to participate in the international forum.[88]

In more recent times, a key development has been the publication of the Asian Yearbook of International Law, supported by the Foundation for the Development of International Law in Asia (DILA) established about 20 years ago (originally in the Netherlands).[89] Then the Asian Society of International Law (ASIL) was set up in 2007.[90] It now organizes periodic conferences for the region where academics and other can have interchanges about developments of International Law.

The Yearbook also has useful section covering recent State practice from the region in annual/biannual survey of activities of the AALCO. There are a number of periodicals dealing with aspects of International Law in the region, including the Asian Journal of International Law.

Catalytic meetings also take place periodically, now organized by ASIL. Interestingly, the World Congress on International Law took place in 2015 in New Delhi with this mission:

---

[86]For more details, see: Simon Chesterman, 'Asia's Ambivalence about International Law and Institutions: Past, Present and Future', *EJIL*, 27(2016)4, pp. 945–78.

[87]Ibid.

[88]In the meantime, Oppenheim was subjecting them to the test of whether they were civilized enough to join:

> ' Persia, Siam, China, Korea, Abyssinia and the like, are civilized, but their civilization has not yet reached a point to enable them to carry out rules of International Law…the example of Japan can show them that it depends entirely upon their efforts to be received as full members into that family. 'Oppenheim, International Law Treaties (1905) cited by Phil. C. W. Chan, 'China's Approach to International Law since the Opium War', *Leiden J. Int. Law*, 27(2014), pp. 859–892; 870.

[89]See further: https://home.heinonline.org/titles/Foreign--International-Law-Resources-Database/Asian-Yearbook-of-International-Law/.

[90]https://www.asiansil.org/ accessed 23 June 2020.

> The objective is to 'confederate' different national and regional societies and other bodies engaged in promotion of study and spread of awareness of International Law under one roof. The idea is to bring together scholars and national and regional International Law bodies drawn from diverse countries from different continents, forge a global network of such bodies devoted to International Law, and deliberate on contemporary issues of International Law as frequently as possible, at least once in every two years. Such get-togethers amongst non-governmental bodies comprising academia, lawyers, diplomats, parliamentarians, policymakers and members of judiciary from different countries, representing a cross-section of International Law academia and practitioners on one platform would provide a continuous framework for exchange of ideas, joint seminars, conferences, workshops, research collaborations between and amongst various national and regional societies, and meeting in some important city in a country willing to host such meetings. Furthermore, this network of International Law societies will hopefully and eventually seek to establish The World Society of International Law.
>
> The objective of the Conference is to examine and discuss the contemporary issues of International Law, which encompass a variety of topics, WTO and International Trade, Investment Law, Arbitration, Intellectual Property Rights, Technology and Development of International Law, National Implementation of International Law and Other Issues.[91]

The spread and diffusion of issues discussed at the Conference and related scholarship provide a barometer of topics of interest in the region: Asian-African approaches to International Law; South Asia and International Law; Non-State Actors and International Law; Climate Change and International Environmental Law; Role of International Courts and Tribunals in the Development of International Law; Foreign Investment and International Taxation; Law of Piracy; Teaching, Research and Practice of International Law.

The subjects taught at University in Asian countries have also proliferated, moving far beyond the more traditional topics of public and private International Law, such as Sources of International Law. This is exemplified by a broad range of courses at one of the Universities in Thailand at the undergraduate level: Law of the Sea, Human Rights, Migration and Refugee Law, International Economic Law, Maritime Law, International Law of Child Rights, International Humanitarian Law, International Criminal Law, Law and Development, Law and Society, European Union Law, ASEAN Law, Law of International Organizations, Seminar on International Law.....[92] FinTech Law has now arrived as a course in the general curriculum.

Education is not divorced from the social conditions at hand. Interestingly, the ageing population in some countries will mean a reduced market for tertiary education in the traditional arrangement of universities catering to students to physically attending in classrooms. There will be more room for online learning. With the advent

[91] https://www.symlaw.edu.in/international-conference accessed 23 June 2020.

[92] Derived from the curriculum at Chulalongkorn University, for example. Interestingly, the UN has organized annual regional training courses on International Law in the Asian region. In 2019, the course included: law of treaties, international environmental law, law of the sea, state responsibility, international peace and security, and settlement of disputes, international human rights law, international humanitarian law, International Law in Asia–Pacific, law of international organisations, diplomatic and consular relations, international trade law, international investment law. https://legal.un.org/poa/rcil/asia/index.html accessed 23 June 2020. Some courses of the curriculum at the national level, as in Thailand, have even more specific focus, such as child rights law.

of COVID-19 in 2020 in many countries, online courses became the rule (at least during the crisis) rather than the exception. Will the range of subjects taught have to change?

Obviously modernistic courses interplaying with today's and future world will be important; the prospects include climate change/the environment and International Law; biotechnology, law and ethics; robots/artificial intelligence and International Law; biotechnology and International Law; digitalization and International Law, including social media, privacy and expression issues, and platform-related dimensions. Prospectively, the 17 Goals of the Sustainable Development Goals (SDGs) provide an entry point for the global agenda till 2030 and International Law is interlinked with all the Goals whether through hard law (such as treaties) and or soft law (such as global and national action plans, and guidelines for action).[93]

The advent of pandemics and the link with the natural environment invite further research and teaching of International Law from the perspective of health and environmental crises. This is likely to snowball with global warming. In a sense, judgement concerning the fate of humanity (via the various challenges of International Law in the Asian region and now COVID-19) may already be at hand.

The study now turns to Chapters addressing the following issues: Sovereignty and Responsibility; Historical Ambiguity and Territoriality; Normativity and Maritime Competitivity; Plights and Human Rights; Trade Liberalization and Inhibition; Regionalism and Eclecticism. The final part of the concluding Chapter offers various projections for the future, particularly on the importance of human inputs such as through peacekeeping and on the issue of inanimate actors, including the UN and the potential for its reform, and the emergence of automation, Artificial Intelligence (AI) and algorithms. There is also perhaps a sense of foreboding, unless we—the animate—remain in command—with a spirit of humanity and humility.

---

[93]See further: https://sustainabledevelopment.un.org/sdgs.

Chapter 2
Sovereignty and Responsibility

Sovereignty implies the state of being Supreme, with power over others under its umbrella and with safeguards for its own parameters from the impingement of others: in the words of a commentator: "local control" and "foreign exclusion".[1] In the context of this book, it is inextricably intertwined with the rise of nation States. It is thus worth recalling that in International Law, there are four main characteristics needed to be a State: permanent territory, population, presence of a Government and the capacity to enter into international relations (with other States and other international legal persons such as international organizations.)[2] Sovereignty is very much linked with the exercise of State power, its competence and jurisdiction. However, there might be particular features conditioned by the political nature of the State. For instance, Iran's sovereignty profile is based upon the hybrid between a theocratic State and people-based underpinnings.[3] Contrast that with pre- Second World War Japan where sovereignty was embodied in the Emperor,[4] while after the War, this shifted to sovereignty resting with the people at large, a welcome testament to democratization.

Configurations

There are at least five configurations underpinning the concept of sovereignty to be explored: temporal, spatial/territorial, personal/jurisdictional and material. A new dimension is this: technological/digital sovereignty.

---

[1] Jenik Radon, 'Sovereignty: A Political Emotion, not a Concept?', *Stan J. Int'l L.*, 40(2004)2, pp. 195–209; 199.

[2] See further: Montevideo Convention on the Rights and Duties of States 1933. https://www.jus.uio.no/english/services/library/treaties/01/1-02/rights-duties-states.xml.

[3] Nasser Ghobadzadeh, 'Electoral theocracy and hybrid sovereignty in Iran', Contemp. Politics, 22(2016)4, pp. 1–19.

[4] Kenneth Colegrove, 'The Japanese Emperor', *Am. Polit. Sci. Rev.*, 26(1932)4, pp. 642–59.

V. Muntarbhorn, *Challenges of International Law in the Asian Region*,
https://doi.org/10.1007/978-981-16-2047-8_2

The temporal component is much linked with the fact that in its origins, that supremacy emerged with the rise of European States via the Treaty of Westphalia and its aftermath during an era when territorial acquisition by conquest and war was still valid. In today's world, particularly after the establishment of the UN, that premise has been invalidated.[5]

Also evident is this institutional development: admission to the UN is evidence of Statehood, with the sovereignty of the admitted State confirmed rather than constrained.[6]

The spatial configuration is tied to the above. With the demise of colonization, the rise of new States has also been subjected to new claims by the peoples on those territories. A critical question is whether in the case of non-colonial States, a group might claim the right to self-determination which could lead to the fragmentation of that space and result in secession or other accommodations. On another front, during the pre-UN days, some spatial aspects were not raised or were merely dormant, but with today's world where different spaces interface, there are prospects of overlaps which have to be dealt with. This is much linked with maritime claims and the need for dialogue and dispute settlement based on some convergent criteria, such as in the case of the treaties on the Law of the Sea and related judicial deliberations.

There is then the personal/jurisdictional angle. A key bone of contention is to what extent a State has criminal jurisdiction over various actions interlinked with individuals and how expansive that jurisdiction should be. Thus, the bases of jurisdiction vary from territorial, to nationality linked, passive and active personality test, security based claims, and universal and international jurisdiction.[7] Where there are extraterritorial implications, there might be a need to compromise through deals agreed upon via treaties. Yet, in some instances, there might be customary rules enabling States to take charge irrespective of whether it reaches an agreement with other States on the issue. A clear case of the latter is universal jurisdiction over an international crime – piracy—with which, for example, a key Asian State, China, agrees and for which it is willing to exercise jurisdiction even in relation to those who are not its nationals and in the case where the misdeeds take place outside Chinese territory.[8]

The material configuration of sovereignty is much linked with how developing countries in the final decades of the 20th Century acted together to claim control over their natural resources and to reject the benefits appropriated economically and commercially by developed countries, often synonymous with ex-colonial masters and multinational corporations (MNCs). This was evident in the various UN GA resolutions on the New International Economic Order (NIEO) when and where the "third world" wished to open up to the issue of expropriation of property held by

[5] Radon, *supra* note 1, pp. 199–200.

[6] Ibid, p. 201.

[7] Ian Brownlie, *Principles of Public International Law* 7th ed (Oxford: OUP, 2008). Part VI, Chapter 15.

[8] Chi Manjiao, 'A Note On China's Legal and Operational Response to International Piracy', *Ocean Dev. Int. Law*, 44(2013)1, pp. 113–22.

companies linked with developed countries on the basis of less stringent conditions.[9] Thus their claim was that compensation should be paid for the "appropriate" sum rather than on a "prompt, adequate and effective" basis.[10]

The word "sovereignty" itself is often tied to another, which becomes a Siamese twin in the form of "State sovereignty".[11] That is much linked with independence and the creation of States in International Law. There is the implication of capacity to enter into relations with other entities on the basis of sovereign equality. There is inherently a nexus with the right to self-determination which has been a wrenching question not only in regard to decolonization but also how non-colonial States deal with the different peoples on their territory in terms of their participation, decision-making and stakeholdership. A more liberal slant towards the integration of popular participation into the process implies democracy and is premised on "popular sovereignty". Yet, many Asian States are non-democracies and are also apprehensive about the claims of indigenous peoples and minorities. There lingers the question: cohesion or fragmentation?

There is a politically charged question which preoccupies many Asian States, transfixing the authorities: how absolute or near absolute is State sovereignty and how broad is its attendant principle of "non-interference in the internal affairs of a State"? As seen below, State sovereignty is not absolute. Indeed, with the turn of the new Millennium, the pendulum has been swinging from the right not to be encroached upon by others, alias non-intervention or "non-interference in the internal affairs of a State", to the State's responsibility to protect the people on its territory and related accountability.

The starting point for its placement in International Law is the UN Charter, particularly Article 2:

1. The Organization is based on the principle of the sovereign equality of all its Members.
2. All Members, in order to ensure to all of them the rights and benefits resulting from membership, shall fulfil in good faith the obligations assumed by them in accordance with the present Charter.
3. All Members shall settle their international disputes by peaceful means in such a manner that international peace and security, and justice, are not endangered.
4. All Members shall refrain in their international relations from the threat or use of force against the territorial integrity or political independence

---

[9] https://www.unescwa.org/new-international-economic-order accessed 21 August 2020. See also: P. N. Agarwala, *The New International Economic Order* (Oxford: Pergamon, 1983).

[10] See resolution: Charter of Economic Rights and Duties of States.
GA Res. 3281(xxix), UN GAOR, 29th Sess., Supp. No. 31 (1974) 50 (12 December 1974).

[11] Radon, *supra* note 1, p. 201; Winston P. Nagan and Craig Hammer, 'The Changing Nature of Sovereignty in International Law and International Relations', *Colum. J. Transnat'l L.*, 43(2004), pp. 141–87.

> of any state, or in any other manner inconsistent with the Purposes of the United Nations.
>
> 5. All Members shall give the United Nations every assistance in any action it takes in accordance with the present Charter, and shall refrain from giving assistance to any state against which the United Nations is taking preventive or enforcement action.[12]

Interestingly, the UN mandate can cover even non-State parties as per Article 2(6) in regard to its power as the guardian of international peace and security, whatever the sovereignty of those non-State parties:

> 6. The Organization shall ensure that states which are not Members of the United Nations act in accordance with these Principles so far as may be necessary for the maintenance of international peace and security.[13]

Importantly, there is Article 2(7) which entrenches State sovereignty by countering any intervention in matters under the domestic jurisdiction of the State as an inherent part of that sovereignty but the UN Charter qualifies it by subjecting it to measures from the UN Security Council (UNSC) per Chapter VII:

> 7. Nothing contained in the present Charter shall authorize the United Nations to intervene in matters which are essentially within the domestic jurisdiction of any state or shall require the Members to submit such matters to settlement under the present Charter; but this principle shall not prejudice the application of enforcement measures under Chapter VII.[14]

While this provides the backbone for the non-interference in the internal affairs of a State as an intrinsic component of State sovereignty, it also implies that such sovereignty is not absolute, particularly with the stipulation that measures under Chapter VII (including sanctions and enforcement measures backed by the UNSC) may prevail over it.[15]

Moreover, Articles 55 and 56 call upon the member States to promote human rights and cooperate with the UN.[16] As for sovereign equality which underpins sovereignty, UN General Assembly (GA) Resolution 2625(XXV))(24 October 1970) unfolds

---

[12]UN Charter: https://www.un.org/en/charter-united-nations/.

[13]Ibid.

[14]Ibid.

[15]https://www.un.org/en/sections/un-charter/chapter-vii/index.html accessed 21 August 2020.

[16]*Supra* note 12.

the panoply by underlining, among other issues, territorial integrity and political independence of each State.[17]

Looking to the Asian region, many States (especially non-democracies) project a broad notion of State sovereignty, especially as linked with the non-interference principle, and they are very hesitant towards claims of human rights which question their authority. Moreover, they are reticent towards UNSC measures which aim to impose sanctions especially in regard to their region. While they might be open to sanctions imposed on the countries of other regions, e.g. against South Africa in the era of apartheid,[18] they are wary of such measures in regard to their Asian neighbours, especially where the latter share a convergent political position or platform with them.[19]

On another front, in the progression of history, the self-justification of European powers in their post Westphalian era was ultimately overturned by the rise of decolonization which increasingly questioned the validity of the principle of territorial acquisition by force or war. This would witness also the advent of self-determination to cast off the colonial yoke. This has been backed by key UNGA Resolutions on the decolonization process and the rise of independent States as sovereign nations anchored in self-determination, especially Resolutions *1514(XV)and 1541.* The former outlines the stakes on the granting of independence to colonial countries and peoples, including the right to self-determination.[20] Resolution 1541 provides the ground work for non-self-governing territories to burgeon into fully independent States or other possible formations/associations, with an international reporting process to monitor such development.[21] Yet, the new States would then be confronted with another aspect of self-determination—not only the internal aspect demanding participation by different groups in the governance of the State but also the external aspect whereby the peoples on the territory might aspire to other arrangements leading also to separatism or secession.[22]

Where States have already cast off colonization, can self-determination lead to territorial fragmentation or secession and if so, on what conditions? The question requires a contextual answer—with which many Asian countries are uncomfortable. First, self-determination is not equivalent to secession or separatism. It may mean many things, including participation. In regard to its external aspect, it might lead

[17] https://treaties.un.org/doc/source/docs/A_RES_2625-Eng.pdf.

[18] For example, UNGA resolution 1761 of 1962 in response to apartheid established by the South African Government.

[19] For instance, ASEAN countries are hesitant towards sanctions against Myanmar. https://www.voanews.com/archive/southeast-asian-nations-oppose-sanctions-against-burma accessed 21 August 2020.

[20] General Assembly resolution 1514 (XV) of 14 December 1960: Declaration on the Granting of Independence to Colonial Countries and Peoples. https://legal.un.org/avl/ha/dicc/dicc.html; https://www.ohchr.org/EN/ProfessionalInterest/Pages/Independence.aspx.

[21] UN GA Resolution 1541 of 15 December 1960. https://www.undocs.org/A/RES/1541(XV).

[22] Ved P. Nanda, 'Self-determination and Secession in International Law', *Denv. J. Int'l L. & Pol'y*, 19(2002–2001)4, pp. 305–26.

to confederation with or other arrangements with other countries and not necessarily secession or separatism. Second, given the fulfilment of certain conditions, there could be situations where self-determination might justify territorial fragmentation or realignment in an extreme situation. This is particularly the case where the Government of the country fails to represent its people and where it is oppressive. Clarification on this sensitive front can be viewed through Article 1 of the International Covenant on Civil and Political Rights (ICCPR)[23] and its accompanying General Comment: ICCPR General Comment No. 12: Article 1—The Right to Self determination of Peoples adopted at the Twenty-first Session of the Human Rights Committee, on 13 March 1984.[24]

The more problematic issue concerns self-determination of those countries which are not colonies or non self-governing territories. In such context, it is thus important to cross refer to GA Resolution 2625(XXV) of 24 October 1970, known as the "Declaration on Principles of International Law concerning Friendly Relations and Co-operation among States in accordance with the Charter of the United Nations", which further elucidates the right to self-determination, as per this paragraph:

> **Nothing in the foregoing paragraphs shall be construed as authorizing or encouraging any action which would dismember or impair, totally or in part, the territorial integrity or political unityof sovereign and independent States conducting themselves in compliance with the principle of equal rights and self-determination of peoples as described above and thus possessed of a government representing the whole people belonging to the territory without distinction as to race, creed or colour. (emphasis added).**[25]

What if a Government does not represent the whole people belonging to the territory and is discriminatory and or oppressive? There could thus be implications for 'action which would dismember or impair .... the territorial integrity or political unity'.[26]

Another key test for the development of International Law is whether indigenous peoples have the right to self-determination and to what extent that might lead to fragmentation of the territory and possible realignment. The message from the sole UN Declaration on the subject is this:

> 'Article 46.
> **1. Nothing in this Declaration may be interpreted as implying for any State, people, group or person any right to engage in any activity or to perform any act contrary to the Charter of the United Nations or construed as authorizing or encouraging any**

[23]Article 1 ICCPR: https://www.ohchr.org/en/professionalinterest/pages/ccpr.aspx accessed 22 August 2020.

[24]UN Human Rights Committee (HRC), *CCPR General Comment No. 12: Article 1 (Right to Self-determination), The Right to Self-determination of Peoples*, 13 March 1984, available at: https://www.refworld.org/docid/453883f822.html accessed 21 August 2020.

[25]https://treaties.un.org/doc/source/docs/A_RES_2625-Eng.pdfaccessed 21 August 2020.

[26]Ibid.

action which would dismember or impair, totally or in part, the territorial integrity or political unityof sovereign and independent States.'[27] **(emphasis added).**

Therefore, the right of indigenous peoples to self-determination is understood not to affect the territorial integrity of the State where they live. A similar position was voiced by the 1993 Vienna Declaration and Programme of Action of the World Conference on Human Rights implying the intangibility of territorial integrity.[28]

With regard to the angle of sovereignty over natural resources, there was a time—some five decades ago—when developing countries from Asia and other parts of the world advocated the NIEO. *Par excellence*, this was propounded by the Resolution adopted by the General Assembly 3201 (S-VI): Declaration on the Establishment of a New International Economic Order of 1 May 1974.[29]

A key target was to retake control over their resources vis a vis multinationals which had held the reins of power over these countries. Consequently, if the latter expropriated property, appropriate compensation, rather than full, prompt and adequate compensation would be paid. This then appeared prominently in the Charter of Economic Rights and Duties of States, with a majority vote from developing countries favouring the mentioned position.[30]

Yet, the momentum of the NIEO faltered and it started to fade. Partly the failure of the NIEO was due to the controversy about whether a notion advanced in a GA resolution could be binding, especially as customary International Law. The advocacy of the NIEO was also not responded to by developed countries and if it were to succeed, there would need to be reform of the Bretton Woods Institutions, such as the World Bank and the International Monetary Fund. At the time, there was no global political will to do so.

The demands in regard to the NIEO became increasingly rhetorical and those earlier demands gave way to other initiatives and the rise of globalization in the mid 1990s. Focus was then shifted to trade liberalization and development related adjustments—with the change from the General Agreement on Tariffs and Trade (GATT) to the World Trade Organization (WTO) and the less vocal role of UN Conference on Trade and Development (UNCTAD). The energy to help developing countries was tapped through various global conferences and commitments from the 1990s such as the Copenhagen Conference on Development.[31] This was also accommodated by the Washington Consensus and after.[32]

---

[27]UN Declaration on the Rights of Indigenous Peoples 2007: https://www.un.org/development/desa/indigenouspeoples/declaration-on-the-rights-of-indigenous-peoples.html accessed 21 Augusts 2020.

[28]https://www.ohchr.org/en/professionalinterest/pages/vienna.aspx accessed 21 August 2020.

[29]https://digitallibrary.un.org/record/218450?ln=en accessed 21 August 2020.

[30]Charter of Economic Rights and Duties of States:
GA Res. 3281(xxix), UN GAOR, 29th Sess., Supp. No. 31 (1974) 50 (12 December 1974). https://www.unescwa.org/charter-economic-rights-and-duties-states.

[31]https://www.un.org/development/desa/dspd/world-summit-for-social-development-1995.html accessed 22 August 2020.

[32]https://www.britannica.com/topic/Washington-consensus accessed 22 August 2020.

There have also been concessions to least developed countries (LDCs) through various global commitments. From the end of the twentieth century till today, the outlet for the voices and claims of developing countries has been through various global frameworks such as the Millennium Developments Goals(MDGs)[33] and from 2015, the Sustainable Development Goals(SDGs).[34]

In this contemporary world, there remains an ironic question concerning the governance of some of the countries after decolonization. While the ills of colonization have to be countered, a number of countries that cast off that yoke fell under undemocratic regimes that have also plundered or are plundering the people's resources. One crime does not justify another. There is now emphasis on not only equitizing the external factor but also democratizing the internal factor, such as not only to claim more development aid from outside but also to institute fiscal reforms and anti-corruption measures inside to share wealth and resources.[35]

At this point in time, one can add that multilateralism is changing—with one key actor, the US during the past few years, withdrawing from it (at least until the new US administration in 2021) while another—China—highlighting the cooperative nature of multilateralism. All this is amidst a rising tide of populism and nationalism that leads to racial segmentation, especially the demonization of minorities and incoming migrants, made more complicated by the trauma of COVID-19.

At another level, various perspectives from two Asian powers—the two most populous countries—should be borne in mind as influential outlooks from the region. For decades, they have been vocal exponents of how they envision the issue of State sovereignty and the interplay with the outer world. Importantly, both China and India expounded in the 1950s their positions. The vision of China is ostensible through its 5 Principles of Peaceful Coexistence:

- 'Mutual respect for each other's territorial integrity and sovereignty
- Mutual non-aggression
- Mutual non-interference in each other's internal affairs
- Equality and mutual benefit
- Peaceful coexistence'[36]

In the historical perspective, China's approach is understandable particularly from the angle that it suffered greatly from the various unequal treaties imposed upon the country by colonial countries.

As commented upon by a key analyst:

'China strongly upholds the principle of sovereignty, because it believes in diversity and mutual respect in international political life. The position rests upon its historical past as well

---

[33]https://www.un.org/millenniumgoals/ accessed 1 September 2020.

[34]https://www.un.org/sustainabledevelopment/sustainable-development-goals/ accessed 22 August 2020.

[35]Fesseha Mulu Gebremariam,' New International Economic Order (NIEO): Origin, Elements and Criticisms', *IJMMU*, 4(2017)3, pp. 22–8.

[36]For China's 5 Principles, see: Andrew Coleman and Jackson Nyamuya Maogoto, ' "Westphalian" meets "Eastphalian" Sovereignty: China in a Globalised World', *AJIL*, 3(2013), pp. 237–69; 244.

as its vision of the future world order...China has adopted a foreign policy of independence and peace. Based upon the Five Principles of Peaceful Coexistence as proclaimed by China together with some other Asian countries in the 1950s, this position has never been changed in China's foreign relations...Of the 5 principles, the essence is the principle of sovereignty'.[37] The comment adds, however, that the global situation has been changing due to the variety of international actors and fragmentation of International Law. It also interrelates with China's current more intensive engagement with the global, multilateral system as well as its own mega-project with transnational reach—the Belt and Road Initiative which is discussed later in this study.

With regard to the other Asian power, in its "Panchsheel" approach, India integrated those principles into various treaties with neighbours (such as the 5 Principles of the Agreement on Trade and Intercourse between the Tibet Region of China and India 1954).[38] Such principles were later incorporated into the Ten Principles of International Peace and Cooperation enunciated in the Declaration issued by the April 1955 Bandung Conference of 29 Afro-Asian countries.[39] Those ten principles are:

1. 'Respect for fundamental human rights and for the purposes and the principles of the Charter of the United Nations.
2. Respect for the sovereignty and territorial integrity of all nations.
3. Recognition of the equality of all races and of the equality of all nations large and small.
4. Abstention from intervention or interference in the internal affairs of another country.
5. Respect for the right of each nation to defend itself singly or collectively, in conformity with the Charter of the United Nations.
6. Abstention from the use of arrangements of collective defense to serve the particular interests of any of the big powers, abstention by any country from exerting pressures on other countries.
7. Refraining from acts or threats of aggression or the use of force against the territorial integrity or political independence of any country.
8. Settlement of all international disputes by peaceful means, such as negotiation, conciliation, arbitration or judicial settlement as well as other peaceful means of the parties' own choice, in conformity with the Charter of the United Nations.
9. Promotion of mutual interests and cooperation.
10. Respect for justice and international obligation.'[40]

The Bandung principles obviously interrelate closely with the UN Charter, with a particular angle from the developing world represented by Asia and Africa.

Yet, there is also a slippery reality in the Asian and other regions. While in the early days of the UN, the external aspect of sovereignty was much linked with repudiating aggression and advocating self determination so that colonial peoples would be able

[37]Xue Hanqin,' Chinese Observations on International Law', *Chinese JIL*, 6(2007)1, pp. 83–93; 85–6.

[38]http://www.mea.gov.in/Uploads/PublicationDocs/191_panchsheel.pdf accessed 22 August 2020.

[39]https://www.britannica.com/event/Bandung-Conference accessed 1 September 2020.

[40]http://www.chinadaily.com.cn/english/doc/2005-04/23/content_436882.htm accessed 22 August 2020.

to rise as new States, as the decades passed, that external dimension has been much voiced by less than democratic Governments as a basis for highlighting the non-interference principle—and often to entrench a status quo, post colonization. It has been a mainstay for non-democracies (regrettably far too many in the Asian region!) to extend their longevity, even though the internal aspect of self-determination—participation in national governance—is overlooked or suppressed.

Next to that ambivalence, the bystander should take note of the global jurisprudence which helps to confirm the stepping stones to decolonization (while recognizing the politico-legal difficulty of grappling with the claims of the secession or other accommodations in non-colonial situations). A seminal Asian case paving the way to decolonization was the Case concerning Right of Passage over Indian Territory (Portugal v India): (Merits) Judgement of 12 April 1960.[41] The case concerned the Right of Passage between Portugal and India and the claimed Right of Passage by Portugal to various enclaves which constituted its colony on the Indian sub-continent.[42]

The ICJ had to look at three issues on the merits: '(1) The existence in 1954 of a right of passage in Portugal's favour to the extent necessary for the exercise of its sovereignty over the enclaves, exercise of that right being regulated and controlled by India; (2) Failure by India in 1954 to fulfil its obligation in regard to that right of passage; (3) In the event of a finding of such failure, the remedy for the resulting unlawful situation.'[43]

The ICJ then found by majority:

- the enclaves are subject to the regulation and control of India, in respect of private persons, civil officials and goods in general;
- Portugal did not have in 1954 such a right of passage in respect of armed forces, armed police, and arms and ammunition;
- India has not acted contrary to its obligations resulting from Portugal's right of passage in respect of private persons, civil officials and goods in general.[44]

The nuance concerning the sovereignty debate has been commented upon: '…While Portugal accused India of "committing an offence to the detriment of Portugal sovereignty", India, in turn, accused Portugal of not complying with the rule of customary International Law requiring her to undertake diplomatic negotiation" before starting the dispute….

(The) ICJ verdict worked both ways; it gave a sense of satisfaction to Portugal by stating that it still had the right of civil passage, and to India by stating that

[41] ICJ, Case concerning Right of Passage over Indian Territory (Portugal v India): (Merits) Judgement of 12 April 1960, *ICJ Reports 1960*. https://www.icj-cij.org/files/case-related/32/032-19600412-JUD-01-00-EN.pdf accessed 22 August 2020.

[42] Ibid., pp. 7–8. See also: Prabhakar Singh, 'India Before and After the Right of Passage Case', *Asian JIL*, 5 (2015), pp. 176–208.

[43] Ibid., p. 34.

[44] Ibid., pp. 43–4.

Portugal could not conduct an armed intervention into affairs which India claimed were internal by nature..'[45]

However, much remains unsettled concerning the claims of groups in non-colonial situations where they advocate self-determination targeted to meaningful participation. They are currently found all over Asia—such as in the regard to dissident groups in the Philippines and Myanmar.

Palestine

The issue of Palestine deserves special treatment as a monumental test for International Law involving the Asian region, no less in regard to the sovereignty issue. Palestinian self-determination and its consequences invite intensive study as one of the most intractable and longstanding issues since the end of the Second World War, certainly for the Asian region and for the world.[46] With seeds sown much earlier, this Asian dilemma was born when after the Second World War, the international community helped to set up the State of Israel in 1948 but failed to establish a State for the Palestinian people (the latter with claims backed especially by Arab States). The contested territory on the tip of the Mediterranean in West Asia has been a hotspot for armed conflicts ever since.

The origins of the Jewish state can be traced back to the Balfour Declaration in 1917 which called for the establishment of a Jewish homeland in Palestine. The plight of Palestinians was, however, neglected. After the formation of Israel, there ensued a number of wars between Israel and Arab countries, resulting in Israeli occupation of various territories beyond the original boundaries of the Israeli State, particularly in regard to the Occupied Territory comprising the Golan Heights (originally Syrian), the Gaza strip, East Jerusalem, and the West Bank, with large scale displacements of the Palestinian people. (There are several million Palestinian refugees in the Gaza Strip and the West Bank). Israel has since then tried to annex the territories, even though there are many UN resolutions calling for its withdrawal from the Occupied Territory. In recent decades, settlers from Israel have also encroached upon these territories and at one stage, Israel built a very long and massive Wall on the occupied land, blocking off Arab land for the sake of Israel's own security, with implications for annexation. This became a bone of contention before the ICJ.

The Asian region has learned much on this front from the ICJ Advisory Opinion on the legality of the Wall built by Israel.[47] It has also been involved with the struggle

---

[45] Singh, *supra* note 42, pp. 194–6.

[46] Se for example a recent report by the UN Secretary General: https://www.un.org/unispal/document/right-of-peoples-to-self-determination-right-of-palestinian-people-to-self-determination-secretary-general-report-to-ga-excerpts/ accessed 22 August 2020.

[47] ICJ, Legal Consequences of the Construction of a Wall in the Occupied Palestinian Territory of 9 July 2004, *ICJ Reports 2004*. https://www.icj-cij.org/en/case/131 accessed 22 August 2020.

to enable Palestine become a member of the UNGA[48], and subsequently the issue of relocation of foreign embassy from Tel Aviv to Jerusalem and the response from the UNGA concerning its illegality.[49] Basically, most Asian countries reject the claim of sovereignty by Israel directly or indirectly in regard to Palestine; its occupation of that territory remains an illegality in International Law. This is bolstered by the developments below. Conversely, there is the rise of Palestine's sovereignty in the eyes of the world.

With regard to the case of the Wall, the question for the ICJ in the referral from the UNGA was as follows: 'What are the legal consequences arising from the construction of the wall being built by Israel, the occupying Power, in the Occupied Palestinian Territory, including in and around East Jerusalem, as described in the report of the Secretary-General, considering the rules and principles of International Law, including the Fourth Geneva Convention of 1949, and relevant Security Council and General Assembly resolutions? '[50] The ICJ delivered its advice underlining the illegality of the Wall, calling upon Israel to give compensation for the damage incurred by construction of the Wall, and calling upon all other States not to recognize that illegality.[51]

On the issue of Palestinian membership of the UNGA, generally Asian countries were supportive of the Resolution validating the request, recognizing the status of non-member observer State for the State of Palestine, per Resolution 67/19.[52] The votes were significant: 138 approval, 9 rejections, 41 abstentions, 5 absent members of the GA. No Asian country voted against this Resolution, although a small number abstained.

As for the issue whether it is legal to relocate an embassy from Tel Aviv to Jerusalem, on 21 December 2017, the UNGA voted for Resolution ES-10/L.22.[53] With 128 votes (including many Asian countries in favour), the GA declared "null and void" any action altering Jerusalem's character. It called on all States not to set up embassies there, as well as to ensure compliance with UNSC resolutions, with the potential of a two State solution for this longstanding conflict between Israel and Palestine.[54]

This issue is interlinked with the next Chapter of this study concerning historical ambiguities and territoriality.

---

[48] https://unispal.un.org/UNISPAL.NSF/0/19862D03C564FA2C85257ACB004EE69B accessed 22 August 2020.

[49] https://www.un.org/press/en/2017/ga11995.doc.htm accessed 22 August 2020.

[50] *Supra* note 47.

[51] Ibid.

[52] GA Resolution A/RES/67/19 on Palestine's Non-Member Observer State Status in the UN of 4 December 2012.

[53] *Supra* note 49.

[54] Ibid.

Digital Sovereignty?

Leaping to modern times with a hint of futurism, digitalization (or digitization) has become all pervasive; there has emerged the issue of technological/digital sovereignty, especially in the race to become technologically superior.[55] From one angle, a key proposition in this competition is that people should be able to control use of data concerning themselves and this is interrelated with their right to privacy which the State should protect. There is another dimension: their right to seek erasure of data concerning them on cyberspace—the right to be forgotten vis a vis those who put such information without their consent on the internet. The challenge interplays with the vast new business sector in the form of digital platforms, Big Data and commercialization. On a related note, there is heated competition between the Superpowers to control the technology interlinked with the digital revolution.

A key exponent of the nexus between digitalization and sovereignty has been Europe itself, with increasingly influence on other regions of the world, including Asia. The context is as follows:

> 'Digital technology provides undeniable benefits across many areas, but the "touchscreen revolution" has bolstered the position of the US tech giants (Google, Apple, Facebook, Amazon, Microsoft - GAFAM) within Europe, with their Chinese counterparts (Baidu, Alibaba, Tencent, Xiaomi - BATX) now not far behind. Coupled with trade, not to mention ethical, practices at stark odds with the principles by which the European Union (EU) sets great store, such a stronghold is posing a major threat in terms of sovereignty.
>
> For the EU, returning sovereignty to the heart of its digital strategy involves restoring and ensuring compliance with the rules of free and fair competition and tackling tax injustice, guaranteeing and shoring up freedom of consent and neutrality online, cracking down on illegal content and narrowing the digital divide. It also involves the EU charting its own way forward, reviving the principles of an open and decentralized internet, supporting European stakeholders in the sector, safeguarding the use of free software and investing in such promising technologies as high performance computing, artificial intelligence, the Internet of Things or blockchain.'[56]

The European region has elaborated upon the right to be forgotten, namely the right of persons to ask those who put personal information concerning them on the internet to take down the information, or at least erase the URL. From case law,[57] this has now been expanded as substantive EU law ensuring more safeguards for data protection unless exceptions are justified on the basis of key criteria such as public interest, scientific and statistical purposes.[58]

---

[55]For instance, re US–China Strategic Competition for Technological Leadership, see: https://www.chathamhouse.org/publication/us-china-strategic-competition-quest-global-technological-leadership accessed 22 August 2020.

[56]https://www.lecese.fr/en/publications/towards-european-digital-sovereignty-policy accessed 11 January 2020.

[57]See, for example, the Costeja case in the European Union: https://epic.org/privacy/right-to-be-forgotten/ accessed 22 August 2020.

[58]REGULATION (EU) 2016/679 OF THE EUROPEAN PARLIAMENT AND OF THE COUNCIL of 27 April 2016 on the protection of natural persons with regard to the processing of personal data

Interestingly, digital sovereignty seems to imply a right vested in the human person linked with privacy in this modernistic scenario of expanding cyber-actors. However, the fact that it needs a State-backed guarantee in the form of law, premised on a regional legal framework vis a vis the new business sector in the form of digital platforms, illustrates well the changing nature of sovereignty. This intermix of stakeholders has had an impact on Asia in the form of new data protection laws, such as the recent legislation in Thailand.[59]

On another front, there is the inter-State competition for control over technology which has impact on not only economic benefits but also national security and military superiority. There is the internal dimension in that non-democracies particularly seek control over technology and digitalization precisely because these elements help to consolidate control over the population and surveillance against dissent. There is the external dimension in that it may impact on not only trade and commercial superiority but also international peace and security, especially from the angle of competition for military and defence predominance internationally. This is evident today in the race to control 5G and the interface (or confrontation) between China and the US, played out expansively through the threat or imposition of trade sanctions to dampen the other side's aspiration to be technologically superior. This is expanded in the later Chapter on Trade Liberalization and Inhibition and in the concluding Chapter.

As illustrations of the intercontinental competitive challenge, this report on the spread of 5G, implying both merits and demerits, is informative:

> 'In late October (2019), Germany and China began commercial-scale rollouts of 5G, the wireless technology infrastructure that is transforming the way the world computes. Machines and people will still talk to each other over the borderless network we call the Internet. But with 5G, a new networking infrastructure is emerging, dependent on the Internet but distinct from it and subject to much more government and private control.
>
> With 5G it is possible to do enormous amounts of computing at very high speeds and without having to connect the input device—a cell phone, say, or a self-driving car—to a wire of any kind. But those high speeds are possible only if the rest of the system (signal towers, base stations, distributed servers, and the mega scale centers that house the data and do a great deal of computing themselves) is physically near enough to these input devices. Having your phone, car, or pacemaker in constant contact with vast computational power in the so-called cloud sounds amazingly untethered and extraterritorial. Yet in its physicality and focus on location, the emerging system is more grounded than the Internet ever was.
>
> Whether control over 5G will be exercised principally by States or companies remains to be seen. But the implications for surveillance, security, and national prosperity are enormous, and yet policymakers and business executives have hardly begun to address them.'[60]

Thus the mutating dimensions of digital sovereignty.

---

and on the free movement of such data, and repealing Directive 95/46/EC (General Data Protection Regulation).

[59]Thai personal data law: https://www.dataprotectionreport.com/2020/02/thailand-personal-data-protection-law/ accessed 22 August 2020.

[60]Scott Malcomson, 'The Real Fight for the Future of 5G. Who Will Patrol the Borders of a New Network?', 14 November 2019. https://www.foreignaffairs.com/articles/2019-11-14/real-fight-future-5g accessed 5 September 2020.

Responsibility

What is the other side of the sovereignty coin? In recent times, there has been advocacy that sovereignty is anchored in an obligation or responsibility towards the people of the State. This eschews or modifies the former personification of sovereignty as a self-justification for actions of the Government of the State and opts for a more population/people-centric rationale.

The turning of the tide was witnessed, *par excellence*, by the emergence of the Responsibility to Protection(R2P) concept at the turn of this new millennium.

Rethinking the concept of sovereignty afresh came with the impetus of the World Outcome Document in 2005. The key was to underline the State's obligation to protect its people for various egregious crimes.[61] The summation of this (re)conceptualization was found in these paragraphs:

> 'Responsibility to protect populations from genocide, war crimes, ethnic cleansing and crimes against humanity
>
> 138. Each individual State has the responsibility to protect its populations from genocide, war crimes, ethnic cleansing and crimes against humanity. This responsibility entails the prevention of such crimes, including their incitement, through appropriate and necessary means. We accept that responsibility and will act in accordance with it. The international community should, as appropriate, encourage and help States to exercise this responsibility and support the United Nations in establishing an early warning capability.
>
> 139. The international community, through the United Nations, also has the responsibility to use appropriate diplomatic, humanitarian and other peaceful means, in accordance with Chapters VI and VIII of the Charter, to help protect populations from genocide, war crimes, ethnic cleansing and crimes against humanity. In this context, we are prepared to take collective action, in a timely and decisive manner, through the Security Council, in accordance with the Charter, including Chapter VII, on a case-by-case basis and in cooperation with relevant regional organizations as appropriate, should peaceful means be inadequate and national authorities manifestly fail to protect their populations from genocide, war crimes, ethnic cleansing and crimes against humanity. We stress the need for the General Assembly to continue consideration of the responsibility to protect populations from genocide, war crimes, ethnic cleansing and crimes against humanity and its implications, bearing in mind the principles of the Charter and International Law. We also intend to commit ourselves, as necessary and appropriate, to helping States build capacity to protect their populations from genocide, war crimes, ethnic cleansing and crimes against humanity and to assisting those which are under stress before crises and conflicts break out.' [62]

That Document incorporated the R2P as a key principle advocating that every State has a responsibility to protect its populations from four egregious violations and mass atrocities, namely, genocide, crimes against humanity, war crimes and ethnic cleansing, including in regard to incitement to such crimes.[63]

---

[61] https://www.un.org/en/development/desa/population/migration/generalassembly/docs/globalcompact/A_RES_60_1.pdf accessed 22 August 2020.

[62] Ibid. Resolution adopted by the General Assembly on 16 September 2005 [without reference to a Main Committee (A/60/L.1)] 60/1. 2005 World Summit Outcome.

[63] http://www.responsibilitytoprotect.org/index.php/component/content/article/383 accessed 22 August 2020.

In brief, genocide can be summarized as actions targeting the destruction of a group, with specific intent against the group, for example, extermination of the group.[64] Crimes against humanity take place in war and in peace and are based upon widespread and systematic attack on the civilian population, with intent, such as the repeated bombings of civilians without distinguishing them from military targets. War crimes take place in times of war (both internal and international armed conflicts) and can be single events, such as an attack on a hospital or killing of a prisoner of war. Ethnic cleansing is understood to cover particularly the situation when the population is coerced to leave their homes *en masse* or cleared from locations forcibly, interlinked with ethnic reasons.

Subsequently the UN Secretary General elaborated upon the R2P by stating that there are three pillars for its operationalization:

- **Pillar One: The protection responsibilities of the State:** 'Pillar one is the enduring responsibility of the State to protect its populations, whether nationals or not, from genocide, war crimes, ethnic cleansing and crimes against humanity, and from their incitement.'[65]
- **Pillar two: International assistance and capacity-building:** 'Pillar two is the commitment of the international community to assist States in meeting those obligations. It seeks to draw on the cooperation of Member States, regional and subregional arrangements, civil society and the private sector, as well as on the institutional strengths and comparative advantages of the United Nations system.'[66] This includes preventive action.
- **Pillar three: Timely and decisive response: '**Pillar three is the responsibility of Member States to respond collectively in a timely and decisive manner when a State is manifestly failing to provide such protection.'[67] Actions may thus cover pacific measures under Chapter VI of the UN Charter, coercive ones under Chapter VII and/or collaboration with regional and subregional arrangements under Chapter VIII. There is thus a range of possibilities which should not be understood narrowly. Ultimately, in International Law, Chapter VII measures can, of course, include enforcement measures (in laypersons' terms: military and other sanctions), but they are subject to the veto powers of the five permanent members of the UNSC.

These are now complemented by two UN advisers working on the prevention of genocide and on the R2P.

---

[64]According to the 1948 Genocide Convention, there are five components all of which constitute genocide: per Art.II: '(a) Killing members of the group; (b) Causing serious bodily or mental harm to members of the group; (c) Deliberately inflicting on the group conditions of life calculated to bring about its physical destruction in whole or in part; (d) Imposing measures intended to prevent births within the group; (e) Forcibly transferring children of the group to another group.' Specific intent against the targeted group also needs to be proved. See further: https://treaties.un.org/doc/publication/unts/volume%2078/volume-78-i-1021-english.pdf.

[65]UN Doc. A/63/677 (12 January 2009), para. 11.

[66]Ibid.

[67]Ibid.

The backdrop for the evolution of the R2P should not be forgotten. Prior to its inception, there was an unsettled global debate on whether a country or organization could send troops unilaterally into another country to help the population against key human rights violations perpetrated by the authorities of the latter, on the basis of "Humanitarian Intervention" (HI).[68] While academic quarters suggested various criteria for its validation, many countries were fearful of impingement by outsiders on their cherished State sovereignty and their sacrosanct notion of non-interference in the internal affairs of a State.[69]

The International Commission on State Sovereignty and Humanitarian Intervention which was tasked with examining this issue prior to the World Outcome Document was ingenious to offer an alternative approach: to project State sovereignty as based upon responsibility towards its people (rather than as an absolute right to non-intervention on the part of the State authorities), as well as to set defined criteria for the R2P with normative content.[70] Thus the constituents noted above:

(1) State responsibility
(2) to protect its populations and.
(3) against four key violations.

It should be noted that rather than being a substantive offence, in International Law, ethnic cleansing tends to be subsumed under the notion of forced mass displacement of the population from their homes (in conflict situations) which is a crime under the laws of war or international humanitarian law.[71]

They are paralleled by the rise of the international criminal responsibility of individuals in regard to four key violations, which overlap largely with the R2P, for which individuals might land up in an international criminal tribunal, especially the International Criminal Court (ICC), namely, genocide, crimes against humanity, war crimes and the crime of aggression.[72] Even when a State is not a party to the Rome Statute of the ICC, its nationals might still be referred to the Court if there is a UNSC resolution backing the cross-referral. Therefore, today, State responsibility and individual criminal responsibility go hand in hand in this broader panorama of responsibility interlinked with accountability.

The normative setting of the R2P through the International Law lens has also to be grounded in political realities. While there was a sense of euphoria at the time of the World Outcome Document that people would be protected under the R2P, the invocation and utilization of the R2P has fluctuated with the times since then.[73]The

---

[68]https://www.britannica.com/topic/humanitarian-intervention accessed 22 August 2020.

[69]See example, Maziar Jamnejad and Michael Wood, 'The Principle of Non-Intervention', *Leiden J. Int. Law*, 22(2009)2, pp. 345–81.

[70]International Commission on Intervention and State Sovereignty, *The Responsibility to Protect* (Ottawa: International Development Research Centre, 2001).

[71]https://ihl-databases.icrc.org/customary-ihl/eng/docs/v2_rul_rule129_sectionc accessed 22 August 2020.

[72]https://www.icc-cpi.int/resource-library/documents/rs-eng.pdf accessed 22 August 2020.

[73]Alex J. Bellamy and Tim Dunne (eds.), The Oxford Handbook of the Responsibility to Protect (Oxford:OUP, 2016).

pinnacle of international operations under the R2P was seen in relation to the Libyan conflict - to counter the Government under Colonel Qaddafi, when UN SC Resolution 1973 in 2011 permitted all "necessary measures" to protect civilians, thus opening up to UN-backed military action in the armed conflict with that Government.[74] This also justified the imposition of a no-fly zone to prevent the latter from resorting to aerial warfare. Individuals linked with that Government were also listed by the UNSC for sanctions and cross referral to the ICC.[75]

Interestingly, a superpower from the East Asian region abstained from the UNSC vote on Resolution 1973, and since then, it has shown hesitation towards the R2P; it has cast its veto or abstained in some of the later situations. This is partly due to the fact that in the Libyan operations, there was critique from some quarters which regarded various actions, such aerial bombardments on the members of that Government and related family (implying perhaps the motive of regime change), as not being congruent with the UNSC Resolution.

In the Appendix B at the back of the book, there is a long Table B.1 which shows a sample of recent votes by Asian countries in the UNSC bearing on R2P, not including the draft resolutions which were blocked by the veto of the permanent five, including China. The tally shows quite a lot of convergence in relation to situations in Africa. In more recent years, many UNSC Resolutions citing the R2P have been in relation to armed conflicts in Africa, particularly to support protection and assistance for the affected civilian population such as in South Sudan. Reference to the R2P in the context of the now longstanding and ferocious armed conflict in Syria, also in the Asian region, has been much more ambivalent. A key draft UNSC resolution to refer cases to the ICC was blocked by the veto exercised by China and Russia.[76] However, other UN Resolutions were agreed upon in regard to backing for Syria's elimination of chemical weapons and ratification of the international Convention to eliminate chemical weapons.[77] Agreement could also be achieved in regard to support for humanitarian assistance to the affected population on the basis that aid agencies would need to notify the Syrian authorities before aid deliveries.[78] Nevertheless, there remains a very intractable and caustic situation, highly instrumentalized by both global and regional Powers.

The bottom line is that it is easier to operationalize the R2P in relation to Pillars 1 and 2, but difficult in regard to Pillar 3 if it is related to Chapter VII enforcement measures. This is definitely the case where there is a very politically charged backdrop involving multiple Powers with manifold vested interests, such as in the decade old conflict in Syria.

---

[74] https://www.un.org/securitycouncil/s/res/1973-%282011%29 accessed 20 August 2020.

[75] Ibid.

[76] https://www.un.org/press/en/2014/sc11407.doc.htm.

[77] UNSC Resolution 2118 - adopted unanimously on 27 September 2013, in regard to the Framework for Elimination of Syrian Chemical Weapons during the Syrian conflict. It also referred to United Nations Security Council Resolutions 1540, 2042 and 2043.

[78] Contrast unanimous vote on resolution 2139 of 2014 with a recent resolution 2533 of July 2020 which passed with China, Russia and one other abstaining.

Another conundrum is this: what if the UN or international community itself is dysfunctional? Is there room for other operations with the risk of unilateralism? Aptly, this invites consideration of the link between the responsibility issue and Asian situations in the vicinity.

Dysfunctionality

A major problem since the inception of the UN has been the (over-)use of the veto by some of the Powers in the UNSC rendering the entity dysfunctional on several occasions.[79] There have thus been efforts in recent years, supported by various Asian countries, to limit use of the veto or "votes against", particularly in regard to action against mass atrocity crimes. There has thus emerged a Code against use of the veto for international crimes in the form of a proposition through the UNGA.[80] Many Asian countries supported this Code.[81] There are three Superpowers missing from the equation—the US, Russia and China, while the United Kingdom and France declared their commitment to the Code.

There remains a dilemma concerning what to do if the UNSC is dysfunctional. Intriguingly, in the early 1950s at the time of the Korean War, the UNGA adopted the Uniting for Peace Resolution to fill in this gap by advocating a role for the UNGA in considering and taking collective measures, such as through emergency special sessions, where there is a blockage in the UNSC: The UNGA

'1. Resolves that if the Security Council, because of lack of unanimity of the permanent members, fails to exercise its primary responsibility for the maintenance of international peace and security in any case where there appears to be a threat to the peace, breach of the peace, or act of aggression, the General Assembly shall

[79]Richard Gowan, *Navigating the Storms at the UN Security Council*, International Crisis Group (ICG) (5 FEBRUARY 2020). https://www.crisisgroup.org/global/navigating-storms-un-security-council accessed 22 August 2020.

[80]A/70/621–S/2015/978 General Assembly Security Council Distribution: General 14 December 2015.

[81]Vote in favour:

Albania Andorra Australia Austria **Bahrain** Belgium Belize Benin **Bhutan** Botswana Bulgaria Cabo Verde Central African Republic Chad Chile Colombia Costa Rica Côte d'Ivoire Croatia **Cyprus** Czech Republic Democratic Republic of the Congo Denmark El Salvador Estonia Finland France Gabon Georgia Germany Ghana Greece Grenada Guatemala Guinea Guinea-Bissau Honduras Hungary Iceland **Indonesia Iraq** Ireland Italy Jamaica **Japan Jordan Kuwait** Latvia **Lebanon** Lesotho Libya Liechtenstein Lithuania Luxembourg Madagascar **Malaysia Maldives** Malta Mexico Monaco **Mongolia** Montenegro Morocco Netherlands New Zealand Niger Norway **Oman** Palau Panama **Papua New Guinea** Paraguay Peru **Philippines** Poland Portugal **Qatar Republic of Korea** Republic of Moldova Romania Samoa Saint Kitts and Nevis San Marino **Saudi Arabia** Seychelles **Singapore** Slovakia Slovenia Somalia Spain Switzerland **Thailand** The former Yugoslav Republic of Macedonia **Timor-Leste** Togo Trinidad and Tobago Tunisia **Turkey** Tuvalu Ukraine **United Arab Emirates** United Kingdom Uruguay Vanuatu **Yemen State of Palestine. (Bolded as Asian).**

consider the matter immediately with a view to making appropriate recommendations to Members for collective measures, including in the case of a breach of the peace or act of aggression the use of armed force when necessary, to maintain or restore international peace and security. If not in session at the time, the General Assembly may meet in emergency special session within twenty four hours of the request therefor. Such emergency special session shall be called if requested by the Security Council on the vote of any seven members, or by a majority of the Members of the United Nations'. [82]

That Resolution has been used several times to support UNGA positions such as on Palestine and to call special sessions for deliberations.[83] Yet, it has not been used to impose binding measures because it is understood that it is only the UNSC which has the power to do so, especially per Chapter VII of the UN Charter. However, there should be advocacy that where the UNSC is dysfunctional and where there are threats to peace and security with key human rights violations, at least some measures should be possible for the UNGA to adopt, especially as it is a more representative body than the UNSC. Today a more proactive role is witnessed to some extent by the setting up of various investigative mechanisms, such as on Syria[84] by the UNGA (and most recently by the UN Human Rights Council on Myanmar[85]) to pursue accountability vis a vis perpetrators of mass atrocity crimes.

The next question is then: why not interpret that Uniting for Peace Resolution for the UNGA to set up ad hoc tribunals address international criminal responsibility, at least, in relation to the egregious crimes committed by individuals, when the path through the UNSC is blocked? Why permit a "protection vacuum", especially when increasingly today sovereignty implies responsibility?

This interlinks with the next Chapter which concerns States' acquisition of territory and their consolidation, anchored in the emergence of Statehood and its claim of sovereignty in the face of history and its ambivalences.

---

[82] UNITING FOR PEACE RESOLUTION: UN General Assembly Resolution 377 (V) A (1950) (3 November 1950).

https://www.google.com/search?q=uniting+for+peace+resolution+pdf&rlz=1C1CHBF_enTH694TH695&oq=Uniting+for+Peace+Resolution&aqs=chrome.1.0l8.9845j0j8&sourceid=chrome&ie=UTF-8 accessed 20 February 2020.

[83] https://en.wikipedia.org/wiki/United_Nations_General_Assembly_Resolution_377.

See further: Keith S. Petersen,' The Uses of the Uniting for Peace Resolution since 1950', *Int. Organ.*, 13 (1959)2, pp. 219–32.

[84] The International, Impartial and Independent Mechanism for the Syrian Arab Republic was established by the UNGA in 2016.

https://iiim.un.org/mandate/ accessed 20 February 2020.

[85] 'The Independent Investigative Mechanism for Myanmar was set up by the UN Human Rights Council in 2018.

https://www.ohchr.org/EN/HRBodies/HRC/IIMM/Pages/Index.aspx accessed 20 February 2020.

Chapter 3
Historical Ambiguity and Territoriality

In the previous chapter, a key part of the sovereignty discussion was related to the rise of States, and a key element of Statehood is that there is defined territory on which it is grounded. It should be admitted, however, that there is much ambiguity concerning how a State acquired its original territory, especially if the State emerged centuries ago. International Law rules tend to cover the acquisition of territory in more recent times, and they tend to concern the acquisition of additional territory rather than the question of title or ownership of the original territory. Thus, it is timely to address the question of whether there are International Law principles and practices which help to provide an element of certainty and compromise, with lessons learned from some instructive cases concerning the Asian region.

In essence, territoriality concerns control, possession, ownership/title and/or jurisdiction over space—different types of space. While traditionally, land, sea and air were at the heart of the issue, today there is the cyberspace or digital "territory" which is all the more challenging. While this chapter deals mainly with the traditional concerns, a later chapter addresses the portal of cyberspace more directly. Ominously or propitiously, this will be the gateway to a phenomenon of all encompassing power—disruptive and transformative—of a forward-looking kind.

The territorial issue, especially concerning land, is an age-old challenge, steeped in the mirage of history, and Asia has more territorial disputes than other regions of the world. This has implications for activities also on the sea and in the air. According to one study, the region is the crucible of some 38% of disputes which have not been settled. This is compared with Africa whose figures are at about half that of Asia,[1] coupled with extensive militarization: 'Militarization of disputes in Asia peaked from the 1950s to the mid 1960s.'[2]

[1] M. Taylor Fravel, 'Territorial and Maritime Boundary Disputes in Asia', in Saadia M. Pekkanen, John Ravenhill and Rosemary Foot (eds.), *The Oxford Handbook of the International Relations of Asia* (Oxford: OUP, 2014), pp. 526–46; 529.

[2] Ibid., p.530.

V. Muntarbhorn, *Challenges of International Law in the Asian Region*,
https://doi.org/10.1007/978-981-16-2047-8_3

Numerous wars have broken out in different parts of the region since the end of the Second World War:

> Since 1945, 7 wars over disputed territories have occurred in Asia. Five of the wars occurred between the late 1940s and mid-1970s, including the 1947–8 India-Pakistan war, the Korean war (1950–3), the China-India Border War (1962), the Vietnam war (1965–75) and 1965 India-Pakistan war.[3]

The volatile situation is exemplified by conflicts in West Asia, especially the Middle East, and this is shown by a number of wars between Israel and Arab countries since the end of the Second World War, much linked with contested territorial claims.[4] The nexus with the Palestine issue should not be overlooked. This is at the heart of the question of self-determination voiced in the previous chapter of this book, with the tug of war concerning the Occupied Palestinian Territory—and related sovereignty. The International Law position on annexation of the Occupied Territory is clear: it is illegal, although annexation or conquest by force was unquestioned in colonial times.

Nor has West Asia been the only flashpoint. In other parts of the Asian region, territorial disputes are numerous, but they can be suspended, tempered or modulated by good neighbourly relations and leadership premised on "rapport" or "entente". Conversely, they can flare up as heated conflicts because of competition for resources, the spread of political invective and nationalistic drumbeats, externalizing grievances for internalized political competition and brinkmanship. There are over a dozen key areas of conflict, actual and potential.[5]

In addition, there have been and remain quite a few civil wars or non-international armed conflicts which still wreak havoc on the region today, with major impact on the concerned territories. These include Afghanistan, Syria, Iraq, Yemen, Myanmar and the Philippines, to name but a few. Incidentally, the Afghan[6] and Iraqi[7] situations have witnessed both international and non-international armed conflicts, while the Syrian situation is a very internationalized non-international armed conflict.[8]

Interestingly, while seaborne issues are very much the contestation of the day between neighbours as seen in the next chapter, in recent times land issues (at least in regard to a major Asian power) have enjoyed a more placid setting. For

---

[3]Ibid., p. 531.

[4]See further: Encyclopaedia Britannica. https://www.britannica.com/event/Arab-Israeli-wars.

[5]Border areas between Kyrgyzstan, Tajikistan and Turkmenistan; between Afghanistan and Pakistan; between China and India; between Thailand and Cambodia; enclaves between India and Bangladesh; demilitarized zone between North and South Korea; various islands between China and Vietnam; between China and Japan; between Japan and Russia; and the Spratly Islands dispute between several Southeast Asian countries, for example. See further: https://www.businessinsider.com/asias-disputed-borders-2016-03.

[6]Annyssa Bellal, Gilles Giacco and Stuart Casey-Maslen, 'International Law and Armed non-State Actors in Afghanistan', *IRRC*, 93(2011)881, pp. 47–79.

[7]Ibrahim J. Gassama, 'International Law at a Grotian Moment: The Invasion of Iraq in Context', 18 *Emory Int'l L. Rev.*, 18(2004)1, pp. 1–52.

[8]See reports of the UN Commission of Inquiry in Syria: ohchr.org https://www.ohchr.org/en/hrbodies/hrc/iicisyria/pages/independentinternationalcommission.aspx.

instance, as noted by a commentator, 'the territory being contested along China's land borders is generally less valuable than offshore islands or homeland territories such as Taiwan…'[9]. Intriguingly also, it is noted that the risk of war between China and neighbours has declined due to the military balance which the former enjoys along its land border.[10] There is also a regional forum where confidence building can take which helps to tone down the potential of conflict: the Shanghai Cooperation Organization (SCO).[11]

Yet, there are vestiges of the past which should not be forgotten. In particular, there are the inequitable consequences of colonization; aspects of International Law advanced by European States from the Treaty of Westphalia placed Asian peoples/countries in a situation of disadvantage from the outset. These were exemplified by the various modes of acquisition of territory, especially relating to land—which were very much drawn from or weighed in favour of the former and which provided a raison d'etre for the spread of their territorial aggrandizement. Perhaps, the most poignant, which is no longer accepted today, is territorial acquisition by war or conquest, alias annexation.[12]

By contrast and as will be dealt with in the next chapter, sea-related claims and actions have enjoyed from olden times some convergent rules which have been concretized into treaties to which Asian countries have ostensibly contributed. Many Asian countries are parties to the various Conventions on the Law of the Sea, in particular the 1982 Law of the Sea Convention (LOS).[13] Yet, some of the most serious hotspots today concern seaborne conflicts, given the rivalries vying for resources.

Anomalies

Reverting to the land issue, it can be remembered that traditionally, the main modes of territorial acquisition were occupation, prescription, cession, accretion and annexation.[14] However, since the end of the Second World War, annexation has been outlawed and any implication of conquest repudiated by the international community. These modes are intersectional in the sense that other factors would be borne in mind by international courts where land-related claims reach that point of contestation. Thus, issues of acquiescence, estoppel and the conduct of the disputants are often determinant. On the other hand, claims linked with title based on historical links

[9]Fravel, *supra* note 1, p. 537.

[10]Ibid., p. 539.

[11]Ibid., p. 540.

[12]https://casebook.icrc.org/glossary/annexation-prohibition accessed 22 August 2020.

[13]https://www.un.org/depts/los/convention_agreements/texts/unclos/unclos_e.pdf accessed 22 August 2020.

[14]Ian Brownlie, *Principles of Public International Law* 7th Edition (Oxford: OUP, 2008). Part 3, Chap. 7. For most recent, James Crawford, *Brownlie's Principles of Public International Law* Revised 8th Edition (Oxford: OUP, 2012).

and contiguity without adequate sovereign acts to validate them have been impugned increasingly by international jurisprudence.[15]

Two rules have a particularly colonial lens as a double-edged sword; while they might be necessary to keep the peace, they are not necessarily just/equitable if gauged from the angle of historical transparency. They can be seen as either anomalies or ambiguities. One is the intertemporal law, whereby the acquisition of territory is to be tested by the rules at the time of its happening rather than the rules of today (the latter being as a kind of ex post facto rationalization).[16] One consequence is that States which have emerged in the post-colonial era are at a disadvantage if they question the happenings of yesteryears.[17]

The other is the principle of *uti possidetis* which entrenches the inviolability/intangibility of frontiers, particularly colonial frontiers. This might be linked to treaties which ultimately have impact on not only colonized territories but also non-colonized territories in their vicinity and which perpetuate asymmetric power relations—to the detriment of the more vulnerable stakeholder. This is all more so if maps drawn up by colonizers are the backbone of this principle and are asserted as conclusive or determinant.

Per a commentator:

> The principle of *uti possidetis* juris developed as an attempt to obviate territorial disputes by fixing the territorial heritage of new States at the moment of independence and converting existing lines into internationally recognized borders, and can thus be seen as a specific legal package, anchored in space and time, with crucial legitimating functions. It is also closely related to the principle of the stability of boundaries and both draws upon and informs a variety of other principles of International Law, ranging from consent and acquiescence to territorial integrity and the prohibition of the use of force against States.[18]

As expanded by another commentator:

> *Uti possidetis*, a principle used to define post colonial boundaries in Latin America, Asia and Africa, is a doctrine under which newly independent States inherit the pre-independence administrative boundaries set by the former colonial power. The doctrine posits that title to the colonial territory devolves to the local authorities and prevails over any competing claims based on occupation. Thus *uti possidetis* is predicated on a rejection of self-determination and assures that internal administrative boundaries are functionality equivalent to international boundaries.[19]

From one angle, there is the rationale geared to international peace and stability. From another angle, there is the sense of a fait accompli, sanctioned by *uti possidetis*, which evokes sentiments of injustice. Matters are made more complicated by unequal power relations and the relevancy of maps when there are competing claims.

[15]Ibid.

[16]T. O. Elias, 'The Doctrine of Intertemporal Law', *AJIL*, 74 (1980)2, pp. 285–307.

[17]Anubhav Bijalwan and Deeksha Gupta, 'Justifying The Unjust: An Analysis Of Intertemporal Law'. http://ijlpp.com/justifying-the-unjust-an-analysis-of-intertemporal-law/ accessed 22 August 2020.

[18]Malcom Shaw, 'The Heritage of States: The Principle of Uti Possidetis Juris Today', *BYIL*, 67(1996), pp. 75–154; 76.

[19]Brian Taylor Sumner, 'Territorial Disputes at the ICJ', *Duke L. J.*, 53(2004)6, pp. 1779-812; 1791.

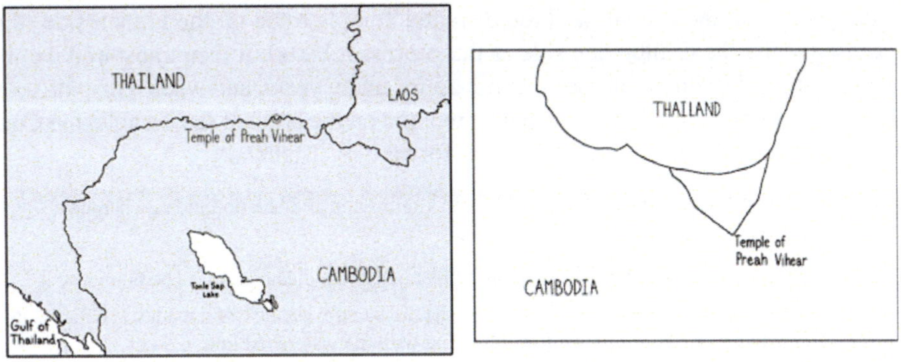

Map 3.1 Thailand, Cambodia and disputed area. *Source* map drawn by author's team adapted from the ICJ, Case concerning Preah Vihear (Cambodia v Thailand), Merits, Judgement of 15 June 1962

The impact on colonies and their neighbours might on occasion be linked with maps which were imposed on peoples/countries at a time when the latter were subjugated by colonial powers or pressured by the latter to make territorial concessions. There may, however, be a question concerning the determinacy of such maps, namely to what extent they are conclusive and confirm or legitimize territorial delimitation or demarcation. Might they give rise to title or at least establish the status quo whereby it is difficult to question the territorial partitioning represented by and validated by such maps?

This emerged poignantly in a classic territorial dispute concerning the Asian region where two countries were affected by the colonial presence in Southeast Asia. In the Temple case between Cambodia and Thailand[20] before the ICJ, there was a dispute between the two countries concerning a Temple situated between them and it was connected with the principle of estoppel, described by Prof. Brownlie as follows:

> In many situations, acquiescence/express admissions are but part of the evidence of sovereignty. Estoppel differs in that if it exists, its suffices to settle the issue because of its unambiguous characterisation of the situation. Resting on good faith and the principle of consistency in state relations, estoppel may involve holding a government to a declaration, which in fact does not correspond to its real intentions.[21]
>
> See Map (3.1).

The origins of the dispute could be traced back to a treaty between Siam (later Thailand) and France dated 1904 which had indicated the "watershed line" as the border between the town countries, while the exact course of the frontier was to be dealt with by a Franco-Siamese Commission. Impliedly, per the watershed line, that line would show the Temple to be on the Thai side of the border. However, in 1907, a map (in Annex I) was drawn up by a technical commission which did not follow

---

[20] ICJ, Case concerning Preah Vihear (Cambodia v Thailand), Merits, Judgement of 15 June 1962, *ICJ Reports 1962*, p. 30. https://www.icj-cij.org/en/case/45/judgments accessed 2 August 2020.

[21] Brownlie, *supra* note 14, p. 153.

the watershed line and showed the disputed Temple to be on the French side (thus subsequently the Cambodian side as the successor State). It then transpired that the Thai authorities did not question that map for many years, and when a dispute arose decades later between Thailand and Cambodia on the issue of the Temple, the Court repudiated the following arguments put forward by Thailand:[22]

- The map was not the work of the Mixed Commission and had no binding character.
- There was an error in the map.
- Thailand never accepted this map or the frontier line indicated on it to be bound by it.
- Alternatively, if she did accept the map, she did so only because of a mistaken belief that the map was correctly drawn to correspond with the watershed line.

The ICJ rejected Thailand's propositions. It raised the question of acquiescence and invoked the principle of estoppel (in French: "preclusion"—also a principle found in the national law of many countries) against Thailand for the country's belated repudiation of the map, reasoning that the country had benefited from the situation as follows:

> Even if there were any doubt as to Siam's acceptance of the map in 1908, and hence of the frontier indicated thereon, the Court would consider, in the light of the subsequent course of events, that Thailand is now precluded by her conduct from asserting that she did not accept it. She has, for 50 years, enjoyed such benefits as the Treaty of 1904 conferred on her, if only the benefit of a stable frontier. France, and then Cambodia, relied on Thailand's acceptance of the map. Since neither side can plead error, it is immaterial whether or not this reliance was based on a belief that the map was correct. It is not now open to Thailand, while continuing to claim and enjoy the benefits of the settlement, to deny that she was ever a consenting party to it.[23]

The ICJ thus decided that Thailand was estopped from questioning a map linked with a treaty between the country and France, the colonial power, such map indicating that the Temple was on Cambodian territory.[24] This was despite the fact that the map did not follow the watershed line which had been stipulated in the treaty and which should have been the border between the two countries.

The Court's rationalization aptly foreshadows the question of maps and how much weight should be accorded to them. This comment from an analyst on the Temple case deserves note:

> This implicit acceptance of maps showing the Temple in what became Cambodia substantiated Cambodia's claim against Thailand. The maps derived their importance from their mandate in the 1904 boundary treaty and the borders that they reflected devolved to Cambodia and Thailand under *uti possidetis*. The Court also rejected Thailand's effective control claim by which it had asserted that acts subsequent to the 1904 treaty manifested its exercise of sovereignty.[25]

---

[22] *Supra* note 20.

[23] Ibid.

[24] Ibid.

[25] Sumner, *supra* note 19, p. 1796.

There is the additional observation that in a case before an international court, the first stepping stone is to look for a treaty as determinant, but if no such document exists, the judicial deliberation is likely to resort to the principle of *uti possidetis*. Beyond that, there would be resort to the issue of effective control and this is linked with the principle of *effectivités* noted below.[26]

In reality, the Temple case went through several phases.[27]

Re Phase 1, the ICJ adjudged in 1962 in favour of Cambodia as follows, visible in the Box below:

Box 3.1 ICJ Judgement in the Temple Case

THE COURT,

by nine votes to three,

finds that the Temple of Preah Vihear is situated in territory under the sovereignty of Cambodia;

by nine votes to three,

that Thailand is under an obligation to withdraw any military or police forces, or other guards or keepers, stationed by her at the Temple, or in its vicinity on Cambodian territory;

by seven votes to five,

that Thailand is under an obligation to restore to Cambodia any objects of the kind specified in Cambodia's fifth Submission which may, since the date of the occupation of the Temple by Thailand in 1954, have been removed from the Temple or the Temple area by the Thai authorities.

Source: Case concerning Preah Vihear (Cambodia v Thailand), ICJ, Merits, Judgement of 15 June 1962.

Concerning Phase 1, even though Thailand (Siam) was found to be estopped from questioning a map which was linked with a treaty between France and Thailand for lack of protest from the latter, what should not be forgotten is the issue of colonial predominance which militated against the possibility of protest and which was raised as follows by this dissent:

---

[26]Ibid., p. 1804.

[27]Case concerning Preah Vihear (Cambodia v Thailand), ICJ, Merits, Judgement of 15 June 1962, *supra* note 20. Later:

ICJ, Request for interpretation of the judgment of 15 June 1962 in the case concerning the temple of Preah Vihear (Cambodia v. Thailand) Request for the Indication of Provisional Measures Order of 18 July 2011, *ICJ Reports 2011*; ICJ, Request for Interpretation of the Judgment of 15 June 1962 in the Case concerning the Temple of Preah Vihear (Cambodia v Thailand) Judgment of 11 November 2013, *ICJ Reports 2013*.

> In determining what inferences may or should be drawn from Thailand's silence and absence of protest regard must, I believe, be had to the period of time when the events we are concerned with took place, to the region of the world to which they related, to the general political conditions existing in Asia at this period, to political and other activities of Western countries in Asia at the time and to the fact that of the two States concerned one was Asian, the other European. It would not, I think, be just to apply to the conduct of Siam in this period objective standards comparable to those which reasonably might today be or might then have been applied to highly developed European States.[28]

The imbalance in power relations underpinned the viewpoint of another dissent:

> 34. It is of course an undisputed fact that both the pavilion in which the French Resident and his associates spent the night and the flag pole on which was hoisted the French national flag had been put up specially for the temporary purpose of welcoming the Siamese Prince. In view of this fact, taken together with the other related circumstances referred to above, it may be reasonable to presume that the French officer's presence had been intended to assert French authority or Cambodia's sovereignty over the Temple area and that the Prince or the Siamese Government must have regarded the episode in itself as constituting a sufficient cause for protest. However, even if this presumption is correct, it does not necessarily follow that they should not have waited for a more propitious occasion to make one than in the actual circumstances prevailing at the time. The reason why "he did not ask the Government to lodge a protest" was eloquently stated by his daughter, Princess Phun Phitsamai Diskul, who went with him during the visit to the Temple, to be as follows:
>
> > It was generally known at the time that we only give the French an excuse to seize more territory by protesting. Things had been like that since they came into the river Chao Phya with their gunboats and their seizure of Chanthaburi.
>
> In view of the history of the relations between Siam and French Indo-China at the time and earlier during the preceding decades, the Princess's explanation seems natural and reasonable. It was a situation not peculiar to Siam. It was, generally speaking, the common experience of most Asiatic States in their intercourse with the Occidental Powers during this period of colonial expansion.[29]

Years later, there was Cambodia's request for interpretation of the earlier judgement which led to a provisional order from the Court to the two sides to abide by a demilitarized zone until final judgement.[30]

In the most recent judgement concerning interpretation of the earlier judgement, at issue was the question concerning the area—promontory—around the Temple and whether this belonged to Cambodia (in addition to the already adjudged Temple itself and related artefacts). The ICJ dispositive clarified that the promontory belonged to Cambodia and Thailand had to withdraw from the area, as follows:

> (1) Unanimously,
>
> *Finds* that it has jurisdiction under Article 60 of the Statute to entertain the Request for interpretation of the 1962 Judgment presented by Cambodia, and that this Request is admissible;

[28]Judgement of 1962, ibid., dissent of Sir Percy Spender, p. 126.

[29]Ibid., dissent of Wellington Koo, pp. 88–9.

[30]Provisional Measures: Request for Interpretation of the Judgment of 15 June 1962 in the Case concerning the Temple of Preah Vihear (Cambodia v. Thailand), *supra* note 27.

(2) Unanimously,

Declares, by way of interpretation, that the Judgment of 15 June 1962 decided that Cambodia had sovereignty over the whole territory of the promontory of Preah Vihear, as defined in paragraph 98 of the present Judgment, and that, in consequence, Thailand was under an obligation to withdraw from that territory the Thai military or police forces, or other guards or keepers, that were stationed there.[31]

On a constructive note, the message is for the two countries to sit down and follow the directions set by the Court. Much depends on the political climate of our times; if the relations between the two countries are good, the actual delimitation issue can be dealt with in a friendly manner—this may mean suspension of the issue for a while or finalization through concrete negotiations.

On the broader front of historical ambiguity and the status (and weightiness?) of maps, fortunately today, there is jurisprudence from the ICJ which rejects maps as the basis for conferring automatic title to the claimed territory (e.g. the Burkina Faso v Mali case).[32]

In the Asian region, it is worth recalling that the seeds for questioning the reliance on maps were sown by an earlier dispute between India and Pakistan. In The Rann of Kutch case,[33] there was a development in the jurisprudential deliberation to promote a shift from relying upon maps to harnessing more tangible acts of administration displaying sovereign power.[34]

In that arbitral award, about 90% of the territory under the dispute was found to be Indian and the rest belonged to Pakistan. It was followed up by joint cooperation between the two countries as part of peaceful settlement between the two neighbours who have had, for years, a delicate and precarious relationship.

Per a commentator, some salient elements from the arbitration were the following:

'On the basis of an appraisal of the evidence concerning the several incidents in the pre-partition period in which the disputed boundary had been in issue (*i.e.,* in the course of correspondence connected with surveys, the constitution of Sind as a Governor's Province, an attempt by Kutch to establish jurisdiction over certain areas used by Sind inhabitants for grazing purposes, etc.), the Tribunal concluded on the first issue that the evidence did not support the conclusion that the disputed boundary was a historically recognized and well-established boundary but indicated on the contrary that such a boundary did not exist at any relevant time.'[35] The tribunal looked

[31]Request for Interpretation of the Judgment of 15 June 1962 in the Case concerning the Temple of Preah Vihear (Cambodia v Thailand), ICJ, Judgment of 11 November 2013, *supra* note 27.

See further: Alexandra C.Traviss, 'Temple of Preah Vihear: Lessons on Provisional Measures', *Chic. J. Int. Law*, 13(2012)1, pp. 317–44; Alessandro Chechi, 'The 2013 Judgement of the ICJ in the Temple of Preah Vihear Case and the Protection of World Cultural Heritage Sites in Wartime', *Asian JIL*, 6(2016)2, pp. 353–78.

[32]https://www.icj-cij.org/en/case/69 accessed 22 August 2020.

[33]Reports of International Arbitral Awards, The Indo-Pakistan Western Boundary (Rann of Kutch) between India and Pakistan (India, Pakistan), 19 February 1968, Vol. XVII, UN, 2006, pp. 1–576.

[34]J. Gillis Wetter, 'The Rann of Kutch Arbitration', *AJIL*, 65(1971)2, pp. 346–57.

[35]Ibid., p. 351.

for evidence of continuous exercise of authority with a measure of effectiveness.[36] As for the maps in the case, they were found not conclusive to support title to the territory.[37]

In essence, in the Rann of Kutch case, while there was resort to maps to support claims, the Tribunal looked rather at the weight of determinant acts to help reach a settlement between India and Pakistan over the disputed territory, presaging the concretization of *effectivités* (discussed below) as a key element of International Law.

Effectivités

Moving beyond the argumentation above, subsequent cases involving Asian countries have contributed to the formulation/strengthening of rules on territoriality, particularly the principle of *effectivités* which is anchored in the unfolding of evidence-based claims, with the more empirical/probative party gaining the upper hand.

In a number of cases involving Asian countries where the legal title is unclear, the issue of effective, sovereign acts (*a titre souverain*), or *effectivités*, seen through consistent or continuous acts carried out on a claimed territory, has been at the forefront of adjudication and (re)iteration. The judicial deliberations below from this region strengthen the position that countries need to provide substantive evidence-based action over a claimed territory, where there is no treaty on the issue; this is what matters to international adjudication when contraposed claims reach the point of contestation and beyond. Even where there is a treaty which offers some clarity of delimitation backing a legal title, *effectivités* might also be invoked to reinforce the positions of contestants. This has been witnessed by various ICJ-related cases concerning title to islands, linking between land and sea issues.

Two Asian cases are of special interest:

The first case concerned sovereignty over Pulau Ligitan and Pulau Sipadan.[38] It involved claims between Indonesia and Malaysia concerning various islands which had to be adjudged on the basis of who could produce the most solid evidence of acts asserting sovereignty.

The ICJ found that Malaysia's actions in regulating the taking of turtle eggs (among others) in regard to those islands were part of the *effectivités* that prevailed, by contrast with the weaker claims of Indonesia whose pleadings were mainly based on the passage of ships nearby. The ICJ added that navigational aids, such as lighthouses, are not necessarily adequate as manifestations of authority to become *effectivités*.

[36] Ibid. p. 353.

[37] Ibid., p. 354: 'The maps relied upon by India therefore were held not to be conclusive support for a positive claim of sovereign title.'

[38] ICJ, Case concerning Sovereignty over Pulau Ligitan and Pulau Sipadan (Indonesia v Malaysia), Judgment of 17 December 2002, *ICJ Reports 2002*.

The following citation exemplifies the Court's reasoning concerning the evidence presented:

> 127. Both Parties claim that the *effectivités* on which they rely merely confirm a treaty-based title. On an alternative basis, Malaysia claims that it acquired title to Ligitan and Sipadan by virtue of continuous peaceful possession and administration, without objection from Indonesia or its predecessors in title. The Court, having found that neither of the Parties has a treaty-based title to Ligitan and Sipadan (see paragraphs 92 and 124 above), will consider these *effectivités* as an independent and separate issue ....
>
> 143. As evidence of such effective administration over the islands, Malaysia cites the measures taken by the North Borneo authorities to regulate and control the collecting of turtle eggs on Ligitan and Sipadan, an activity of some economic significance in the area at the time. It refers in particular to the Turtle Preservation Ordinance of 1917, the purpose of which was to limit the capture of turtles and the collection of turtle eggs "within the State [of North Borneo] or the territorial waters thereof". The Court notes that the Ordinance provided in this respect for a licensing system and for the creation of native reserves for the collection of turtle eggs and listed Sipadan among the islands included in one of those reserves.
>
> Malaysia adduces several documents showing that the 1917 Turtle Preservation Ordinance was applied until the 1950s at least. In this regard, it cites, for example, the licence issued on 28 April 1954 by the District Officer of Tawau permitting the capture of turtles pursuant to section 2 of the Ordinance. The Court observes that this licence covered an area including "the islands of Sipadan, Ligitan, Kapalat, Mabul, Dinawan and Si-Amil". Further, Malaysia mentions certain cases both before and after 1930 in which it has been shown that administrative authorities settled disputes about the collection of turtle eggs on Sipadan.
>
> 144. Malaysia also refers to the fact that in 1933 Sipadan, under section 28 of the Land Ordinance, 1930, was declared to be "a reserve for the purpose of bird sanctuaries".
>
> 145. The Court is of the opinion that both the measures taken regulate and control the collecting of turtle eggs and the establishment of a bird reserve must be seen as regulatory and administrative assertions of authority over territory which is specified by name.
>
> 146. Malaysia further invokes the fact that the authorities of the colony of North Borneo constructed a lighthouse on Sipadan in 1962 and another on Ligitan in 1963, that those lighthouses exist to this day and that they have been maintained by Malaysian authorities since its independence. It contends that the construction and maintenance of such lighthouses is "part of a pattern of exercise of State authority appropriate in kind and degree to the character of the places involved".
>
> 147. The Court observes that the construction and operation of lighthouses and navigational aids are not normally considered manifestations of State authority *(Minquiers and Ecrehos, Judgment, I.C.J. Reports 1953,* p. 71). The Court, however, recalls that in its Judgment in the case concerning *Maritime Delimitation and Territorial Questions between Qatar and Bahrain (Qatar* v. *Bahrain)* it stated as follows:
>
> "Certain types of activities invoked by Bahrain such as the drilling of artesian wells would, taken by themselves, be considered controversial as acts performed a *titre de souverain.* The construction of navigational aids, on the other hand, can be legally relevant in the case of very small islands. In the present case, taking into account the size of Qit'at Jaradah, the activities carried out by Bahrain on that island must be considered sufficient to support Bahrain's claim that it has sovereignty over it." *(Judgment, Merits, I.C.J. Reports 2001,* pp. 99–100, para. 197.) The Court is of the view that the same considerations apply in the present case.[39]

[39] Ibid.

The Court also noted the absence of protest from the Dutch side (impacting on Indonesia as the successor State) as another piece of evidence for the jigsaw. [40] The ICJ was thus found for Malaysia: sovereignty over Pulau Ligitan and Pulau Sipadan belonged to Malaysia.[41]

The other seminal case involved Malaysia and Singapore: Case concerning Sovereignty over Pedra Branca/Pulau Batu Puteh, Middle Rocks and South Ledge (Malaysia/Singapore).[42] *Effectivités* through evidence adduced were also authoritative, and the case illustrates well the probative weighing by the Court. One piece of evidence was UK legislation over Pedra Branca and Pulau Batu Puteh as part of sovereign authority; in this case, there was a regulation over a lighthouse, to which Singapore succeeded. There were also other acts such as investigations and measures of control by the UK in the area. By contrast, there was a lack of activities from the Malaysian side.[43] These excerpts exemplify the weighing of the evidence:

'168. Singapore, in support of its contention that it has continuously exercised state and sovereign authority over Pedra Branca/Pulau Batu Puteh, refers to legislation which it and its predecessors in title enacted specifically relating to the island. The legislation regulated the defraying of costs of establishing and operating the lighthouse, vesting control of it under various governmental bodies, and regulating the activities of persons residing, visiting and working on Pedra Branca/Pulau Batu Puteh. All the measures were open and notorious and drew no protests from Malaysia....

274. The conduct of the United Kingdom and Singapore was, in many respects, conduct as operator of Horsburgh lighthouse, but that was not the case in all respects. Without being exhaustive, the Court recalls their investigation of marine accidents, their control over visits, Singapore's installation of naval communication equipment and its reclamation plans, all of which include acts à titre de souverain, the bulk of them after 1953. Malaysia and its predecessors did not respond in any way to that conduct, or the other conduct with that character identified earlier in this Judgment, of all of which (but for the installation of the naval communication equipment) it had notice.

275. Further, the Johor authorities and their successors took no action at all on Pedra Branca/Pulau Batu Puteh from June 1850 for the whole of the following century or more. And, when official visits (in the 1970s for instance) were made, they were subject to express Singapore permission. Malaysia's official maps of the 1960s and 1970s also indicate an appreciation by it that Singapore had sovereignty. Those maps, like the conduct of both Parties which the Court has briefly recalled, are fully consistent with the final matter the Court recalls. It is the clearly stated position of the Acting Secretary of the State of Johor in 1953 that Johor did not claim ownership of Pedra Branca/Pulau Batu Puteh. That statement has major significance.

[40]Ibid.

[41]*Supra* note 38. See also Sumner, *supra* note 19, p. 1800.

[42]ICJ, Case concerning Sovereignty over Pedra Branca/Pulau Batu Puteh, Middle Rocks and South Ledge (Malaysia/Singapore) Judgement of 23 May 2008, *ICJ Reports 2008*.

[43]Ibid.

276. The Court is of the opinion that the relevant facts, including the conduct of the Parties, previously reviewed and summarized in the two preceding paragraphs, reflect a convergent evolution of the positions of the Parties regarding title to Pedra Branca/Pulau Batu Puteh. The Court concludes, especially by reference to the conduct of Singapore and its predecessors à titre de souverain, taken together with the conduct of Malaysia and its predecessors including their failure to respond to the conduct of Singapore and its predecessors, that by 1980 sovereignty over Pedra Branca/Pulau Batu Puteh had passed to Singapore.'[44]

Thus, Singapore was adjudged to have sovereignty over Pedra Branca/Pulau Batu Puteh. As for the case of Middle Rocks, from the evidence, Malaysia was found to have succeeded to its title from the Sultan of Johor.[45] In regard to South Ledge, which related to low-tide elevation,[46] the court found that it was in the territorial waters of Singapore and Malaysia, depending on its location.[47]

The key lesson learned is that proof of sovereign activities is all important. This is also evolving as an issue linked with how Asian countries have contributed to (or at times undermined) rules and practices concerning maritime areas and how they have endeavoured to settle disputes, in some cases more successfully than others, as configured in the next chapter.

On the downside perhaps, it can be observed that on territorial issues, there have been few instances of dispute settlement by judicial means and/or arbitration involving Asian countries, although there have been some seminal cases involving Asian countries as shown in the next chapter on the Law of the Sea.[48] This might hint at the preferred track of many Asian States—it is the political art of diplomatic

---

[44]Ibid.

[45]Ibid.

[46]Article 13 of the United Nations Convention on the Law of the Sea provides as follows:

> 1. A low-tide elevation is a naturally formed area of land which is surrounded by and above water at low tide but submerged at high tide. Where a low-tide elevation is situated wholly or partly at a distance not exceeding the breadth of the territorial sea from the mainland or an island, the low-water line on that elevation may be used as the baseline for measuring the breadth of the territorial sea.
>
> 2. Where a low-tide elevation is wholly situated at a distance exceeding the breadth of the territorial sea from the mainland or an island, it has no territorial sea of its own.

[47]*Supra* note 42.

[48]Tommy Koh, 'International Law and the Peaceful Resolution of Disputes: Asian Perspectives, Contributions, and Challenges', *Asian JIL*, I(2011)1, pp. 57–60; 59:

> (2) According to the record of the ICJ, there have been only fifteen disputes involving an Asian state or states in the court's history .... Although China and Japan have nationals who are judges, neither country has brought a case to the ICJ. Nor has South Korea. In contrast, of the ten ASEAN countries, 5 have brought cases to the ICJ: Cambodia, Indonesia, Malaysia, Singapore and Thailand.

negotiations (and/or wait and see approach) rather than definitive judicial settlement or the equivalent which has often prevailed. Or simply let the issue lie dormant.

This connects nicely with the next chapter with many hotspots in Asia today. What then is the maritime situation in principle and in practice—and are we all at sea?

Chapter 4
Normativity and Maritime Competitivity

In recent decades, it has become obvious that Asian States (as well as other States) are competing more assertively for resources, especially the riches found at sea. One commentator has noted that there are at least three main areas of conflict: the oil factor, competition on fisheries and freedom of navigation issues (including whether warships and submarines can pass through the territorial sea without notifying or seeking permission from the coastal state).[1]

This should not underestimate the fact that the region itself has been instrumental throughout history in laying the groundwork for the building of norms as the basis of the Law of the Sea (in the form of international treaties as well as custom), which contrasts with the state of flux in regard to claims on land. *En passant*, it can be noted that Grotius, forefather of the Law of the Sea, took his inspiration partly from links with Asia. He worked for the Dutch East India Company and had access to the various contemporary practices in the Southeast Asian region visible at the time. These also provided an anchor for the emergence of a rules-based Law of the Sea, particularly freedom of the high seas and related principles which became the bedrock of his Mare Liberum:

> Martine Julia van Ittersum, in Profit and Principle: Hugo Grotius, Natural Rights Theories and the Rise of Dutch power in the East Indies (1595–1615), argues that "Dutch expansion overseas in the early modern period is literally inconceivable without Grotius' natural law and natural rights theories, i.e. that unimpaired "freedom of trade and navigation was a natural right, innate to all peoples, including Dutch merchants and their indigenous trading partners", that the natural law principle "pacta sunt servanda" [treaties must be honoured) forges the contractual obligations and their enforcement between the Dutch East Asia Company (VOC)] and the Asian rulers', and that "right to self-defense" entitles "each private person" to resume "his sovereign powers" and execute "judgement in his own cause".[2]

[1]Mark J. Valencia, 'Asia, The Law of the Sea and International Relations', *Int. Aff.* (Royal Institute of International Affairs, 73(1997)2, pp. 263–82.

[2]As cited by: Robert Feenstra (ed.), *Hugo Grotius Mare Liberum 1609–2009*, (Leiden/Boston: Brill, 2009) p. XI.

V. Muntarbhorn, *Challenges of International Law in the Asian Region*,
https://doi.org/10.1007/978-981-16-2047-8_4

In the competitive maritime environment, it is reassuring that Asian countries have contributed to the forging of rules—normativity—to regulate sea-based claims. As illustrated below, this is seen *par excellence* by the emergence of various norms advocated by Asian interlocutors and integrated into the UN Convention on the Law of the Sea (UNCLOS or LOS). At least five positive inputs from a number of Asian countries can be identified in the formulation of the LOS and its aftermath: the notion of archipelagic states, rules concerning international straits, concern for landlocked states, the challenge of exploitation of deep sea bed resources and related technology transfer, and principles concerning maritime delimitation as linked with equidistance and equity.

On the other hand, parts of the region are hotspots which are both unsettled and unsettling. As will appear later, even though there have been efforts to use peaceful dispute resolution with success on some fronts, acute claims particularly in the South China Sea have led to confrontation between key actors, needing not only rules but also political will and resourcefulness to help settle disputes peacefully. Having said that, the LOS provisions only provide a limited reference to the issue of environmental protection and some maritime developments sound the alarm for more attention reaching beyond the LOS in this regard. The world will inevitably have to deal with more future-oriented issues such as plastic waste and pollution, global warming, biomass and automation/artificial intelligence on the seas, such as unmanned vessels.

Progression

As a backdrop for such developments, the first observation is that there has been extensive ratification of the LOS by Asian countries as part of the commitment to norms, with the exception of Central Asian States, as in this Table 4.1.

At the negotiations which later led to the LOS, there were various groups joined by Asian countries which interlinked well with the contributions which would emerge with LOS itself. Per a commentator:

- Coastal States group: Fiji, India and Pakistan
- Landlocked and geographically disadvantaged States Group: Bahrain, Iraq, Nepal, Singapore and UAE.
- Straits States Group: Fiji, Indonesia and the Philippines.[3]

The Chairs of various drafting committees, particularly in regard to the deep seabed regime and the negotiations leading to the later 1994 Agreement on deep sea mining and related technology transfer, came from Asia.

It can first be noted that contribution to the concept of archipelagic States came from, among others, Indonesia and the Philippines, premised on the special features

[3]Robert Beckman, 'Law of the Sea and Asian States', in Simon Chesterman, Hisashi Owada and Ben Saul (eds.), *The Oxford Handbook on International Law in Asia and the Pacific* (Oxford: OUP, 2019), pp. 205–36; 207.

Table 4.1 Ratification of Law of the Sea (LOS) Convention by Asian countries

Country/Convention	United Nations Conventions on the Law of the Sea 1982	
	Signature	Ratification
East Asia		
China	10 Dec. 1982	7 Jun. 1996
Democratic People's Republic of Korea (DPRK)	10 Dec. 1982	
Japan	7 Feb. 1983	20 Jun. 1996
Mongolia	10 Dec. 1982	13 Aug. 1996
Republic of Korea (ROK)	14 Mar. 1983	29 Jan. 1996
Southeast Asia		
Brunei Darussalam	5 Dec. 1984	5 Nov. 1996
Cambodia	1 Jul 1983	
Indonesia	10 Dec. 1982	3 Feb. 1986
Lao People's Democratic Republic (PDR) (Laos)	10 Dec. 1982	5 Jun. 1998
Malaysia	10 Dec. 1982	14 Oct. 1996
Myanmar	10 Dec. 1982	21 May 1996
Philippines	10 Dec. 1982	8 May 1984
Singapore	10 Dec. 1982	17 Nov. 1994
Thailand	10 Dec. 1982	15 May 2011
Timor-Leste		8 Jan 2013 (a)
Viet Nam	10 Dec. 1982	25 Jul. 1994
South Asia		
Afghanistan	18 Mar. 1983	
Bangladesh	10 Dec. 1982	27 Jul. 2001
Bhutan	10 Dec. 1982	
India	10 Dec. 1982	29 Jun. 1995
Iran[a]	10 Dec. 1982	
Maldives	10 Dec. 1982	7 Sep. 2000
Nepal	10 Dec. 1982	2 Nov. 1998
Pakistan	10 Dec. 1982	26 Feb. 1997
Sri Lanka	10 Dec. 1982	19 Jul. 1994
Central Asia		
Kazakhstan		
Kyrgyzstan		
Tajikistan		
Turkmenistan		
Uzbekistan		

(continued)

Table 4.1 (continued)

Country/Convention	United Nations Conventions on the Law of the Sea 1982	
	Signature	Ratification
West Asia		
Bahrain	10 Dec. 1982	30 May 1985
Iraq	10 Dec. 1982	30 Jul. 1985
Israel		
Jordan		27 Nov. 1995 (a)
Kuwait	10 Dec. 1982	2 May 1986
Lebanon	7 Dec. 1984	5 Jan. 1995
Oman	1 Jul. 1983	17 Aug. 1989
Palestine		2 Jan. 2015 (a)
Qatar	27 Nov. 1984	9 Dec. 2002
Saudi Arabia	7 Dec. 1984	24 Apr. 1996
Syria		
United Arab Emirates(UAE)	10 Dec. 1982	
Yemen	10 Dec. 1982	21 Jul. 1987

Source Table by author's team derived from https://treaties.un.org/pages/ViewDetailsIII.aspx?src=TREATY&mtdsg_no=XXI-6&chapter=21&Temp=mtdsg3&clang=_en accessed 20 August 2020.
(a) denotes accession
[a]Iran may be categorized as part of South Asia or West Asia for the purpose of this study

and geographies of the two maritime countries, replete with thousands of islands straddling their archipelago. The advocacy of the special features of these States led to the integration of the notion of archipelagic states in the 1982 LOS Convention with the configurations outlined in its Articles 46–47. Basically, these archipelagic countries enjoy the totality of the lands and waters of the archipelago with some conditions attached. While the mass of the area belongs to the archipelagic State, that State should designate a lane for the passage of ships (and aircraft) from other states under a regime known as archipelagic sea lanes passage (ASLP)—maritime passage to be traversed without the need to seek permission from the archipelagic State, benefiting both ships and aircraft.[4]

The ASLP above is different from the right of innocent passage linked with the general law on the "territorial sea" (TS) which enables passage without the need to ask for permission from the coastal state in regard to ships but not aircraft (the latter still needing to ask for permission for overflight). Thus, ASLP enables ships and aircraft to pass continuously and without impediment, without having to ask for permission from the archipelagic State (Other areas are, of course, subject to other general rules, such as the right of innocent passage).

[4]LOS, *Article53.*

Second, there is the issue of international straits and the regime of transit passage. Singapore and Indonesia both contributed to the law on this subject in relation to the LOS, particularly to help ships, aircraft and even submarines to pass through international straits on a continuous basis without the need to seek permission from the coastal State and in the case of submarines, to remain submerged while enjoying the unimpeded passage, as per Articles 37–38. Various duties for ships and aircraft are stated, including the need to pass through the strait without delay.[5]

Third, Asian countries contributed to the concretization of principles to help geographically disadvantaged states, especially land-locked states, several of which are in Asia. For instance, both Nepal and Laos are land-locked states, thus being constrained in relation to access to the high seas. In regard to the LOS, provisions on such States underline freedom to transit through other States with access to maritime areas (subject to negotiations), as per Articles 124–125.

Fourth, there were Asian inputs in regard to how to enable access to technology to exploit the deep sea bed resources. The LOS Convention originally faltered on this issue, and it was due to a subsequent agreement that fairer terms were agreed upon to appease the fear of developed countries, namely the qualm that they might be forced to transfer technology to developing countries. For example, this is visible from the poignant US view which sees itself as pressured and disadvantaged by the LOS which it has not joined:

> The Law of the Sea Treaty requires extensive transfers of data and technology – at least some of which could be highly detrimental to America's industrial competitiveness (including in fields far removed from maritime-related activities) and to the national security. For example:
>
> - The Law of the Sea Treaty (LOST) LOST's Article 266 mandates that states "cooperate in accordance with their capabilities to promote actively the development and transfer of marine science and marine technology on fair and reasonable terms and conditions" and "endeavour to foster favourable economic and legal conditions for the transfer of marine technology."
> - Article 268 requires states to "promote the acquisition, evaluation and dissemination of marine technological knowledge and facilitate access to such information and data."
> - Article 269 calls for parties to "establish programs of technical cooperation for the effective transfer of all kinds of marine technology to States which may need and request technical assistance." …
> - Compulsory dispute settlement mechanisms afford further opportunities to obtain sensitive technology and information. Article 6 of Annex VII requires that parties to a dispute "facilitate the work of the arbitral tribunal and … provide it with all relevant documents, facilities and information." It can therefore be expected that countries may bring the United States or its businesses before arbitral tribunals—without expectation of a favourable result, solely for the purpose of obtaining sensitive technology information.[6]

In 1994, there was an additional agreement to modify those provisions of the LOS and balance the interests of developed and developing countries by providing that

[5]LOS, Article 39.

[6]https://www.unclosdebate.org/argument/662/us-would-be-obligated-transfer-technology-under-unclos accessed 21 July 2020.

such technology would be acquired on fair market terms on the open market (rather through compulsory transfer, express or implied) by the commercial arm set up by the Authority looking after the sea bed area—the Enterprise—to explore/exploit deep sea bed resources.[7] (This is seen per section 5 of the Annex to the 1994 Agreement.)

Fifth, there have been key cases from Asia in recent years concerning development of the equidistance method and its link with that of equitable solution or equity, bearing in mind special circumstances, in relation to maritime delimitation which have provided greater clarity on how to carry out the delimitation—amidst potential and actual conflicts, and helping to contain such conflicts, albeit not always successfully as seen later in the case of the Spratlys.[8] In essence, the equidistance method for maritime delimitation is based on the median line which is used for dividing the geography between two or more neighbouring States. Meanwhile, the pursuit of an equitable solution opens the door to other factors, not necessarily based on the median line, with added attention for relevant circumstances (such as particular geographic features). While the median line is not an absolute binding method, cases from the Asian region have validated its use as a starting point and enable it to be complemented by the quest for equity to adjust the line for delimitation, especially in regard to the Exclusive Economic Zone (EEZ) and the Continental Shelf (CS). At times, this may lead to a single line being drawn for both the EEZ and the CS.

To understand these nuances, there is a need to distinguish between the TS, the EEZ and the CS (rather like concentric circles seaward from land) and the LOS guides the delimitation of the various zones and maritime areas; while the starting point for dealing with overlapping territorial sea is to apportion on the basis of equidistance, the basis in regard of the EEZ and CS is equity—or rather, an equitable solution.[9]

The evolution of judicial and arbitral cases, several involving Asian countries, suggests that in regard to the EEZ and CS, there is now a mix between the equidistance method and other adjustments, such as the call of special circumstances. Before the ICJ case: Maritime Delimitation in the Black Sea (Romania v. Ukraine)[10] (The Black Sea case), an important case which laid down an even more structured three part test below, the mixed method as tested in Asia was propounded by an Asian case—the Qatar v Bahrain case where the Parties requested the Court, 'to draw a single maritime boundary between their respective maritime areas of seabed, subsoil and superjacent waters'.[11] The ICJ found that some areas belonged to Qatar while others belonged

---

[7] https://www.un.org/Depts/los/convention_agreements/texts/agreement_part_xi/agreement_part_xi.htm accessed 22 August 2020.

[8] The Chapter will examine two recent cases below.

[9] See LOS: Article 15: Delimitation of the territorial sea between States with opposite or adjacent coasts; Article 74: Delimitation of the exclusive economic zone between States with opposite or adjacent coasts; Article 83: Delimitation of the continental shelf between States with opposite or adjacent coasts.

[10] ICJ, Maritime Delimitation in the Black Sea (Romania v. Ukraine), JUDGMENT OF 3 fEBRUARY 2009, *ICJ Reports 2009*. The case concerned the two countries seeking the Court's help to establish a single line to delimit both the EEZ and CS in the Black sea.

[11] Maritime Delimitation and Territorial Questions between Qatar and Bahrain (Qatar v. Bahrain), Merits, Judgment, I.C.J. Reports 2001, p. 101, para. 204.

to Bahrain and it decided that the single maritime boundary that divides the various maritime zones of the State of Qatar and the State of Bahrain would be drawn as indicated in (paragraph 250 of) the Judgment.

A three part test has since evolved for delimiting the Continental Shelf and the Exclusive Economic Zone, namely: the first stepping stone is to use the equidistance principle provisionally, then secondly to adjust it if necessary in the pursuit of equitable result, bearing in mind relevant circumstances such as the concave coast which produces a cut-off effect on the seaward projection, and then thirdly to adjust further if there is disproportionality in regard to the ratios of the lengths of the coasts. As already mentioned, the seminal case laying down this method was the Black Sea delimitation case of the ICJ: Maritime Delimitation in the Black Sea case: (Romania v. Ukraine) Judgment of 3 February 2009.[12]

Some Asian countries have resorted to the International Tribunal on the Law of the Sea (ITLOS) or arbitration peacefully and connected positively with dispute settlement on such matters, strengthening the three part test mentioned. The following cases from the Asian region illustrate the evolution of maritime delimitation in recent years, particularly re the EEZ and CS, and the three part test. In this endeavour, the courts do not refashion geography and the quest to equitize here is not to share resources more fairly nor to give more to the poorer party.

The two seminal cases are as follows: the first involved Bangladesh and Myanmar before ITLOS, and the second involved the former and India before an Arbitral Tribunal.

Re Dispute concerning Delimitation of the Maritime Boundary Between Bangladesh and Myanmar in the Bay of Bengal (Bangladesh/Myanmar)2012:[13] The dispute concerned the delimitation of the maritime boundary between Bangladesh and Myanmar in the Bay of Bengal with respect to the territorial sea, the exclusive economic zone and the continental shelf. The judgement concerned, in part, delimitation of the territorial sea and the equidistance principle which per the LOS prevailed in regard to the TS.

With regard to the EEZ and CS within 200 miles, the two parties agreed to let the Tribunal draw a single line. The judgement of the Tribunal built upon the international jurisprudence of the three part test, starting with a provisional equidistance line, then adjusted to take into relevant circumstances (e.g. the configuration of the coast) geared to an equitable result, followed by a further possible adjustment influenced by the disproportionality of the ratios between the various maritime features so as to ensure an equitable result. A particular consideration in the adjustment was the concave nature of Bangladesh's coastline, inviting attention to achieve an equitable result.

---

[12] Its deliberations and three part test are noted by analysts: Abdullah Al Faruque, 'Judgement in Maritime Boundary Dispute between Bangladesh and Myanmar: Significance and Implications under International Law', 18 *Asian yearb. int. law* (2012), pp. 62–84; 76; Tafsir Malick Ndiaye, 'The judge, maritime delimitation and the grey areas', *IJIL*, 55(2015), pp. 493–533; 502–503.

[13] ITLOS, Dispute concerning Delimitation of the Maritimes Boundary between Bangladesh and Myanmar in the Bay of Bengal (Bangladesh/Myanmar) Judgment of 14 March 2012. https://www.itlos.org/cases/list-of-cases/case-no-16/ accessed 1 September 2020.

These excerpts illustrate the operationalization of the methodology in the Box below.

Box 4.1 Bangladesh/Myanmar case: ITLOS: Three Part Test

Relevant coasts

233. In the Black Sea case, the ICJ built on the evolution of the jurisprudence on maritime delimitation. In that case, the ICJ gave a description of the three-stage methodology which it applied. At the first stage, it established a provisional equidistance line, using methods that are geometrically objective and also appropriate for the geography of the area to be delimited. "So far as delimitation between adjacent coasts is concerned, an equidistance line will be drawn unless there are compelling reasons that make this unfeasible in the particular case" (Maritime Delimitation in the Black Sea (Romania v. Ukraine), Judgment, I.C.J. Reports 2009, p. 61, at p. 101, para. 116). At the second stage, the ICJ ascertained whether "there are factors calling for the adjustment or shifting of the provisional equidistance line in order to achieve an equitable result" (ibid., at pp. 101, para. 120). At the third stage, it verified that the delimitation line did not lead to "an inequitable result by reason of any marked disproportion between the ratio of the respective coastal lengths and the ratio between the relevant maritime area of each State by reference to the delimitation line" (ibid., at p. 103, para. 122).

234. The Tribunal notes that, as an alternative to the equidistance/relevant circumstances method, where recourse to it has not been possible or appropriate, international courts and tribunals have applied the angle-bisector method, which is in effect an approximation of the equidistance method. The angle bisector method was applied in cases preceding the Libyan Arab Jamahiriya/ Malta judgment, namely, Continental Shelf (Tunisia/Libyan Arab Jamahiriya) [Judgment, I.C.J. Reports 1982, p. 18, at p. 94, para. 133 (C) (3)], Delimitation of the Maritime Boundary in the Gulf of Maine Area (Judgment, I.C.J. Reports 1984, p. 246, at p. 333, para. 213), and Delimitation of the Maritime Boundary between Guinea and Guinea-Bissau (Decision of 14 February 1985, ILR, Vol. 77, p. 635, at pp. 683–685, paras. 108–111). It was more recently applied in the case concerning Territorial and Maritime Dispute between Nicaragua and Honduras in the Caribbean Sea (Nicaragua v. Honduras) (Judgment, I.C.J. Reports 2007, p. 659, at p. 741, para. 272 and at p. 746, para. 287)....

238. The Tribunal notes that jurisprudence has developed in favour of the equidistance/relevant circumstances method. This is the method adopted by international courts and tribunals in the majority of the delimitation cases that have come before them.

239. The Tribunal finds that in the present case the appropriate method to be applied for delimiting the exclusive economic zone and the continental shelf between Bangladesh and Myanmar is the equidistance/relevant circumstances method.

240. In applying this method to the drawing of the delimitation line in the present case, the Tribunal, taking into account the jurisprudence of international courts and tribunals on this matter, will follow the three stage-approach, as developed in the most recent case law on the subject. Accordingly, the Tribunal will proceed in the following stages: at the first stage it will construct a provisional equidistance line, based on the geography of the Parties' coasts and mathematical calculations. Once the provisional equidistance line has been drawn, it will proceed to the second stage of the process, which consists of determining whether there are any relevant circumstances requiring adjustment of the provisional equidistance line; if so, it will make

> an adjustment that produces an equitable result. At the third and final stage in this process the Tribunal will check whether the line, as adjusted, results in any significant disproportion between the ratio of the respective coastal lengths and the ratio of the relevant maritime areas allocated to each Party ....
>
> 324. The Tribunal recalls that it has decided earlier in this Judgment (see paragraph 297) that the concavity which results in a cut-off effect on the maritime projection of Bangladesh is a relevant circumstance, requiring an adjustment of the provisional equidistance line.
>
> Source: Dispute concerning Delimitation of the Maritimes Boundary between Bangladesh and Myanmar in the Bay of Bengal (Bangladesh/Myanmar), ITLOS, 2012, pp. 66–87.

However, there was disagreement on whether the Tribunal could delimit the CS beyond the 200 miles, with Bangladesh in favour and Myanmar against. The Tribunal proceeded to so by rejecting the principle of natural prolongation of the CS for the delimitation and by underlining the outer edge of the continental margin as key.[14] The judgement thus built upon the three part test and utilized it to establish a single demarcation line for the EEZ and CS within 200 miles, while extending the delimitation to the CS beyond 200 miles also.

Another case advanced the above methodology progressively: Bay of Bengal Arbitration between Bangladesh and India 2014 (Bangladesh/India).[15] The Arbitral Tribunal constituted under Annex VII of the United Nations Convention on the Law of the Sea in the Bay of Bengal Maritime Boundary Arbitration (Bangladesh/India) rendered its Award. The Award laid down the maritime boundary line between Bangladesh and India in the territorial sea, the exclusive economic zone and the continental shelf within and beyond 200 nautical miles. Both had asked the Tribunal to draw a maritime boundary delimiting their respective territorial seas, exclusive economic zones and the continental shelf within and beyond 200 nm in the area in question. The Tribunal confirmed the three steps equidistance/relevant circumstances approach for the CS and EEZ, while rejecting Bangladesh's proposal to use the bi-sector approach premised on straight lines as linear approximations of the coasts.[16]

The Arbitration addressed the issue of the relevant coasts and relevant area for delimitation beyond the territorial sea.[17] It rationalized the methodology for the delimitation of the EEZ and CS within 200 nautical miles (nm).[18] The arbitration then rounded off with the issue of delimitation of the continental shelf beyond 200 nm, confirming that entitlement relates to the outer edge of the continental margin rather

[14] Ibid., paras. 371–462.

[15] PCA, in the Matter of the Bay of Bengal Maritimes Boundary Arbitration between—The People's Republic of Bangladesh and the Republic of India—Award of 7 July 2014. https://pcacases.com/web/sendAttach/383 accessed 24 February 2020.

[16] Ibid.: paras. 191–248.:

[17] Ibid., paras. 277–9.

[18] Ibid.

than natural prolongation from the coast and that 'the final step in the delimitation process involves a test to ensure that the delimitation line does not yield a disproportionate result. The disproportionality test compares the ratio of the relevant maritime space accorded to each Party to the ratio of the Parties' relevant coastal lengths.'[19] Thus the case builds upon the three part test from the Black Sea case based upon peaceful dispute settlement as a possible "win-win" situation for disputants where both sides benefit from the adjudication.

Flashpoint

On a less placid front, there is intra-Asian competitivity which has led to potentially explosive conflicts. While there are many sea-related flashpoints in the Asian region (e.g. in Northeast Asia also), the conflict *par excellence* must be that surrounding the South China Sea. Is dispute prevention/settlement possible? Most piquant is the case of the Spratly Islands where there are overlapping claims between China, Vietnam, Malaysia, Brunei and the Philippines. (In the vicinity, China also has a dispute with Vietnam over the Paracel Islands.)

The conflict concerning this most famous hotspot came to a head in the case of Arbitration between the Philippines and China discussed below. The geographic backdrop is thus:

> 3. The South China Sea is a semi-enclosed sea in the western Pacific Ocean, spanning an area of almost 3.5 million square kilometres…. The South China Sea lies to the south of China; to the west of the Philippines; to the east of Viet Nam; and to the north of Malaysia, Brunei, Singapore, and Indonesia. The South China Sea is a crucial shipping lane, a rich fishing ground, home to a highly biodiverse coral reef ecosystem, and believed to hold substantial oil and gas resources. The southern portion of the South China Sea is also the location of the Spratly Islands, a constellation of small islands and coral reefs, existing just above or below water, that comprise the peaks of undersea mountains rising from the deep ocean floor. Long known principally as a hazard to navigation and identified on nautical charts as the "dangerous ground", the Spratly Islands are the site of longstanding territorial disputes among some of the littoral States of the South China Sea.[20]

Map 4.1 provides a silhouette of the area concerned.

Against its will, China was taken to Arbitration by the Philippines. The findings of the Tribunal provide many lessons which are not necessarily conclusive (at least in political terms). Yet, it can also be asserted that it is preferable to have a process/channel/mechanism offering peaceful dispute settlement. The findings from the case also offer standards of preferred implementation, while there can, of course, be differences of opinion in regard to its rationalization.

---

[19] Ibid., para. 481. See also: paras. 438–458.

[20] PCA, Case No 2013–19 in the Matter of the South China Sea Arbitration—before an Arbitral Tribunal Constituted under Annex VII to the 1982 Convention on the Law of the Sea—between the Republic of the Philippines and the People's Republic of China—Award of 12 July 2016. https://www.pcacases.com/pcadocs/PH-CN%20-%2020160712%20-%20Award.pdf accessed 1 September 2020.

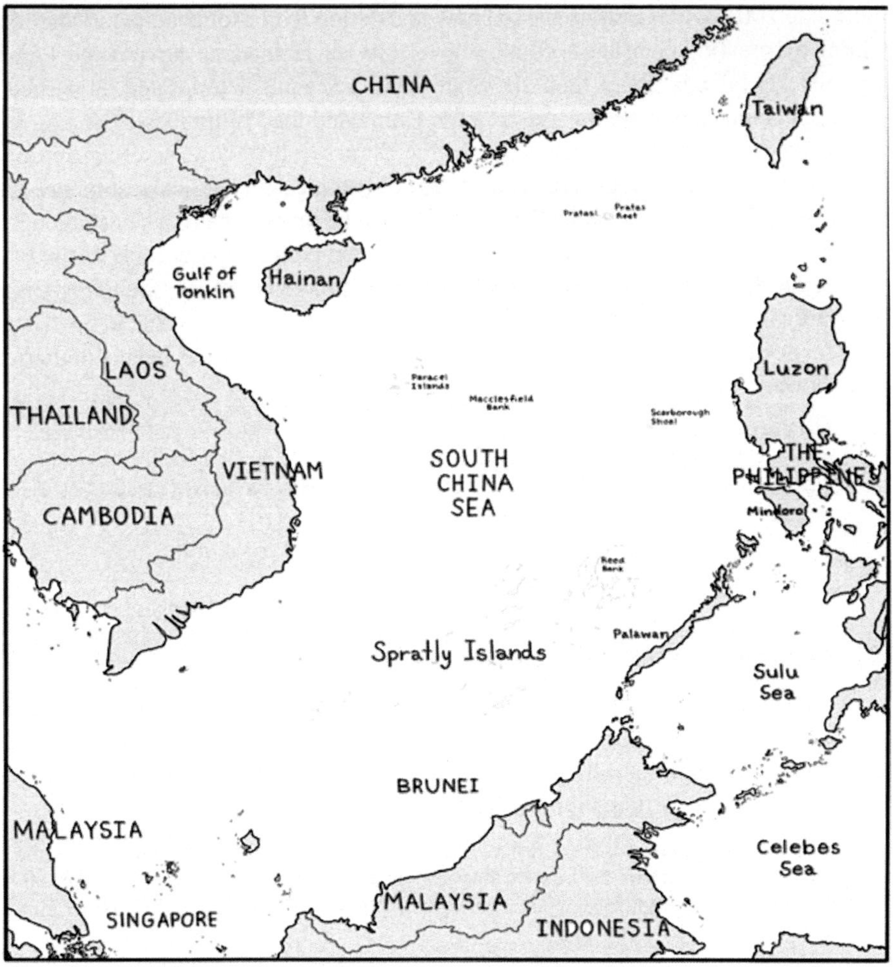

Map 4.1 Spratly Islands. *Source* map drawn by author's team adapted from map in the Arbitral Tribunal Award, Case No 2013–19 in the Matter of the South China Sea Arbitration—before an Arbitral Tribunal Constituted under Annex VII to the 1982 Convention on the Law of the Sea—between the Republic of the Philippines and the People's Republic of China—Award of 12 July 2016. (copyright of PCA)

The delicate background deserves note. In relation to much of the South China Sea, China claims historic rights and applies its " Nine-Dash line" to encompass much of that maritime area on this basis. However, the area has many claimants, with intricacies noted by various commentators. [21] ' The South China Sea remained stable

[21]Zheng Wang, 'Chinese Discourse on the Nine Dashed Line', *Asian Surv.*, 55(2015)3, pp. 502–24;505. See further: Zhiguo Gao and Bing Bing Jia, 'The Nine-Dash Line in the South China Sea: History, Status and Implications', *AJIL, 107(*2013)1, pp. 98–124; 108; Xavier Furtado, 'International Law and the Dispute over the Spratly Islands: Whither UNCLOS?', 21 *Contemp.Southeast Asia*, 21(1999)3, pp. 386–404; 388.

until late 2007, when Beijing passed new legislation to consolidate its jurisdictional claim by creating Sansha, a country level city in Hainan, to govern the Paracel and Spratly Islands. Since then, the South China Sea has deteriorated, in particular between China and Vietnam and between China and the Philippines'.[22]

While, in a sense, it is understandable that China would take an assertive approach over the area on the basis of historical ties and economic cum political resurgence after centuries of being disadvantaged by outside powers, there remains a key challenge of compatibility and compliance with what the global community accepts as the basic law of the sea—in the form of the LOS to which most countries, including China, are parties.

The position of China in relation to the seas in its vicinity has been summarized as follows:

> Its land territory includes the mainland and offshore islands, Taiwan and all islands appertaining thereto, including the Diaoyu Islands, the Pengu Islands, the Dongsha (Pratas) Islands, the Xisha (Paracel) Islands, the Zhongsha Islands and the Nansha (Spratly) Islands, as well as all the other islands that belong to China.[23]

And on dispute settlement:

> The Government of the PRC does not accept any of the procedures provided for in section 2 of Part XV of the Convention with respect to all the categories of disputes referred to in para. 1(a)(b) and (c) of Article 298 of the Convention.[24]

China prefers to settle issues over bilateral dialogue and shuns judicial settlement.

Nevertheless, the controversy over Chinese actions in the South China Sea led to Philippines' invocation of the Arbitral Tribunal to hear its case vis a vis China, even in the face of non-participation by the latter:

> 2. This arbitration concerns disputes between the Parties regarding the legal basis of maritime rights and entitlements in the South China Sea, the status of certain geographic features in the South China Sea, and the lawfulness of certain actions taken by China in the South China Sea.[25]

---

[22]Mike Weissman, 'The South China Sea: Still no war on the horizon', *Asian Surv.*, 55(2015)3, pp. 596–617; 602.

See further: Ekrem Korkut and Woo Hyun Kang, 'China's Nine Dash Line Claim in Light of the Ruling by the Permanent Court of Arbitration (12 July 2018)', *Penn.St.J.L. & Int'l Aff.*, 5(2017)2, pp. 425–63; 455–6:

'In its note verbal of 2011, China said its Nansha (Spratly) Islands are "fully entitled to territorial sea, exclusive economic zone and continental shelf without differentiating low-tide elevations, rocks or islands from each other. Since these insular features include low-tide elevations, rocks and islands, they cannot produce the same maritime zones. The Arbitral Tribunal in the South China Sea Arbitration conclude that the high tide elevations in the Spratlys were not capable of sustaining human habitation or economic life of their own, because they were rocks. Indeed most of the features in the South China Sea are low tide elevations.' Also: Stein Tonneson, 'The South China Sea: Law Trumps Power', *Asian Surv.*, 55(2015)3, pp. 455–77.

[23]Zou Keyuan, 'China and the UNCLOS: Recent Developments and Prospects', *Ocean Yearb.*, 26(2012), pp. 161–80; 161.

[24]Ibid., p. 169.

[25]Permanent Court of Arbitration (PCA) Case No 2013–19 in the Matter of the South China Sea Arbitration—before- an Arbitral Tribunal Constituted under Annex VII to the 1982 Convention on

What is clear from the outset is that in exercising jurisdiction, the Tribunal saw itself as not deciding on delimitation of maritime boundaries but rather addressing the claim of historic rights advocated by China. This is all the more important as, before the time of the dispute, China had already excluded compulsory dispute settlement in regard to delimitation issues (Map 4.2).

In regard to the jurisdiction issue, the Tribunal recognized that a state party can exclude certain issues, such as delimitation, from compulsory dispute settlement, but that the claims presented by the Philippines did not concern sovereignty and sea boundary delimitation—rather, they were concerned with claimed entitlements, and

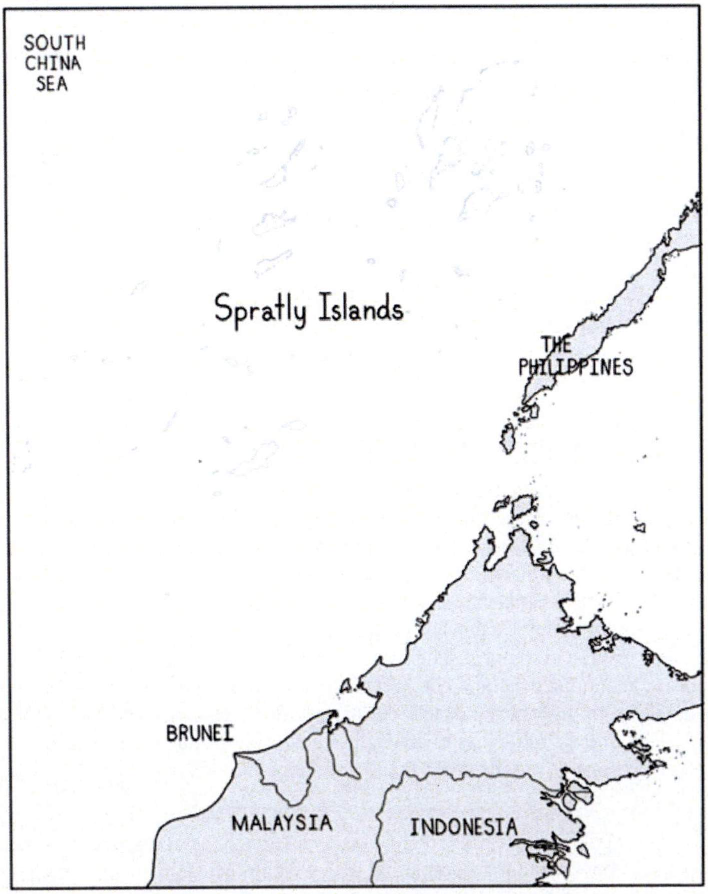

Map 4.2 Spratlys—disputed area. *Source* map drawn by author's team adapted from map in the Arbitral Tribunal Award, Case No 2013–19 in the Matter of the South China Sea Arbitration—before an Arbitral Tribunal Constituted under Annex VII to the 1982 Convention on the Law of the Sea—between the Republic of the Philippines and the People's Republic of China—Award of 12 July 2016. (copyright of PCA)

---

the Law of the Sea—between—the Republic of the Philippines—and—the People's Republic of China (2016), *supra* note 20.

were not, therefore, subject to the exception to the dispute settlement provisions of the Convention. The Tribunal acknowledged China's objections as follows:

> 153. The Tribunal next considered whether there is a dispute between the Parties concerning the interpretation or application of the Convention, which is the basis for the dispute settlement mechanisms of the Convention. In so doing, the Tribunal considered two objections set out in China's Position Paper: first, that the Parties' dispute is actually about sovereignty over the islands of the South China Sea and therefore not a matter concerning the Convention, and second, that the Parties' dispute is actually about the delimitation of the maritime boundary between them and therefore excluded from dispute settlement by an exception set out in the Convention that States may activate by declaration.[26]

It countered them with this reasoning:

> 154.... The Tribunal also emphasized that "[t]he Philippines has not asked the Tribunal to rule on sovereignty and, indeed, has expressly and repeatedly requested that the Tribunal refrain from so doing.
>
> 155. With respect to the latter objection, the Tribunal noted that a dispute concerning whether a State possesses an entitlement to a maritime zone is a distinct matter from the delimitation of maritime zones in an area in which they overlap.[27]

It noted and rebutted China's claims to historic rights as conflicting with the LOS to the extent that those claims exceeded China's maritime zones—which was the case here. Moreover, claims to historic rights were superseded by the entry into force of the LOS. The rationalization of the Arbitral Tribunal is seen in the Box below.

Box 4.2 The issue of Historic Rights before the Arbitral Tribunal

232. The Tribunal has already indicated that it understands, on the basis of China's actions, that China claims historic rights to the living and non-living resources in the waters of the South China Sea within the "nine-dash line", but that China does not consider that those waters form part of its territorial sea or internal waters (other than the territorial sea generated by islands). Such a claim would not be incompatible with the Convention in any areas where China already possesses such rights through the operation of the Convention. This would, in particular, be the case within China's exclusive economic zone and continental shelf. However, to the extent that China's claim to historic rights extends to areas that would be considered to form part of the entitlement of the Philippines to an exclusive economic zone or continental shelf, it would be at least at variance with the Convention....

RE FEATURES:

252 .... The Tribunal also notes that China's position, as asserted during the negotiation of the Convention, is incompatible with a claim that China would be entitled to historic rights to living and non-living resources in the South China Sea that would take precedence over the exclusive economic zone rights of the other littoral States. China never advanced such a claim during the course of the negotiations, notwithstanding that the South China Sea and the question of sovereignty over the Spratly

---

[26]Ibid.

[27]Ibid.

Islands was raised on several occasions in exchanges between China and the Philippines during the work of the Seabed Committee and between China and Viet Nam during the Third UN Conference….

261. For all of the reasons discussed above, the Tribunal concludes that China's claim to historic rights to the living and non-living resources within the 'nine-dash line' is incompatible with the Convention to the extent that it exceeds the limits of China's maritime zones as provided for by the Convention. This is apparent in the text of the Convention which comprehensively addresses the rights of other States within the areas of the exclusive economic zone and continental shelf and leaves no space for an assertion of historic rights. It is also reinforced by the negotiating record of the Convention where the importance of adopting a comprehensive instrument was manifest and where the cause of securing the rights of developing States over their exclusive economic zone and continental shelf was championed, in particular, by China.

262. Accordingly, upon China's accession to the Convention and its entry into force, any historic rights that China may have had to the living and non-living resources within the 'nine-dash line' were superseded, as a matter of law and as between the Philippines and China, by the limits of the maritime zones provided for by the Convention.

263. The Tribunal has held, in the preceding Section, that the entry into force of the Convention had the effect of superseding any claim by China to historic rights to the living and non-living resources within the 'nine-dash line' beyond the limits of China's maritime zones as provided for by the Convention. This conclusion would, in one sense, suffice to decide the dispute presented by the Philippines' Submissions No. 1 and 2. The Tribunal nevertheless considers it important, for the sake of completeness, to distinguish among China's claims to historic rights and to separate those that are, in fact, in excess of and incompatible with the Convention, from those that are not. The Tribunal considers that, in ratifying the Convention, China has, in fact, relinquished far less in terms of its claim to historic rights than the foregoing conclusion might initially suggest ….

270 … In practice, to establish the exclusive historic right to living and non-living resources within the 'nine-dash line', which China now appears to claim, it would be necessary to show that China had historically sought to prohibit or restrict the exploitation of such resources by the nationals of other States and that those States had acquiesced in such restrictions. In the Tribunal's view, such a claim cannot be supported. The Tribunal is unable to identify any evidence that would suggest that China historically regulated or controlled fishing in the South China Sea, beyond the limits of the territorial sea. With respect to the non-living resources of the seabed, the Tribunal does not even see how this would be theoretically possible. Seabed mining was a glimmer of an idea when the Seabed Committee began the negotiations that led to the Convention ….

Source: Permanent Court of Arbitration (PCA) Case No 2013–19 in the Matter of the South China Sea Arbitration—before- an Arbitral Tribunal Constituted under Annex VII to the 1982 Convention on the Law of the Sea—between—the Republic of the Philippines—and—the People's Republic of China (2016), pp. 98–114. (copyright of PCA)

The Tribunal then proceeded to deal with the status of maritime features—islands, high-tide and low-tide elevations, and rocks—particularly to clarify whether they could give rise to some maritime entitlements around them. This was despite the lack of inputs from China since it had already rejected the Tribunal's jurisdiction. The Arbitration deduced that since a low-tide elevation beyond the territorial sea next to the coast of a State has no territorial sea of its own, this norm being expressly stated by Article 13(2) of the LOS, it also has no continental shelf and exclusive economic zone in such situation. Another key implication is the principle that the mere fact that a State builds on low-tide elevations does not give rise to additional entitlements; construction thereon does not change the submerged nature of those elevations.[28]

With regard to the status of islands and rocks, the Tribunal posited some interesting findings. It distinguished between "fully entitled islands" and "rocks", using the former term to cover rocks which can sustain human habitation or economic life of their own. The latter term "rocks" is used by the Tribunal to cover maritime features without such elements. Mere military presence does not prove that a feature can sustain human habitation. The implication is also that "rocks" do not give rise to entitlements in regard to the continental shelf and exclusive economic zone. They cannot be transformed into a full entitled island by land reclamation. Moreover, an island is not defined by its geological origins.[29]

While the Tribunal also had to deal with other issues such as effect of fishing rights, environment, occupation of reef(s), the main issues were as above: in essence, the Tribunal reasoned that this was not an issue about sovereignty, nor was it about delimitation of maritime areas, but the fact that the claim of historic rights in this context was contrary to the LOS and further that it had been superseded by the LOS. It also went further by ordering China not to aggravate the issue.[30]

Implications

Non-participation by China on basis of rejection of compulsory dispute settlement (as allowed by the scope of the exception in Article 298(1)(a)(i) of the Convention LOS) did not preclude the Tribunal's jurisdiction.[31]

Inevitably, compliance after the Award will be difficult. Of course, as with several other international judgements against major powers, one does not need to be disingenuous to believe that it will be followed necessarily by the losing party. Yet, some of the principles noted above are important, for instance: rejection of historic rights and the implication that piling construction on a low-tide elevation does not convert it into a high tide elevation with additional maritime claims.

[28] Ibid.

[29] Ibid. On Islands and rocks: para. 386 ff.

[30] Ibid.

[31] Ibid., paras. 202–6.

The Award has become the subject of divergent views and analyses; some are not totally settled internationally. A counterargument includes: if the LOS did not deal with the issue of historic rights, why should the Arbitral Tribunal have jurisdiction to deal with it? Moreover, despite the claim on the part of the Tribunal that its findings were not about delimitation, it is not difficult to understand that its findings do have impact on delimitation, precisely because the Award indicates encroachments on maritime areas belonging to one of the litigants. In effect, it delegitimizes some of the claims to delimitation. Moreover, the Tribunal's deliberations on the various features such as islands, fully formed islands, high-tide elevations, low-tide elevations and "rocks" were inevitably interconnected with entitlements and delimitation issues, especially in regard to the TS, EEZ and CS, if not beyond. The Tribunal's power to order non-aggravation by the losing party is also open to debate in a context of ambivalence.

Per a commentator:

> The Tribunal in the Philippines v China case distinguishes the status of the features from their implication for maritime delimitation….it is unprecedented for an international judicial body to draw what seems an artificial distinction, given the intimate connection between the 2 issues, and one might question whether the Tribunal was right to go ahead at all on this basis. But it is submitted that the Tribunal's formulation misstates the question; any decision about the status of a feature inevitably raises a question about the applicability of Articles 74 and 83 and is thus covered by Article 298(1)(a)(i).[32]

Moving beyond the Spratlys, other unsettled disputes include in Northeast Asia: the conflict between Japan and China over the Senkaku (or Diayu in Chinese) islands in the East China Sea and between South Korea and Japan over Dokdo (or Takeshima in Japanese).[33]

---

[32] Chris Whomersley,' The Award on the Merit in the Case brought by the Philippines against China relating to the South China Sea: A Critique', *Chinese JIL*, 16(2017)3, pp. 387–423; 396.

See further: Dustin E. Wallace, 'An Analysis of Chinese Maritime Claims in the South China Sea', *Nav. Law Rev.*, 63(2014), pp. 128–159.

[33] Michael C. Davis, 'Can International Law help resolve the conflicts over uninhabited islands in the East China Sea', *Denv. J. Int'L & Pol'y*, 43(2015), pp. 119–163; 120.

See also: Phoebe Gan, 'Shifting Winds in the East: A Legal Analysis and Case Comparison of the Diaoyu/Senkaku Island Dispute', *South. Calif. Interdiscip. Law J.*, 25(2016), pp. 685–720;

Melissa H. Loja, 'Status Quo Post Bellum and the Legal Resolution of the Territorial Dispute between China and Japan over the Senkaku/Diaoyu Islands', *EJIL*, 27(2017), pp. 979–1004;

Zhang Yixing, 'A Deconstruction of the Notion of Acquisitive Prescription and its Implications for the Diaoyu Islands Dispute', *AJIL*, 2 (2012), pp. 323–38;

Hitoshi Nasu & Donald R. Rothwell,' Re-Evaluating the Role of International Law in Territorial and Maritimes Disputes in East Asia', *Asian JIL*, 4(2014), pp. 51–79;

Lee Chang-Wee, 'Legal and Political Aspects of the Dokdo Issue- Interrelationship between International Law and International Relations', *KYIL*, 1(2013), pp. 49–69;

Sean Fern, 'Dokdo or Takeshima: The International Law of Territorial Acquisition in the Japan-Korea Island Dispute', *SJEAA*, 5(2005)1, pp. 78–89;

Rosalyn Higgins, 'The ICJ Dispute Settlement in the Asian Seas: An Assessment', *Am. Soc'y Int'l Proc*, 107(2014), pp. 53–56;

Stephen Wakefield Smith, 'ASEAN, China and the South China Sea: Between a Rock and a Low-Tide Elevation', *U.S.F. Mar.L.J.*, 29(2016), pp. 29–40; 31–32.

Yet, despite the hotspots, some instances of convergence can be identified. Obviously while adjudication is the last resort, most countries would resort to a political solution first. There may also be a regional framework which helps to prevent, mitigate or even resolve a conflict. One arrangement in Southeast Asia is the move towards a regional Code of Conduct which would bridge between the 10 ASEAN countries and China. In relation to the South China Sea, the ASEAN Group has become a portal between the contestants. A starting point is its Declaration on Conduct of the Parties in the South China Sea which advocates freedom of navigation, peaceful dispute settlement, self-restraint, and cooperation at sea, and the stepping stones towards a more authoritative Code of Conduct on the South China Sea.[34]

The Philippines has been the ASEAN coordinator for dialogue with China since 2018. An intriguing question is this: can the Code on the South China Sea be finalized by 2021 when the term of the Philippines ends? The current administration has opted for a softer engagement, eyeing possibly some economic returns.

According to diplomatic sources, China has three basic demands regarding the code of conduct: It should not be covered by the UNCLOS treaty; joint military exercises with countries outside the region must have the prior consent of all parties to the agreement; and no resource development should be conducted with countries outside the region.

ASEAN cannot accept these demands because they would invalidate the tribunal's ruling on China's nine-dash line, and because they are aimed at curtailing the regional influence of the U.S. and Europe.[35]

On a welcome note, further North, South Korea and Japan reached 2 agreements in 1974: on the Continental Shelf: 'delimiting a median line Continental Shelf boundary in the Northern part of the Korea Strait' and Joint Development agreement in East China Sea.[36] Japan and South Korea also reached a Fisheries agreement in 1998.[37]

Other cooperative activities between East Asian countries include the Joint Development Area between Thailand and Malaysia which has worked well for decades to share overlapping resource. There is also the Sino Vietnam Agreement: Beibu Gulf 2000, with common exploration and development zone, and a maritime boundary delimitation and Sino-Vietnam Cooperation in the Gulf of Tonkin (1994–2016).[38]

[34] https://asean.org/?static_post=declaration-on-the-conduct-of-parties-in-the-south-china-sea-2 accessed 24 August 2020.

[35] Toru Takahashi, 'What Beijing really wants from South China Sea code of conduct.' August 12, 2019.

https://asia.nikkei.com/Spotlight/Comment/What-Beijing-really-wants-from-South-China-Sea-code-of-conduct accessed 24 August 2020.

[36] See: Michael C. Davis, op. cit. note 36, p. 153; John Donaldson and Alison Williams, 'Understanding Maritime Jurisdictional Disputes in The East China Sea', *J. Int'l Aff.*, 59(2005)1, pp. 135–56;145.

[37] Ibid.

[38] Zou Keyuan, 'Implementing the UN Convention on the Law of the Sea in East Asia: Issues and Trends', *SYBIL*, 9(2005), pp. 37–54; 48, 50.

Moreover, there is a Malaysia Vietnam Memorandum of Understanding (MOU) 1992 concerning the Gulf.[39]

Finally, conservation issues have also come to the fore, and adjudication has been helpful to settle claims and make the situation more transparent. Another peaceful pairing of Southeast Asian countries is illustrative of the need for more emphasis on this critically important issue in an era of global warming: exemplified by the case of Malaysia v Singapore before ITLOS.[40] It was Malaysia that took Singapore to the ITLOS to address the environmental impact of land reclamation by the latter. The Tribunal ordered the two sides to cooperate, in particular to establish a group of experts to study the issue and possible measures to address adverse effects from the project and requiring both sides to report back to the Tribunal.

Last but not least, from a regional and extra-regional perspective, linking land and sea, there is the emerging issue of the implications of China's own immense Belt and Road Initiative. Could this be a platform for cooperation cum development or does it presage a more ambivalent scenario? The later Chapter on regionalism explores the momentous voyage on this modern Silk Road and its multidirectional journey. More immediately, the next Chapter concerns pressing (and at times depressing) human issues of rights and wrongs.

On China Vietnam cooperation: common exploration and development zone: Benoit de Treglode, 'Maritime Boundary Delimitation and Sino-Vietnam Cooperation in the Gulf of Tonkin (1994–2016)', *China Perspect.*, 3(2013), pp. 33–41.

Other examples of cooperation include Japan and Korea joint development area:

John Donaldson and Alison Williams, *supra* note 36, p. 145;

Reinhard Drifte, *Japanese-Chinese Territorial Disputes in the East China Sea—Between Military Confrontation and Economic Cooperation*, Working Paper 24, London School of Economics (LSE), London, 2008, p. 16.

Robert Beckman, 'The UN Convention on Law of the Sea and the Maritime Disputes in the South China Sea', *AJIL*, 107(2013)1, pp. 142–63.

[39]Keyuan, ibid, p. 41: Malaysia Vietnam MOU 1992 concerning joint development in the Gulf of Thailand.

[40]Case concerning Land Reclamation by Singapore in and around the Straits of Johor (Malaysia v Singapore): List of cases: No. 12 Provisional Measures Order of 8 October 2003. https://www.itlos.org/cases/list-of-cases/case-no-12/

(See also on Whaling: Australia v Japan case before the ICJ: Whaling in the Antarctic (Australia v Japan: New Zealand intervening) Judgement of 31 March 2014, *ICJ Reports 2014*. The court found against Japan's whaling in the Antarctic and this contributed in part to protection of the resources of the seas from an environmental angle. See further: Michael Johnson, 'Whaling in the Antarctic—the ICJ decision and its consequences for further special permit whaling', *AYBIL*, 32(2014), pp. 87–96.)

Chapter 5
Plights and Human Rights

The twenty-first century has been touted as the Asian Century.[1] However, the disruption caused by COVID 19 in 2020 was massive—resulting in marked recession/contraction in the region and beyond. While the claim of the Asian Century might be true in the progressive, longitudinal sense of demographic predominance, politico-geographic weight and economic development in and from many parts of the region, the region is also the crucible of many conflicts and instability.

The most serious challenge is that it is the whirlpool of major wars and forced migrations. At the time of writing this chapter, the armed conflict in Syria was still raging in West Asia and the refugee numbers together with internally displaced persons was about 13 million people: the biggest caseload globally.[2] The situation was all the more complex because of the multiple actors involved in warfare, including Government troops, non-government armed groups, terrorists and regional and international powers behind the conflagration. The region was also faced with multiple violations of the laws of war or international humanitarian law (IHL), ranging from attacks on civilians to decimation of hospitals and the use of chemical weapons. Concomitantly, that scenario called into play the increasingly important issue of accountability and the rise of international criminal law and its applicability in the region. In UN circles, there was a convergence of emphasis on the need to address rampant IHL and human rights violations, as well as the relevance of international refugee law.[3]

---

[1] Institut Francais des Relations Internationales (French Institute of International Relations) (IFRI), *The Asian Century: What International Norms and Practices* (Paris: IFRI, 2014); Federation Internationale des Droits de l'homme (FIDH), *Demystifying Human Rights Protection in Asia* (Paris: FIDH, 2015); https://www.weforum.org/agenda/2019/10/has-world-entered-asian-century-what-does-it-mean/; https://www.ft.com/content/520cb6f6-2958-11e9-a5ab-ff8ef2b976c7; https://asiancenturyinstitute.com/online-courses/20-asia-and-the-world-in-the-asian-century accessed 25 August 2020.

[2] https://www.unhcr.org/syria-emergency.html accessed 25 August 2020.

[3] https://www.ohchr.org/Documents/Publications/Chapter05-MHRM.pdf accessed 25 August 2020.

V. Muntarbhorn, *Challenges of International Law in the Asian Region*,
https://doi.org/10.1007/978-981-16-2047-8_5

In the vicinity, after so many decades, the Israel and Palestine issue was still unresolved. One should not forget also the fractious and protracted Indochina war of the 1950s–70s in Southeast Asia.[4]. More recently, the warfare in Yemen witnessed manifold violations impinging on IHL, international criminal law, human rights and refugee law. Nearby, there were ongoing conflicts in Iraq and Afghanistan, rendered more complex by the plurality of actors involved—both Statal and non-Statal.[5] Further east, the Myanmar issue remained explosive, not only with a non-international armed conflict relating to different groups but also the massive outflow of the Muslim group known as Rohingyas, as well as the spectrum of genocide, crimes against humanity and war crimes.[6] A sprinkle of other conflicts was visible in the Southeast Asian region, including in the Philippines and Southern Thailand. The tension between India and Pakistan was high, with a shut down in Kashmir, while China's spreading influence, especially at sea, was met with tense incidents in the region. The situation facing masses of detainees in Xinjiang was dire. In Northeast Asia, the wargames of the totalitarian State—North Korea (DPRK)—which had seen a major armed conflict in the early 1950s were still testing international patience to the limit.

The importance of International Law, epitomized by IHL, human rights, international criminal law and refugee law to address plights deriving from abuses of power and egregious violations cannot be overstated. At this juncture, it may be asked: what is the current commitment of Asian countries to those elements of International Law. In this upcoming section, one can look at how the checks and balances offered by IHL, international criminal law and international refugee law are now being provided for, with the rather illusory mirage of how they are practised (or not). This connects with the issue of human rights and the broader vistas of civil, political, economic, social and cultural rights can be purviewed.

Check and Balances

All countries, including from Asia, are parties to the four Geneva Conventions 1949 which are the backbone of IHL, visible in Table C.1 in Appendix C.[7] The record

[4]Jayo Mayda, 'The Vietnam Conflict and International Law', *Nordisk Tidsskrift Int'l Ret*, 38 (1968) 7, pp. 7–17.

[5]Ramesh Thakur, 'Global Norms and International Humanitarian Law: An Asian Perspective', *IRRC*, 841 (March 2001), pp. 1–12; Corri Zoli, Emily Schneider& Courtney Schuster, 'Armed Conflict and Compliance in Muslim State, 1947–2014: Does Conflict Look Different under International Humanitarian Law?', *N. C. J. Int'l L. & Com. Reg.*, 40 (2014) 3, pp. 679–738; Alex Bellamy, 'International Law and the War in Iraq', *Melb. J. Int'l* L., 4 (2003) 2, pp. 497–520.

[6]Independent International Fact-Finding Mission on Myanmar. https://www.ohchr.org/en/hrbodies/hrc/myanmarffm/pages/index.aspx.

[7]The four Geneva Conventions of 1949 are: (I) the Convention for the Amelioration of the Condition of the Wounded and Sick in Armed Forces in the Field, (II) the Convention for the Amelioration of the Condition of the Wounded, Sick, and Shipwrecked Members of Armed Forces at Sea, (III)

of ratification of their three Protocols is variable. Implementation, however, is not guaranteed in practice.

Also, intriguing is the commitment of Asian countries to the Statute of the International Criminal Court—the major treaty on international criminal law.[8] The number of ratifications is low as seen in Table D.1 in Appendix D. For instance, in Southeast Asia, only Cambodia and Timor Leste are a party thereto, the Philippines having now withdrawn. In Northeast Asia, Japan, Mongolia and South Korea are parties. In West Asia, in addition to Jordan, interestingly Palestine is a party, and this has implications for accountability in the Middle East.

What of the participation of Asian countries in their ratification of the international instruments on international refugee law?[9] There is again a limited number of ratifications, as seen in Table E.1 in Appendix E. In Southeast Asia, only Cambodia, Philippines and Timor Leste are parties to the key treaties. In Northeast Asia, China, Japan and South Korea are parties to them. Central Asia has the largest number of ratifying countries.

The membership of Asian countries in regard to human rights treaties is dealt with later in this chapter, as seen in Table F.1 in Appendix F.

International standards are essential as they offer a buffer against abuse of power which is at the heart of violations. Yet, clearly whatever the commitment to international standards, the challenge is their implementation in practice. A major lapse is in regard to impunity. Whatever the pressures for transparency and accountability, it is still difficult to ensure State responsibility and individual criminal responsibility for serious violations. Particularly, in regard to refugee law instruments, to be fair, some countries which are not parties thereto do not fare badly in providing temporary refugee to asylum-seekers. Conversely, some countries which are parties to those instruments do not implement them too well! Alas, what is desired is both ratification and implementation—which would offer predictability of rules, certainty of victim classification and identification, and international cooperation and shared responsibility in addressing the phenomenon. This is not to forget the need for political will and the fact that major powers meddle in the region, often for their own interests.

The scenario is closely linked to the fact that many of the conflicts are backed directly or indirectly by Superpowers and regional powers. No advocacy of the law can be adequate unless the political backdrop is addressed, and this is also shaped by the (dys)functionality of the UNSC. Meanwhile, at the time of writing, the work of the ICC was becoming more precarious in the face of non-cooperation from many

---

the Convention Relative to the Treatment of Prisoners of War, and (!V) the Convention Relative to the Protection of Civilian Persons in Time of War. In brief, they are known as: Geneva Convention (GC) I, Geneva Convention (GC) II, Geneva Convention (GC) III and Geneva Convention(GC) IV. They are complemented by three Protocols. See further:

https://www.icrc.org/en/doc/assets/files/other/what_is_ihl.pdf.

[8] https://www.icc-cpi.int/resource-library/documents/rs-eng.pdf accessed 25 August 2020.

[9] https://www.unhcr.org/publications/legal/3d4aba564/refugee-protection-guide-international-refugee-law-handbook-parliamentarians.html.

actors. Regrettably, the Philippines withdrew from the Statute of the ICC, heralding another episode of opacity in the face of violations from the region.[10]

Rights

On the more general issue of human rights in times of peace and their place amidst constraints in times of war, the spectrum of human rights is usually shaped by three precepts. Their universality, indivisibility and inalienability. The first is much linked with international standards, particularly human rights declarations and treaties. The second is anchored in the totality of civil, political, economic, social and cultural rights which should be promoted and protected, rather than one without the other. The third is the premise that we are all born with human rights; the State does not give us rights but has the primary responsibility to guarantee our rights.

Those three windows are opened by Asian countries to various degrees which do not necessarily represent a common approach from all of them. They are also shaped by the fact that regrettably several Asian States are not democratic and have a tendency to undermine political rights while they might be favourable to economic rights. Nor do Governments and civil society necessarily share the same views. To be fair, however, it should not be forgotten that some of the world's biggest democracies are in Asia, in particular, India and Indonesia.

The barometer for those sensibilities were seen most visibly in the lead up to the most recent World Conference on Human Rights—the 1993 World Conference on Human Rights in Vienna.[11] Asian governments congregated and adopted the Asia Pacific (Bangkok) Declaration on Human Rights,[12] while non-governmental organizations from the region also congregated at a meeting to adopt their Asia Pacific (Bangkok) NGO Declaration on human rights,[13] highlighting the contrasts, with the former voicing various "particularities" from this region which might differ from international standards and which might override them, as seen below.

Perhaps the well-worn path can be addressed in the following way in this chapter: Was there some Asian contribution to the Universal Declaration of Human Rights, that genesis of international human rights standards post World War II? What is the case for Asian Values? What are the key human rights challenges facing the Asian region today?

---

[10] https://www.icc-cpi.int/philippines accessed 25 August 2020.

[11] https://www.ohchr.org/EN/AboutUs/Pages/ViennaWC.aspx.

[12] https://www.hurights.or.jp/archives/other_documents/section1/1993/04/final-declaration-of-the-regional-meeting-for-asia-of-the-world-conference-on-human-rights.html accessed 25 August 2020.

[13] https://digitallibrary.un.org/record/170675?ln=en accessed 24 August 2020.

Declaration

The Universal Declaration of Human Rights, a seminal Declaration adopted by the UN General Assembly in 1948, is now over 70 years old.[14] This instrument has spawned a number of international instruments, particularly nine core human rights treaties ("Conventions") which followed in its wake, and it has inspired a vast range of actions worldwide to protect human rights on the basis of equality and non-discrimination.

The UN Charter which established the UN immediately after the Second World War stipulated the promotion of respect for human rights and fundamental freedoms as one of its key tasks. The Declaration helped to give content to that commitment by charting, in a concise document of thirty provisions, those rights which are universal and inherent in all of humanity, ranging from civil and political rights, such as the right to life and right to freedom of expression, to economic social and cultural rights, such as the right to an adequate standard of living and right to education. Then and now, it acts as an all-embracing framework of basic minimum benchmarks for all countries.

The drafting of the Declaration was led by a nine member committee headed by Eleanor Roosevelt, and there were two Asians on board with inputs from this region: Pen Chun Chang (Chinese) and Charles Malik (Lebanese).[15] The former member is credited for laying down a step-by-step approach, starting with the non-binding Declaration to be followed later by binding treaties and implementation measures, with the package now known as the International Bill of Human Rights. He also balanced the emphasis on individual rights derived from some Western countries with influences from the East, particularly Confucian thinking. Notions of benevolence and harmony, not only through law but also ethics, were raised and these were incorporated into the Declaration via references to "morality" and "conscience".[16]

The latter member of the committee evoked Middle Eastern philosophy, while highlighting also civil and political rights interlinked with personal liberties, such as freedom of thought, conscience and religion. He noted the relationship between the individual and the family and was an intermediary in the debate concerning whether the Declaration should be grounded on deistic attribution.[17] In the final draft, the reference to "God" was omitted, and the Declaration has secular underpinnings based on nature and reason as part of the universal project.

Along the way to its adoption by the UNGA, representatives from various Asian countries provided key contributions. There were inputs from representatives of India and Pakistan who called for more emphasis on women's rights, and this had an impact

[14] https://www.un.org/en/sections/universal-declaration/history-document/index.html accessed 24 August 2020.

[15] https://research.un.org/en/undhr/draftingcommittee accessed 24 August 2020.

[16] Sun Pinghua, 'Peng Chun Chang's Contributions to the Drafting of the Universal Declaration of Human Rights', *JCLS*, 5 (2016) 5, pp. 209–217.

[17] https://research.un.org/en/undhr/draftingcommittee accessed 25 August 2020.

on the concretization of the right to marry and the right to have a family.[18] When the Declaration was adopted, twelve Asian countries, namely Afghanistan, Burma (later Myanmar), China, India, Iraq, Iran, Lebanon, Pakistan, the Philippines, Syria, Turkey and Siam (later Thailand), voted in favour, while only one country (Saudi Arabia) abstained.[19]

The abstention was related to the issue of marriage and family, impliedly women's rights. Altogether forty eight countries voted for the Declaration. There was no dissenting vote, although there were eight abstentions.

Of course, the Declaration has to be viewed through the evolving lens and dynamics of time. There has been much progress in some settings which would justify its celebration. Today, there is a range of human rights treaties with international human rights bodies monitoring their implementation. All Asian countries are parties to the Convention on the Rights of the Child (CRC)[20] and a large number are parties to the other Conventions, such as the Convention on the Elimination of All Forms of Discrimination against Women (CEDAW)[21] and the Convention on the Rights of Persons with Disabilities (CRPD[22]). Well over half of the Asian region are parties to the International Covenant on Civil and Political Rights (ICCPR)[23] and the International Covenant on Economic, Social and Cultural Rights (ICESCR).[24] The relevant ratifications can be seen in Table F.1 which is in Appendix F. All countries have engaged with the UN Human Rights Council's Universal Periodic Review system which acts as peer review of implementation at the national level.[25] However, there are some visible gaps. Some countries in the Middle East and the ASEAN region have kept their distance from those treaties. While China has ratified the latter Covenant, it has signed but not yet ratified the former Covenant.[26]

While the region does not have an intergovernmental human rights system, several parts of the region ranging from Southeast Asia to West Asia have undertaken various initiatives on human rights (admittedly more linked with human rights promotion rather than human rights protection) such as through various human rights mechanisms (for instance, the ASEAN intergovernmental Commission on human rights—AICHR) and treaties or declarations (such as the Arab Charter on human Rights and ASEAN Human Rights Declaration) discussed below. While South Asia has some treaties touching on human rights (such as the Convention against human trafficking

[18] https://www.ohchr.org/EN/NewsEvents/Pages/TheRoleWomenShapingUDHR.aspx accessed 25 August 2020.

[19] https://www.npr.org/2018/12/10/675210421/its-human-rights-day-however-its-not-universally-accepted; Abdulaziz M. Alwasil, 'Saudi Arabia's engagement in, and interaction with, the UN human rights system: an analytical review', *Int. J. Hum. Rights*, 14 (2010) 7, pp. 1072–1091.

[20] https://www.ohchr.org/en/professionalinterest/pages/crc.aspx.

[21] https://www.ohchr.org/EN/ProfessionalInterest/Pages/CEDAW.aspx.

[22] https://www.ohchr.org/en/hrbodies/crpd/pages/conventionrightspersonswithdisabilities.aspx.

[23] https://www.ohchr.org/en/professionalinterest/pages/ccpr.aspx.

[24] https://www.ohchr.org/en/professionalinterest/pages/cescr.aspx.

[25] https://www.ohchr.org/en/hrbodies/upr/pages/uprmain.aspx accessed 25 August 2020.

[26] https://tbinternet.ohchr.org/_layouts/15/TreatyBodyExternal/Treaty.aspx?CountryID=36&Lang=EN accessed 25 August 2020.

and the Convention on child welfare arrangements),[27] it still lacks a (sub)regional intergovernmental mechanism to protect human rights where there are no remedies at the national level. There are no such mechanisms in Central Asia and Northeast Asia, regions often neglected by the need for effective action, if not discourse, on human rights protection.

The fact is that there has been regression in parts of the region, particularly with impediments facing democracy, civil and political rights, and constraints imposed on civil society. Undemocratic regimes predominate in various countries. Some less than democratic governments still voice various particularities, such as "Asian values" below, which they claim should prevail over international standards. This plays into the hands of those who wish to limit the rights of individuals, particularly the right to freedom of expression and peaceful assembly, in the face of the omnipotent State. This is compounded by expansive notions of national security and public morals/morality which are instrumentalized to curb dissidence in the name of the collective interest, at times in the guise of overly broad anti-terrorist laws and policies. Xenophobia and hate speech rear their ugly heads in several countries as populism and nationalism are used to prop up various regimes, especially against minorities. Needless to say, this is not necessarily an Asian phenomenon but also appears in other parts of the world, including in some developed, democratic countries.

It is also increasingly realized that the human rights entry point is inadequate if it neglects the nexus with the environment and sustainable development. With climate change, there will be more disasters facing this region, consequentially with huge displacements and disruption. While there has been great buy-in among Asian countries in their acceptance of the UN's Sustainable Development Goals (SDGs) 2015–30 as a complement to human rights, and while there has been notable progress on tackling poverty in some parts of the region, UN assessment discussed below indicates backsliding in key areas, including on aspects of human rights.

Another intriguing development is that in a recent case, human rights became an inter-State issue in West Asia—the Gulf region, the subject of deliberation in the ICJ: the case between Qatar and United Arab Emirates (UAE).[28] The conflict between them had led to difficulties faced by Qatari nationals, such as students, in the UAE. Qatar thus sought provisional measures to protect those nationals. Concurrently, it also made a complaint to the Committee of the Convention on the Elimination of Racial Discrimination (CERD) claiming discrimination against its nationals by UAE

---

[27] https://childhub.org/en/child-protection-online-library/south-asian-association-regional-cooperation-saarc-2002-saarc; https://www.jus.uio.no/english/services/library/treaties/02/2-05/child-welfare-asia.xml accessed 26 August 2020.

[28] ICJ, Application of the International Convention on the Elimination of All Forms of Racial Discrimination (Qatar v. United Arab Emirates) Request for the Indication of Provisional Measures Order of 23 July 2018, *ICJ Reports 2018. https://www.icj-cij.org/files/case-related/172/172-20180723-ORD-01-00-EN.pdf*.

ICJ, Application of the International Convention on the Elimination of All Forms of Racial Discrimination (Qatar v. United Arab Emirates) Request for the Indication of Provisional Measures Order of 14 June 2019, *ICJ Reports 2019.* https://www.icj-cij.org/files/case-related/172/172-20190614-ORD-01-00-EN.pdf accessed 26 August 2020.

actions. In response, the UAE sought provisional measures to order Qatar to withdraw its communication to the CERD, as it claimed that this was a double channel creating an injustice affecting UAE's right to procedural fairness. The UAE also claimed that it was Qatar which was obstructing UAE's efforts to help Qatari citizens. The ICJ ordered provisional measures as requested by Qatar to protect its citizens, while rejecting the request for provisional measures lodged by the UAE.[29]

One way of viewing the case is that the claim of the former is about protection of humans while the claim of the latter is mainly about protection of the State—the message thus implies and vindicates the position that human rights are intrinsically about protection of humans rather than the State. Of course, one can add the reality that human rights cannot be divorced from politics, and the case was steeped in intricate pressures at different levels.

Might this mean that States of West Asia—the Middle East/the Gulf States—are more willing to advocate human rights, at least on some fronts? (Perhaps the answer lies in the politics of it all!).

Values

Since the 1990s, there has been much discussion of the claim that Asia has a set of values different from universal standards. Taken further, different from "Western" standards. As claimed, those values include deference to authority, accent on family values as a collectivity and the Asian growl of being more diligent than other regions, especially in the heyday of the early 1990s when the region was doing very well economically. Underneath that canopy of "Asian values",[30] there was/is inherently an element of ethnocentrism or cultural relativism, and mistrust of civil and political rights while highlighting economic, social and cultural rights as the priority for the region. Those claims subsided to some extent later in the 1990s due to the economic crash in the region. Periodically, since then, they have emerged in various forms, at times mutating into other metaphors such as "ASEAN values", now coupled with a narrow approach concerning what constitutes the "family" (the narrow approach excludes gender diversity) and more recently the push for a cooperation-based approach to human rights rather than rights advocacy and accountability.

Matters came to a head in 1993 in the march towards the most recent World Conference on Human Rights. There seemed to be a clash between the particularity of the Asian region and the universality of human rights. The contraposed positions were seen in the rather cloistered view of Asia Pacific States embodied in the Bangkok

[29] Ibid.

[30] https://www.britannica.com/topic/Asian-values; So Yong Kim, 'Do Asian Values Exist? Empirical Tests of the Four Dimensions of Asian Values', *J. East Asian Stud.*, 10 (2010) 2, pp. 315–344; Leigh Jenco, 'Revisiting Asian Values', *J. Hist. Ideas*, 74 (2013) 2, pp. 237–258; Alfred Boll, 'The Asian Values Debate and its Relevance to International Humanitarian Law', *IRRC*, 841 (2001), pp. 1–6.

Declaration of those States as in Article 8.[31] Note, in particular, the spectrum of particularities which might override universal human rights.

By contrast, NGOs from the region defended the universality of human rights as follows in their Asia Pacific (NGO) Declaration on Human Rights 1993 ("Bangkok NGO Declaration") advocated as follows:

'There is emerging a new understanding of universalism encompassing the richness and wisdom of Asia-Pacific cultures. As human rights are of universal concern and are universal in value, the advocacy of human rights cannot be considered an encroachment upon national sovereignty.

We affirm our commitment to the principle of indivisibility and interdependence of human rights, be they economic, social and cultural or civil and political rights. There must be a holistic and integrated approach to human rights. One set of rights cannot be used to bargain for another'.'[32]

The compromise between the various positions was seen in Vienna through the Declaration and Programme of Action of the World Conference on Human Rights as follows in the Box below:

Box 5.1 (Vienna) Declaration and Programme of Action of the World Conference on Human Rights 1993

1. The World Conference on Human Rights reaffirms the solemn commitment of all States to fulfil their obligations to promote universal respect for, and observance and protection of, all human rights and fundamental freedoms for all in accordance with the Charter of the United Nations, other instruments relating to human rights, and International Law. The universal nature of these rights and freedoms is beyond question.

In this framework, enhancement of international cooperation in the field of human rights is essential for the full achievement of the purposes of the United Nations.

Human rights and fundamental freedoms are the birthright of all human beings; their protection and promotion is the first responsibility of Governments…..

5. All human rights are universal, indivisible and interdependent and interrelated. The international community must treat human rights globally in a fair and equal manner, on the same footing, and with the same emphasis. While the significance of national and regional particularities and various historical, cultural and religious backgrounds must be borne in mind, it is the duty of States, regardless of their political, economic and cultural systems, to promote and protect all human rights and fundamental freedoms. (emphasis by the author).

Source: https://www.ohchr.org/en/professionalinterest/pages/vienna.aspx.

---

[31] '8. **Recognize that while human rights are universal in nature, they must be considered in the context of a dynamic and evolving process of international norm-setting, bearing in mind the significance of national and regional particularities and various historical, cultural and religious backgrounds'. Source:** https://www.hurights.or.jp/archives/other_documents/section1/1993/04/final-declaration-of-the-regional-meeting-for-asia-of-the-world-conference-on-human-rights.html.

[32] Source: https://digitallibrary.un.org/record/170675?ln=en.

This para. 5 of the Vienna Declaration indicates that if there is a conflict between universal standards and national/regional particularities, the former prevails. So goes the theory, but the national/universal contrapositions are often intractable.

In reality, the preferred message in dissecting the issue is not to generalize too much. It is essential to identify which right, which particularity is being discussed, and whether there is a real conflict between the national/regional and universal/international.

If this approach is taken, it is possible to find that on many fronts, Asian countries converge well with universal standards. On other fronts, they diverge from international standards, and in this regard, some practices in the Asian region are lower than international standards while others are or might be higher. Thus, the test of the relationship between universality and particularity would be: it is best to identify which practices abide by universal standards, which practices are substandard and need modification/rectification, and which practices are higher than universal standards and help to elevate the latter.

At the international level, the common ground is seen where Asian countries agree with and/or accede to international human rights instruments and international humanitarian law treaties. The simple fact is that they accept (more or less) the UDHR and are all parties to the CRC and most are parties to the CEDAW and CRPD. Increasingly, they are becoming parties to the other core human rights treaties and participate in the UPR. (Also all are parties for the four Geneva Conventions which are the backbone of international humanitarian law as above.) The long Table F.1 in Appendix F indicates ratifications of the nine core human rights treaties by Asian countries.

While a host of issues might be explored in terms of the positive and negative, perhaps the most practical in terms of space and time is to comment on some key aspects of civil and political rights, and some aspects of economic, social and cultural rights, with particular relevance and poignancy, testing the cohabitation and tension between universality and particularity, to and from the Asian region.

The positive is manifested by the fact that the region has come a very long way in terms of economic development and is likely to be the leading powerhouse in the twenty-first century; it has done well on economic rights. While it is true that there was an economic crash in 1997, the region managed to revive and when another global crash took place in and around 2008, the Asian region was less affected than America and Europe. Thus, at least outwardly and until recently with the damage created by COVID-19, the prospects for the attainment of economic rights were good.[33] However, this does not mean that wealth is well shared in terms of equity.

[33]https://thediplomat.com/2020/06/asia-and-the-global-economys-covid-19-plunge/ accessed 26 August 2020.

Universal health care (at least in the sense of comprehensive coverage of and for their nationals) is well established in some Asian countries,[34] more comprehensively than found in some developed countries. It should not be forgotten also that notions of peace—Ahimsa and peaceful protest such as hunger strikes were advanced by some great Asian exponents such as Mahatma Gandhi.[35] Matters of the spirit offering empathy for fellow humans, animals and nature are also fostered by various beliefs and practices from Asia—while universal human rights standards rarely talk about the spiritual dimension of human rights.[36] In 2020, however, the arrival of the global pandemic—COVID-19 which started in Asia—dented the economic progress with unpredictable consequences.[37] On another front, many Asian countries are non-democratic and have major problems with political rights, especially freedom of expression, assembly and association. The poignant issue of self-determination was dealt with in an earlier chapter. Various specifics can thus be seen through the following lens.

Variability

1. Civil and Political Rights:

– Death penalty

Contrary to the growing international trend to ban the death penalty outright (or at least have a moratorium on it), unfortunately many Asian countries have the death penalty on the Statute books, at times for secular reasons, at times for religious reasons. It might be helpful to state that International Law does not prohibit the death penalty absolutely, even though there is a trend in that direction. The main standard on the issue is Article 6 of the ICCPR which prohibits that penalty in some situations, particularly in regard to pregnant women and children (under 18).[38] In general, the parameter is set as follows:

Article 6 (2): 'In countries which have not abolished the death penalty, sentence of death may be imposed only for the most serious crimes in accordance with the law in force at the time of the commission of the crime and not contrary to the provisions of the present Covenant and to the Convention on the Prevention and Punishment

---

[34] https://www.who.int/southeastasia/health-topics/universal-health-coverage; Vivian Lin, Gabriel Leung and Bronwyn Carter, 'Asia-Pacific Countries Moving Toward Universal Health Coverage', *Health Systems and Reform*, 2 (2019) 1, pp. 1–6.

[35] https://www.lifegate.com/mahatma-gandhi-non-violence accessed 26 August 2020.

[36] https://www.un.org/press/en/1998/19980427.SGSM6541.html; https://www.ohchr.org/Documents/Publications/HandbookParliamentarians.pdf accessed 26 August 2020.

[37] https://www.unescap.org/resources/impact-and-policy-responses-covid-19-asia-and-pacific accessed 26 August 2020.

[38] https://www.ohchr.org/EN/Issues/DeathPenalty/Pages/DPIndex.aspx.

of the Crime of Genocide. This penalty can only be carried out pursuant to a final judgement rendered by a competent court.'[39]

Thus, if the penalty is to be applied, it should only be for the most serious crimes—and this has been interpreted by the monitoring body, the Human Rights Committee, not to cover drugs related offences.[40]

In reality, many countries from the Asian region have a wide variety of offences which can lead to the penalty, and they have correctly been impugned. The offences include drugs related crimes, anti-blasphemy laws, economic crimes, national security- and terrorism-related violations and penalties against various forms of violence. Moreover, extra-judicial killings linked with officialdom and not sanctioned by judicial decisions often undermine the right to life in both democratic and non-democratic countries. Many are exacerbated by armed conflicts due to civilians being targets attacked by both government elements and non-state armed groups.

– Torture and other violence

Various threats to the right to life, right to physical integrity and freedom from violence are rampant in Asia. They vary from arbitrary detention to enforced disappearances, extra-judicial executions and lack of access to justice and equal treatment before the law, compounded by over use of emergency laws. There is a gender perspective in that women are at times subjected to multiple forms of violence ranging from domestic violence to systemic violence, linked with harmful traditions such as female genital mutilation and early marriage. There is the broader angle of threats to gender diversity, in particular transgender identity and same sex relations in a number of Asian countries. Like other parts of the world, generally Asian countries have legal provisions against torture and related practices. However, not all are parties to the CAT[41] and even States members might have an all too narrow interpretation of torture as violence used to extract confessions, while internationally, the definition is broader and should be incorporated into national law:

'1. For the purposes of this Convention, the term "torture" means any act by which severe pain or suffering, whether physical or mental, is intentionally inflicted on a person for such purposes as obtaining from him or a third-person information or a confession, punishing him for an act he or a third person has committed or is suspected of having committed, or intimidating or coercing him or a third person, or for any reason based on discrimination of any kind, when such pain or suffering is inflicted by or at the instigation of or with the consent or acquiescence of a public official or other person acting in an official capacity. It does not include pain or suffering arising only from, inherent in or incidental to lawful sanctions.'[42]

---

[39]International Covenant on Civil and Political Rights. However, under one of its Protocols, membership of the Protocol would ban the death penalty absolutely.

[40]General Comment No.36, https://www.ohchr.org/Documents/HRBodies/CCPR/GCArticle6/GCArticle6_EN.pdf.

[41]https://www.ohchr.org/en/hrbodies/cat/pages/catindex.aspx accessed 26 August 2020.

[42]https://www.ohchr.org/EN/ProfessionalInterest/Pages/CAT.aspx.

An elusive challenge is impunity whereby officials and non-State actors commit such crimes without accountability. This is further inhibited by emergency laws and broad notions of national security which exempt officials for responsibility and/or make it difficult for complainants to seek justice in the face of a State-centred notion of security which diverges from democratic practices.

– Limits on freedom of expression, assembly and association

A key area of concern is the w ndow for expression, peaceful assembly and association, especially where the democratic space is constrained. International guidance on the scope and parameter of the rights pertaining thereto is found in the ICCPR in the Box attached:

Box 5.2 ICCPR Articles on Freedom of Expression, Assembly and Association

Article 19

1. Everyone shall have the right to hold opinions without interference.
2. Everyone shall have the right to freedom of expression; this right shall include freedom to seek, receive and impart information and ideas of all kinds, regardless of frontiers, either orally, in writing or in print, in the form of art, or through any other media of his choice.
3. The exercise of the rights provided for in para 2 of this article carries with it special duties and responsibilities. It may therefore be subject to certain restrictions, but these shall only be such as are provided by law and are necessary:

(a) For respect of the rights or reputations of others;

(b) For the protection of national security or of public order (ordre public), or of public health or morals.

Article 20

1. Any propaganda for war shall be prohibited by law.
2. Any advocacy of national, racial or religious hatred that constitutes incitement to discrimination, hostility or violence shall be prohibited by law.

Article 21

The right of peaceful assembly shall be recognized. No restrictions may be placed on the exercise of this right other than those imposed in conformity with the law and which are necessary in a democratic society in the interests of national security or public safety, public order (ordre public), the protection of public health or morals or the protection of the rights and freedoms of others.

Article 22

1. Everyone shall have the right to freedom of association with others, including the right to form and join trade unions for the protection of his interests.

2. No restrictions may be placed on the exercise of this right other than those which are prescribed by law and which are necessary in a democratic society in the interests of national security or public safety, public order (ordre public), the protection of public health or morals or the protection of the rights and freedoms of others. This article shall not prevent the imposition of lawful restrictions on members of the armed forces and of the police in their exercise of this right....

Source: https://www.ohchr.org/EN/ProfessionalInterest/Pages/CAT.aspx.

Importantly, while these rights are not absolute and are derogable, with possible limitations such as in regard to national security, the authorities imposing limitations on these rights must prove that those limitations abide by the principle of legality (namely, the action is backed by law and not by arbitrariness), necessity (i.e. there are credible risks which justify the constraints) and proportionality (i.e. the constraints to be imposed are proportionate to the risks). One might add also the principle of legitimacy to test those limitations against what other democracies do (or not do). General Comment No. 34 from the Human Rights Committee also underlines the principles of non-discrimination and human rights universality.[43]

– Threats to human rights defenders

The role of human rights defenders, often members of civil society and/or non-governmental organizations, has been increasingly recognized and the need for their protection is voiced in the UN Declaration on Human Rights Defenders.[44] There is also a UN Special Rapporteur on the theme who can take complaints of violations and interact with States and other stakeholders to press for transparency and redress.[45]

In an era where business and human rights have been converging as a global agenda, the issue of Strategic Litigation against Public Participation (SLAPP) is recurrent in the region with cases concerning both Governments and the private sector acting against human rights defenders[46]. Often they are based on defamation, including under new computer crimes and cyber security laws, and/or national security-related claims against human rights defenders, e.g. for revealing the names of alleged offenders publicly in an attempt to protect vulnerable groups or for raising alarm on environmental harm.

[43]General Comment of HRC No.34: https://www2.ohchr.org/english/bodies/hrc/docs/gc34.pdf accessed 10 February 2020.

[44]Declaration on the Right and Responsibility of Individuals, Groups and Organs of Society to Promote and Protect Universally Recognized Human Rights and Fundamental Freedoms 1998.

[45]https://www.ohchr.org/EN/Issues/SRHRDefenders/Pages/SRHRDefendersIndex.aspx accessed 26 August 2020.

[46]https://www.business-humanrights.org/en/latest-news/strategic-lawsuits-against-public-participation-increasingly-used-by-companies-to-silence-human-rights-defenders-says-journalist/ accessed 26 August 2020.

Moreover, there has been a trend by less than democratic States to compel civil society organizations to register and to subject them to surveillance.[47] A common argument used by some Governments is that NGOs should not take foreign funding and that they undermine the work of the Government. Such attitude is contrary to the spirit of the UN Declaration on human rights defenders which sees civil society/human rights defenders, including NGOs, as key stakeholders in human rights protection.[48] Their access to a variety of resources should be respected—just as Governments themselves seek foreign funding at times (even in less than transparent environments).

– Impunity

A pervasive issue is the lack of remedy for violations and the fact that the perpetrators go unpunished. As a corollary, some who commit violations exercise their weight to shield themselves from accountability by means of self-amnesty decrees or other modalities.

Given the high position of various perpetrators and the lack of local remedies, the only viable though difficult channel may have to be the international channel through fact-finding and international criminal tribunals, ad hoc or permanent. The case of the Khmer Rouge Tribunal illustrates this directly, even though there have been critiques of its expense and paucity of cases and convictions.[49]

More recently, the case of Myanmar has been instructive. Its persecution of the Rohingya community in the country has led to the outflow of a million people, replete with massive violations along the way. There have been several entry points for accountability—from softer to harder. There is monitoring by the UN Special Rapporteur on Myanmar.[50] There is documentation of cases by the international fact-finding body,[51] with follow up by a further investigative mechanism under the UN.[52] There is investigation of the responsibility of individuals (especially military leaders) under the ICC,[53] and there is an inter-State case linked with the Genocide Convention, instituted by the Gambia against Myanmar, before the ICJ which has led to the imposition of provisional measures ordering Myanmar to protect the Rohingyas.[54]

---

47 https://reliefweb.int/sites/reliefweb.int/files/resources/ACT3096472019ENGLISH.PDF accessed 26 August 2020.

48 *Supra.* note 44.

49 https://www.eccc.gov.kh/en/node/39457 accessed 26 August 2020.

50 https://www.ohchr.org/en/hrbodies/sp/countriesmandates/mm/pages/srmyanmar.aspx.

51 https://www.ohchr.org/en/hrbodies/hrc/myanmarffm/pages/index.aspx#:~:text=In%20March%202017%2C%20the%20United,%2C%20and%20abuses%2C%20in%20Myanmar.

52 https://www.ohchr.org/EN/HRBodies/HRC/IIMM/Pages/Index.aspx.

53 https://www.icc-cpi.int/Pages/item.aspx?name=pr1495 accessed 3 September 2020.

54 ICJ, Application of the Convention on the Prevention and Punishment of the Crime of Genocide (The Gambia v. Myanmar) Order of 23 January 2020, *ICJ Reports 2020*. https://www.icj-cij.org/files/case-related/178/178-20200123-ORD-01-00-EN.pdf accessed 3 October 2020.

More recently, the internal mechanism set up by Myanmar to investigate mass atrocity crimes has concluded that there have been war crimes and serious human rights violations committed by some of the military vis a vis the Rohingya community.[55] This internal mechanism has not made a finding of genocide, and this diverges from the well-documented work of the UN backed international fact-finding body which has found violations tantamount to genocide, crimes against humanity and war crimes.[56] While the main bulk of the violations emanates from the authorities, other violations have been committed by non-State actors.

The ICJ also took into account the UN-related international fact-finding work in issuing the provisional measures to protect the Rohingyas.[57] In its provisional order to Myanmar, the ICJ requires the country to take measures to prevent genocide as well as to reporting on the measures taken.[58] The provisional order does not state that genocide has actually taken place, and it remains to be seen what the final outcome will be when a more complete judgement is issued.

Needless to say, International Law leans towards objectivity in assessing serious violations. This has implications for the credibility (or lack of credibility) of internal mechanism(s)which are seen as more subjective. This is all the more so where they have to interface with international mechanism(s) which are independent and impartial under the umbrella of the UN with detailed methodology to collect evidence, offering deeper probing, even to the extent of corroboration paralleling the methods adopted in relation to criminal cases before a Court of law.

2. Economic, Social and cultural rights:

- Poverty and Equity

A key aspect of the issue is poverty in the Asian region. While there are some very rich countries, there are also some very poor countries. Yet, the march to overcome poverty has been motivated in part by the Millennium Development Goals (MDGSs) (2000–2015)[59] and now Sustainable Development Goals (SDGs) (2015–2030).[60] In Asia, there has been progress in the reduction of poverty, evident in many parts of the region, but especially with the impact of COVID-19, recently, there has also been regression on some fronts with implications for human rights, and this includes the wider gap between the rich and the poor linked with the issue of equity.[61]

---

[55] https://www.icoe-myanmar.org/.

[56] *Supra* note 51.

[57] *Supra* note 54.

[58] Ibid.

[59] https://www.un.org/millenniumgoals/.

[60] Resolution A/RES/70/1 adopted by the UN General Assembly on 25 September 2015: Transforming our world: the 2030 Agenda for Sustainable Development.

[61] https://www.asia-pacific.undp.org/content/rbap/en/home/sustainable-development-goals/goal-10-reduced-inequalities.html.

Some countries have done well in reducing poverty, and the targets on this front (Goal 1) are now guided by the SDGs which has 17 Goals. In a report from the UN Economic and Social Commission for Asia and the Pacific (ESCAP) in 2018, it was found, however, that in Southeast Asia, there was regression at least in regard to 2 Goals—Goal 10 on inequality and Goal 16 on peace and justice—this being much linked with human rights.[62] This has to be set against the background of the more recent challenge of COVID-19 and its severe repercussions. The UN ESCAP report for 2019, for example, finds failings in regard to the fulfilment of the whole range of SDGs.[63]

3. Development and Environment:

Two other aspects deserve note: the right to development and the emerging environmental storm. With regard to the former, that right has been espoused actively by some Asian countries, and it is found in the ASEAN Human Rights Declaration below. Yet, there has been a tendency by some Asian countries to view that right from the angle of economic, social and cultural development rather than from a more holistic angle including political development. Thus, the stipulations from the UNGA Resolution on the Right to Development "all human rights" in its Article 1 should not be forgotten.[64] A key angle which needs underlining is vulnerabilities affecting women, often linked with discrimination and violence, as in Article 8 of the resolution on the Right to Development, and the quest for equity as part of social justice, particularly to overcome disparities and spread wealth and other resources.

On the environmental front, many Asian countries have participated well in multilateral environmental protection treaties, but there is the challenge of implementation which is essential in a sustained inter-generational process. Accession by Asian countries to the Paris Agreement on Climate Change targeting the cap on global warming at not more than 2 degree celsius (and hopefully less), with each State committing to nationally determined contributions, is shown in the Table G.1 in Appendix G. Some forty (plus) Asian countries are parties thereto, which shows a constructive record, although tested by the need for effective implementation.

---

[62] https://www.unescap.org/sites/default/files/publications/ESCAP_Asia_and_the_Pacific_SDG_Progress_Report_2019.pdf; https://www.unescap.org/sites/default/files/publications/ESCAP_Asia_and_the_Pacific_SDG_Progress_Report_2020.pdf.

[63] ESCAP, *Asia and the Pacific SDG Progress Report 2019* (Bangkok: ESCAP, 2020), p. 2. https://www.unescap.org/sites/default/files/publications/ESCAP_Asia_and_the_Pacific_SDG_Progress_Report_2019.pdf.

[64] Declaration on the Right to Development adopted by General Assembly resolution 41/128 of 4 December 1986. https://www.ohchr.org/en/professionalinterest/pages/righttodevelopment.aspx accessed 20 Jan 2021.

4. Implications of COVID-19:

The pandemic sheds a new light on the face of human rights in the region. It is wreaking havoc on many fronts, especially in the economic, social and cultural domain for the following reasons.[65] First, access to health care is being tested to the limit with the spread of the disease, with the poor and marginalized relegated to the periphery in many settings. Second, there is the socio-economic impact in terms of increased poverty and loss of jobs, especially for those in the informal sector and those who earn their living on a daily basis. The return of jobs is but a distant future which requires much effort from the authorities to provide social support in the meantime, pending regeneration of the economy.

Third, there is the issue of protection for vulnerable groups; that vulnerability is being compounded by the pandemic. For instance, migrant workers are generally not covered by the social support schemes which countries are offering to their own nationals to mitigate the impact of the pandemic. There is the issue of intersectionality in that people suffer because of several vulnerabilities which may lead to multiple forms of discrimination or violence, for instance, women migrant workers who lose their jobs or women refugees might be threatened more easily by criminal elements involved in trafficking and exploitation. The social plight is aggravated by the constraints imposed in the political domain, such as closed borders, lockdowns, quarantine, curfews and constraints on expression and assembly. All of this is enmeshed with States' invocation of national security and public health which are well nigh impossible to question. The impact of the pandemic on civil and political rights should thus not be underestimated. In all countries, there has been much accumulation of power in the Executive branch of the Government, at times with a weakening of checks and balances against abuse of power.

Instruments/Mechanisms

What of human rights instruments and mechanisms from the Asian region, including on a smaller scale in terms of the various corners of the vast continent? The latter could perhaps be called "subregional". This is set against the backdrop of the lack of an Asian-wide intergovernmental human rights system, unlike in Europe, Africa and the Americas.[66]

At the subregional level, there are a variety of entry points and two will be singled out—Southeast Asia and West Asia, or the ASEAN (sub)region and the Arab (West Asia) (sub) region. Naturally, they have to be tested from the angle of their value added as well as from the perspective of whether they are congruent with international standards.

---

[65] https://www.un.org/sites/un2.un.org/files/sg_report_socio-economic_impact_of_covid19.pdf; https://www.un.org/sites/un2.un.org/files/sg_policy_brief_on_people_on_the_move.pdf accessed 26 August 2020.

[66] https://sur.conectas.org/en/schematic-comparison-regional-human-rights-systems/.

(1) ASEAN Instruments and Mechanisms

Numerous instruments and mechanisms have emerged from ASEAN. The main instrument is the ASEAN Human Rights Declaration 2012, reviewed below. This is coupled with the only Convention from the subregion interlinked with human rights: the ASEAN Convention against human trafficking discussed below. As for mechanisms, ASEAN now has the ASEAN Intergovernmental Commission on Human Rights (AICHR) as well as a sectoral body on women and children: the ASEAN Commission on the Rights of Women and Children (ACWC). There is also a body that deals with cooperation on migrant workers, but this is more of a bureaucratic liaison than a mechanism to protect human rights.

i. ASEAN Human Rights Declaration (AHRD)[67]

One of the first tasks of the AICHR after its establishment was to draft the AHRD, as this had been envisioned by its Terms of Reference (TOR). The Declaration was adopted in 2012, and it consists of 40 articles, structured as follows: general principles; civil and political rights; economic, social and cultural rights; right to development; right to peace; cooperation in the promotion and protection of human rights. It has some innovative elements, such as the call to protect persons with HIV/AIDS, and advocacy of the right to development and peace. These elements complement and may help to elevate international standards, if well implemented.

However, parts of the AHRD have been heavily criticized by analysts as not being consistent with international standards. The stumbling blocks include the appearance of regional particularities in the text which might undermine universally recognized human rights. These include the overt mentioning of "duties/obligations" (of persons) instead of paramount emphasis on human rights, and reference to "national and regional context" which might override universal standards, with components of cultural relativism.[68] The ominous shadow of the latter is found particularly in the wording in the General Principles: Principle 7:

'All human rights are universal, indivisible, interdependent and interrelated. All human rights and fundamental freedoms in this Declaration must be treated in a fair and equal manner, on the same footing and with the same emphasis. At the same time, the realization of human rights must be considered in the regional and national context bearing in mind different political, economic, legal, social, cultural, historical and religious backgrounds.'[69]

There are also omissions of various internationally guaranteed rights, particularly the right to freedom of association; overly broad limitations on human rights in the guise of "morality"; emphasis on "non-confrontation" which interplays with the ASEAN governmental attachment to national sovereignty and their claim that human rights-related action should not interfere in the internal affairs of States; and subjection of human rights, particularly the right to seek asylum, to national law

[67] https://www.asean.org/storage/images/ASEAN_RTK_2014/6_AHRD_Booklet.pdf accessed 2 September 2020.

[68] Ibid.

[69] Ibid.

(bearing in mind that most ASEAN States are not parties to the international refugee agreements).[70]

Problems concerning the text were borne out by the fact that the ASEAN leaders had to issue the Phnom Penh Statement[71] in 2012 to accompany the AHRD, underlining that implementation of the latter had to be in accordance with international standards, cited below.

ii. ASEAN Convention against Trafficking in Persons, especially Women and Children (ACTIP)

The only Convention or Treaty emerging from the ASEAN with bearing on human rights, to date, is the ACTIP 2015 (accompanied by its ASEAN Plan of Action).[72] While it is an anti-crime instrument, the elements of protection and recovery offered to victims invite a human-rights-oriented approach. The provisions of this regional Convention underline a broad definition of human trafficking based on "exploitation", the need for criminalization of the trafficking, criminalization of related money-laundering, obstruction of justice and corruption, possible universal jurisdiction, prevention measures, cross-border cooperation, protection of victims such as measures on victim identification, medical and other assistance, safety of return, effective law enforcement, confiscation of assets of the culprits, mutual legal assistance and cooperation.

While more commitment to help victims of human trafficking is welcome, it is important to note that the ACTIP itself omits the issue of refugee protection which is covered by the international treaty on human trafficking—The Protocol to Prevent, Suppress and Punish Trafficking in Persons, especially Women and Children (Palermo Protocol) attached to the UN Convention against Transnational Organized Crime,[73] to which most ASEAN countries are parties. There is a large number of other Declarations and Plans of Action with bearing on human rights.[74]

iii. AICHR and ACWC

The idea for a regional human rights mechanism, supported by Governments, was sown by the Foreign Ministers of the ASEAN after the 1993 World Conference on Human Rights held in Vienna. The Ministers issued a communiqué indicating the possibility of establishing an "appropriate regional mechanism on human rights".[75]

---

[70]Ibid.

[71]Ibid.

[72]https://asean.org/asean-convention-against-trafficking-in-persons-especially-women-and-children/ accessed 2 September 2020.

[73]https://www.ohchr.org/EN/ProfessionalInterest/Pages/ProtocolTraffickingInPersons.aspx.

[74]Vitit Muntarbhorn, 'ASEAN Instruments and Mechanisms as Pathways to Human Rights Protection?', in FORUM ASIA, *A Decade in Review: Assessing the Performance of the ASEAN Intergovernmental Commission on Human Rights (Volume 2)* (Bangkok/Jakarta: Forum Asia, 2019), pp. 25–35. https://www.forum-asia.org/uploads/wp/2019/10/AICHR10vol2FA.pdf.develop strategies for the promotion.

[75]https://www.bic.moe.go.th/images/stories/AICHR_What_you_need_to_Know_ASEAN_50th_Anniversary_Edition_A_Compendium.pdf accessed 26 August 2020.

However, the issue was not taken up seriously for many years. In the mid-1990s, it was the non-governmental sector which pressed hard for a regional mechanism, voicing various possibilities, ranging from a regional Commission to a regional human rights court, or simply a network of human rights activities. The approach then and now has been to see the regional mechanism as a necessity and not as a substitute for effective national mechanisms. Both are needed, and both have their value added. At the end of the 1990s, the Working Group for an ASEAN human rights mechanism, a civil society group, even drafted a document which it then submitted to the ASEAN Foreign Ministers laying down the details of a possible regional mechanism—an ASEAN human rights commission.[76]

There was a lull until the adoption of the ASEAN Charter (effectively the mini-Constitution for the region) in 2007. The more enlightened drafters of that Charter inserted into its provisions the setting up of a regional human rights "body".[77] A high-level panel was then constituted to draft the Terms of Reference (TOR) for the entity, and this resulted in the formation of the AICHR in 2009.[78]

The following are its stipulated functions, as in the Box below, covering mainly promotion activities.

Box 5.3 Functions of AICHR

4.1. To develop strategies for the promotion and protection of human rights and fundamental freedoms to complement the building of the ASEAN community;

4.2. To develop an ASEAN Human Rights Declaration with a view to establishing a framework for human rights cooperation through various ASEAN conventions and other instruments dealing with human rights.

4.3. To enhance public awareness of human rights among the peoples of ASEAN through education, research and dissemination of information;

4.4. To promote capacity building for the effective implementation of international human rights treaty obligations undertaken by ASEAN Member States;

4.5. To encourage ASEAN Member States to consider acceding to and ratifying international human rights instruments;

4.6. To promote the full implementation of ASEAN instruments related to human rights;

4.7. To provide advisory services and technical assistance on human rights matters to ASEAN sectoral bodies upon request;

---

[76] http://aseanhrmech.org/publications/index.html.

[77] https://asean.org/wp-content/uploads/images/archive/publications/ASEAN-Charter.pdf.

[78] https://www.asean.org/storage/images/archive/publications/TOR-of-AICHR.pdf accessed 26 August 2020.

4.8. To encourage in dialogue and consultation with other ASEAN bodies and entities associated with ASEAN, including civil society organizations and other stakeholders, as provided for in Chapter V of the ASEAN Charter;

4.9. To consult, as may be appropriate, with other national, regional and international institutions and entities concerned with the promotion and protection of human rights;

4.10. To obtain information from ASEAN Member States on the promotion and protection of human rights;

4.11. To develop common approaches and positions on human rights matters of interest to ASEAN;

4.12. To prepare studies on thematic issues of human rights in ASEAN;

4.13. To submit an annual report on its activities, or other reports deemed necessary, to the ASEAN Foreign Ministers Meeting, and

4.14. To perform any other tasks as may be assigned to it by the ASEAN Foreign Ministers Meeting.

Source: https://www.asean.org/storage/images/archive/publications/TOR-of-AICHR.pdf.

The members of the Commission (numbering one per State) are "representatives" rather than independent experts. They meet several times annually (at least twice) and may also engage in consultations with other actors per the TOR. Their three year term of office is renewable once.

In form, the underlying rationale of the body is to promote and protect human rights. However, there is no explicit provision for a protection role in the sense of undertaking investigations, receiving complaints/communications/petitions from those affected negatively by the human rights situation, making findings of violations, and offering remedies, especially where the national system is unable or unwilling to act.[79] Since its inception, in substance, the Commission has thus been more involved with promotion-related activities, e.g. conferences and studies, coupled with the current orientation towards more standard setting rather than addressing human rights issues from a protection angle. This is one of the key challenges for review of its functions projected for 2020 (which has yet to take place in 2021).

Its principal product is the ASEAN HRD. Problems concerning the text were borne out by the fact that the ASEAN leaders had to issue the Phnom Penh Statement in 2012 to accompany the AHRD, underlining that implementation of the latter had to be in accordance with international standards and reaffirming the Universal Declaration of Human Rights, the Vienna Documents and the human rights treaties (instruments) as follows:

---

[79] Muntarbhorn, *supra* note 74.

'1. ADOPT the ASEAN Human Rights Declaration (AHRD);

2. AFFIRM our commitment to the full implementation of the AHRD to advance the promotion and protection of human rights in the region; and

3. REAFFIRM further our commitment to ensure that the implementation of the AHRD be in accordance with our commitment to the Charter of the United Nations, the Universal Declaration of Human Rights, the Vienna Declaration and Program of Action, and other international human rights instruments to which ASEAN Member States are parties, as well as to relevant ASEAN declarations and instruments pertaining to human rights.'[80]

That commitment to international standards is to cushion against the regressive impact of the AHRD. An example of how the AHRD is of a lower standard than international standards is that there is no stipulation of the right to freedom of association in the AHRD. The threat of "particularities" inherent in the AHRD also looms to dilute international standards, as noted earlier.

From AICHR's current Workplan,[81] the directions are increasingly clear: AICHR will undertake more promotion-related activities (e.g. more information sharing, discourse, training and conferencing), more capacity building for itself and with its partners, more research and study for reflection and self-reflection, singling out themes rather than countries and more standard setting, possibly with more ASEAN declarations and treaties. These are all cooperative activities, based on the ASEAN praxis of consensus—building, avoiding confrontation as part of the governmental "ASEAN way."

On another front, the ACWC came into existence just after the AICHR although the seeds for its establishment date back to an earlier commitment through an Action Programme adopted by ASEAN leaders in Vientiane in 2004.[82] The purposes and functions of the ACWC are stated as in its TOR to promote and protect human rights of women and children, interlinked directly with various international instruments such as the CEDAW and CRC.[83] Perhaps, the most important activity undertaken by the ACWC, to date, has been the push for The Declaration on the Elimination of Violence Against Women and Elimination of Violence Against Children in ASEAN, with plans of action for strengthening implementation measures, in 2013[84]. While this Committee has also been involved in many promotion-related activities, such as through training sessions and seminars, and standard setting, it has targeted more practical programming, such as improving standards for service delivery.[85]

---

[80] *Supra* note 67.

[81] https://aichr.org/key-documents/ accessed 26 August 2020.

[82] https://www.asean.org/storage/images/archive/VAP-10th%20ASEAN%20Summit.pdf.

[83] Source: https://www.asean.org/wp-content/uploads/images/2012/Social_cultural/ACW/TOR-ACWC.pdf.

[84] https://violenceagainstchildren.un.org/sites/violenceagainstchildren.un.org/files/documents/political_declarations/east_asia_and_pacific/declaration_on_the_elimination_of_violence_against_women_and_elimination_of_violence_against_children_in_asean.pdf.

[85] https://www.asean.org/storage/images/2015/November/27th-summit/ASCC_documents/ASEAN%20Regional%20Plan%20of%20Action%20on%20Elimintation%20of%20Violence%20Against%20WomenAdopted.pdf.

(2) Arab Instruments and Mechanisms

As linked with West Asia and overlapping with another region (particularly North Africa), there is the Arab (sub)region with its own initiatives on human rights. The conceptualization of the issue can be traced to the League of Arab States (LAS) and the adoption of the Cairo Declaration on Human Rights in Islam, projecting an Islamic approach to human rights.[86] This gradually led to the Arab Charter on Human Rights, paralleled by various mechanisms—starting off with an advisory body (the Permanent Committee), followed by a treaty based monitoring body (Arab Human Rights Committee), and more recently by the establishment of a (sub)regional judicial body in the form of a Court, discussed below. The perennial question is to what extent they provide a value added rather than a platform for a culturally relativistic approach.

i. Arab Charter on Human Rights

In 1998, there appeared the first version of the Arab Charter on Human Rights. It has been adjusted by the 2004 version.[87] The Charter now has 53 articles and sets up a monitor in the form of the Arab Human Rights Committee. There are some traditional stipulations such as the right of peoples to self-determination. Some improvements, such as a provision on non-discrimination and limits on derogations, are acknowledged:

'Overall, the Charter is rightly considered an improvement to its predecessor since it includes a number of human rights which were missing in the previous one:

Broad anti-discrimination clause, including the prohibition on ground of disabilities (Article 3 (1)),

Obligation of States to take measures for effective equality, and extra measures for equality between men and women (Article 3 (3)),

Freedom to manifest religion or beliefs (Article 30); protection of minorities' cultural rights (Article 25),

Redress, compensation and rehabilitation for victims of torture or cruel treatment (Article 8 (2))

Rights to participate in public life spelled out more clearly, including freedom to form associations, etc. (Article 24),

No derogation possible for a large number of rights, for example fair trial guarantees cannot be lifted in times of emergency, including the right to challenge detention before a competent court (Articles 13, 14 (6)).'[88]

However, there are some provisions which might be seen as ambivalent and/or lower than international standards. These include the possibility of subjecting children to the death penalty, limiting several rights to citizens rather being open to all persons without discrimination, limits imposed on various political rights

---

[86] http://hrlibrary.umn.edu/instree/cairodeclaration.html accessed 26 August 2020.

[87] https://digitallibrary.un.org/record/551368?ln=fr.

[88] *The Arab Human Rights System*

Annex to the ABC of Human Rights for Development Cooperation, GIZ, pp. 2–3. https://www.institut-fuer-menschenrechte.de/fileadmin/user_upload/Publikationen/E-Info-Tool/e-info-tool_abc_of_hr_for_dev_coop_the_arab_hr-system.pdf accessed 26 August 2020.

such as freedom of expression which diverge from international standards and the constrained status of women as linked with possibly narrower religious interpretation. There are also several provisions which depend upon protection under national law (which might be substandard), and there is no procedure for communications from individuals to the Committee.[89]

Less known is that there is also the 1983 Charter of the Rights of the Arab Child which by limiting it to the Arab child excludes others who are not Arab.

'As evidenced by its title, it does not cover minority children living under the jurisdiction of Arab States, for example children of Kurdish or Amazigh background.

The Charter lays out the main rights for the Arab child including the right to be raised in a family, the right to identity and nationality, the right to education, health care and social security. To guarantee these rights, States are obliged to strengthen the legislative framework: through amending the relevant laws affecting children and comprehensive policies and programmes to benefit children's development and well-being. All measures should be guided by the best interest of the child. In 2009, the Permanent Arab Committee on Human Rights ...discussed updating the Charter.'[90]

Moreover, there is The Arab Convention on the Status of Refugees in Arab Countries 1994 which is not in force. 'The Arab League has been engaged in a process of redrafting the Convention to be consistent with international standards, in close collaboration with UN High Commissioner for Refugees. But a revised draft that went to a committee of representatives of interested Arab States in 2012 has not resurfaced.'[91]

ii. Arab Human Rights Committee and Permanent Arab Committee on Human Rights

In a role paralleling other monitoring bodies under human rights treaties, the Arab Human Rights Committee was established by the said Arab Charter. Like international treaty bodies, it receives reports from States which it then vets and after which it offers recommendations. However, there is no provision for it to take into

[89] Samples from the Charter include:

'Article 3.

3. Men and women are equal in respect of human dignity, rights and obligations within the framework of the positive discrimination established in favour of women by the Islamic Shariah, other divine laws and by applicable laws and legal instruments. Accordingly, each State party pledges to take all the requisite measures to guarantee equal opportunities and effective equality between men and women in the enjoyment of all the rights set out in this Charter....

Article 7.

Sentence of death shall not be imposed on persons under 18 years of age, unless otherwise stipulated in the laws in force at the time of the commission of the crime.

The death penalty shall not be inflicted on a pregnant woman prior to her delivery or on a nursing mother within two years from the date of her delivery; in all cases, the best interests of the infant shall be the primary consideration.' For text: *supra* note 87.

[90] *The Arab Human Rights System: Annex to the ABC of Human Rights for Development Cooperation*, *supra* note 88, p. 3.

[91] Ibid., p. 3.

account the shadow reports from civil society, and access by individuals to complain of violations (even where local remedies have been exhausted) is not provided for.[92]

En passant, it should be noted that the Arab League also has a political body—The Permanent Arab Committee on Human Rights (or as translated the Arab Human Rights Commission) to advise on human rights matters. This is an intergovernmental mechanism. There are some links with civil society and national human rights institutions.[93]

iii. **Arab Court of Human Rights**[94]

This is certainly the first judicial body of its kind on human rights in the Asian region. However, its formation has been beset with difficulties, particularly the fact that it is viewed by analysts as a body which would not be accessible to individuals and whose deliberations might diverge from universal standards due to the somewhat ethnocentric nature of the Arab Charter mentioned. The Statute establishing the Arab Court of Human Rights was completed and open for membership in 2014.[95] Its location is in Bahrain. The 7 member Court has power to address contentious proceedings as well as to give advisory opinion with this jurisdiction:

> Article 16
>
> The Jurisdiction of the Court
>
> The Court shall have jurisdiction over all suits and conflicts resulting from the implementation and interpretation of the Arab Charter of Human Rights, or any other Arab convention in the field of Human Rights involving a member State.
>
> The Court shall decide any dispute related to jurisdiction in examining suits, petitions or cases at hand.[96]

And on access:

> Article 19
>
> The Right to access the Court
>
> The State Party whose citizen claims to be a victim of a human rights violation has the right to access the Court, provided that both the claimant State and the Defendant State are party to this Statute, or they have accepted the jurisdiction of the Court as determined by Article 20 of the Statute.
>
> States Parties can accept, when ratifying or acceding to the Statute or at any time later, that one or more non-governmental organizations (NGOs) that are accredited and working in

---

[92]Ibid,. p. 4.

[93]Ibid., p. 5.

See further: Armis Sadri,' The Arab human rights system: achievements and challenges', *Int. J. Hum. Rights*, 23 (2019) 7, pp. 1166–182;

Zaid Eyadat and Hani Okasheh, 'Human Rights Mechanisms in the Arab World: Politics and Protection', in Gerd Oberleitner (ed.), *International Human Rights Institutions, Tribunals, and Courts* (Heidelberg: Springer, 2018), pp. 511–526.

[94]Mervat Rishmawi, *Proposed Arab Court of Human Rights: Rewind the process and get it right*, FIDH—International Federation for Human Rights/ICJ- International Commission of Jurists Policy Paper March 2014. https://www.fidh.org/IMG/pdf/20140320_arab_ct_pp_en.pdf.

[95]https://acihl.org/texts.htm?article_id=44&lang=ar-SA accessed 3 September 2020.

[96]Ibid.

> the field of human rights in the State whose subject claims to be a victim of a human rights violation has access to the Court.[97]

Under the Statute, it is thus open to a member State to complain against another member State on behalf of its citizen, and a select group of NGOs can also complain. However, there is no channel for individuals to complain directly. It is not difficult to surmise that access to justice for individuals will be difficult. Much is dependent upon the role of the State Party vested with the power to claim on behalf of its citizen—but this does not include non-nationals. Access to complain is only granted to accredited NGOs complaining on behalf of victims. Yet, it is uncertain whether the requirements of accreditation are too demanding and might be applied to screen out the more vocal NGOs. Moreover, all these channels are subject to the general principle of the need to exhaust local remedies. (To date, Saudi Arabia has become a party and operationalization of the Court is awaited.)[98] One could add that in the region concerned, most countries are non-democratic, adding another obstacle to any aspiration to respect and realize the international Rule of Law.

Realities

In the meantime, there is no gainsaying that it is not possible currently to depend upon regional or subregional mechanisms from the Asian region for effective human rights protection from the angle of receiving communications from individuals and civil society, and related investigations, in the quest for accessible and effective remedies. At best, some of these mechanisms offer some openings for human rights promotion, but there is not yet much room in terms of genuine human rights protection.

In sum, in the overall panorama of human rights in the region, the positive is manifested by the fact that the region has come a very long way in terms of economic development and is likely to be the lead powerhouse in the twenty-first century; it has done well on economic rights. Thus, at least outwardly and until recently, the prospects for the attainment of economic rights were good. Some countries also have high-quality social services, such as on health care, and have progressed on poverty reduction. However, this does not mean that wealth has been well shared in terms of equity. COVID-19 is an unexpected impediment which now means regression for many States and peoples in the near future. With regard to political rights, however, a longstanding problem is that many Asian countries are non-democratic, and there are major obstacles facing freedom of expression, assembly and association. Thus, at the microscopic level, the region witnesses constraints for many advocates of

---

[97] Ibid.

[98] *The Arab Human Rights System*

Annex to the ABC of Human Rights for Development Cooperation, *supra* note 88, p. 5; Konstantinos Magliveras and Gino Naldi, 'The Arab court of human rights: a study in impotence', *Revue québécoise de droit international*, 29 (2016) 2, pp. 147–172. See further: Tabet Koraytem, 'Arab Islamic Developments of Human Rights', *Arab Law Q.*, 16 (2001) 3, pp. 255–262.

human rights regrettably. A less sanguine outlook, premised on the democracy deficit, might further argue that there is quite a lot of human rights language cooptation and cosmeticization from parts of the region for national, regional and international consumption.

The study will now turn to more macroscopic matters concerning trade and commerce to assess the nexus with the Asian region and identify key lessons learned.

Chapter 6
Trade Liberalization and Inhibition

At the beginning of 2020, after a period of acerbic confrontation between the US and China—the so-called Trade War, embodying more and not less protectionism due to the imposition of major tariff increases, and other measures and countermeasures, there was a truce between the two parties.[1] Underlying the heated debate was the grievance of a big trade deficit and limited market access facing the former in relation to the latter, complaints of intellectual property violations, and competition for techno-superiority with the advent of the 5G digital revolution.[2]

In reality and collaterally, the global community had been suffering in recent years from the fallout between the two commercial superpowers which had converted the gains from convergent rules based International Law-making linked with the World Trade Organization (WTO) in the past quarter of a century into one of rattled nerves, strained relations and intransigent nationalistic/populistic policy trading inhibition rather than liberalization. Matters were aggravated by the fact that the WTO Dispute Settlement system was being prevented from functioning due to the emergence of inter-State obstacles blocking the appointment of new members to the Appellate Body under the Dispute Settlement Body (DSB)—in essence, politics inhibiting economics.

---

[1] https://thediplomat.com/2020/07/where-the-us-china-trade-war-should-go-from-here/ accessed 27 August 2020; Mari Pangestu, 'Responding to the Trade War: an ASEAN perspective' https://www.rieti.go.jp/en/events/18120601/summary.html accessed 27 August 2020.

[2] https://thediplomat.com/2020/03/how-the-us-can-compete-in-5g/; Nicol Turner Lee, Navigating the US-China 5 G Competition, April 2020. https://www.brookings.edu/wp-content/uploads/2020/04/FP_20200427_5g_competition_turner_lee_v2.pdf accessed 27 August 2020.

V. Muntarbhorn, *Challenges of International Law in the Asian Region*,
https://doi.org/10.1007/978-981-16-2047-8_6

Despite that regression, if one looks back to the role of Asiancountries, with the birth of the WTO, there has been substantial positive participation from the region in regard to the formulation of rules on trade liberalization on several fronts, bearing in mind that States differ on how they integrate them into the national setting.[3] They have become more actively involved in their commitment to—and use of the dispute settlement mechanism, discussed later in the chapter, bringing the Rule of Law to bear on economic and global liberalization.[4] The participation of Asian countries in the liberalization process under the WTO has contributed markedly to the economic rise of the region, at the heart of globalization. This is exemplified *par excellence* by China's impressive GDP growth in recent times due to its membership of the WTO, export orientation, access to markets, favourable trade balance and the spread of its investments in many parts of the world, converting insularity into globality. Having said that, to be fair, it should not be forgotten that GDP growth does not necessarily mean that wealth is shared more equitably at the local level, unless there are effective distribution and social protection policies and practices.

This does not mean, however, that all Asiancountries have been convergent on every issue in regard to the WTO and related negotiations, nor are they without blemish. This is a natural phenomenon because trade liberalization can cover so many elements and while many countries can agree on many aspects, it would be disingenuous to believe that they have a consensus on most or all matters. In real terms, the challenging variability at the global, regional and multilateral levels cannot escape from these key drivers of trade and the quest to liberalize: goods, services, persons/workers, investment, capital. And more recently, information, communications, protection of intellectual property, trade facilitation, technology/digitalization and e-commerce. During the days of the General Agreement on Tariffs and Trade(GATT), the predecessor of the WTO, liberalization was more about goods. The forward advance of the WTO has been to encompass goods and services, and intellectual property, with services and intellectual property emerging at the same time, followed by other cogs in the wheel of trade. Intriguingly, that liberalization has not covered the freedom of movement of workers, though skilled workers have to some extent benefited from the liberalization of services. Nor does the WTO have rules on investment generally.

In reality, there have been lapses at the national level particularly in regard to intellectual property protection, as seen in some cases below, as well as hidden distortions and protectionism despite the WTO rules. Environmental and labour rights issues are only dealt with cursorily in the WTO context, and the coverage and importance

[3]Jean-Pierre Lehmann, 'Asian Approaches to the International Trade System', in IFRI, *The Asian Century*, (Paris: IFRI, 2014), pp. 55–60; Thomas Cotler, 'The Role of Domestic Courts in the Implementation of WTO Law. The Political Economy of Separation of Powers and Checks and Balances in International Trade Regulation', in Amrita Narlikar, Martin Daunton, and Robert M. Stern (eds.), *The Oxford Handbook on the World Trade Organization* (Oxford: OUP, 2012), pp. 607–631.

[4]Dukgeun Ahn, 'WTO Dispute Settlements in East Asia', in Takatoshi Ito and Andrew K. Rose (eds.), *International Trade in East Asia*, NBER-East Asia Seminar on Economics, Vol. 14 (Chicago and London: University of Chicago Press, 2005), pp. 287–327.

of International Law beyond WTO rules, such as environmental treaties and labour rights and human rights treaties, should not be underestimated to fill in gaps in the spectrum of trade and commerce.

At this juncture, it may be asked: where have Asian countries converged most, thus providing a contribution to trade liberalization? And conversely, where least (or less so)?

Engagement

Asia's engagement with the global liberalization can be seen as follows:

(a) **Values and Rules**

One can observe that the idea or values of free or freer trade also had its origins in the Asian region, embellished by the romance of the Silk Road:

'Likewise, in the Tang Dynasty (AD 618–907), trade with foreign kingdoms expanded dramatically so much so that many foreign traders, such as Persians and Arabs, even formed their own residential communities called fanfang ('barbarian districts') in large cities. Functioning as 'nodes of trade diasporas', these communities networked with their home producers and channelled foreign products into local markets in China. The Tang Dynasty allowed these communities to self-govern in accordance with their own cultural and religious customs. In this accommodating environment, foreign commerce, in the form of both trade and investment, flourished in ancient China.'[5]

An interesting conjecture is also that some situations involving the Asian region have provided an avenue to emphasize the human face behind the trade which should not be forgotten.[6] Asian States have been agreeable to the basic precepts and concepts of free trade posited by the GATT and developed by the formation of the WTO through the various accords adopted at the end of the Uruguay Round of Trade Negotiations in Marrakesh, particularly the principles of Most Favoured Nation Treatment (MFN) and National Treatment, both based on non-discrimination between countries.[7] The former implies that a favour granted to one country must also be enjoyed by other members of the WTO. The latter implies that imports and local products must be treated equally. Another important rule is that customs tariffs rates should be capped (not to be increased) and countries are required to pledge to "bindings" to ensure predictability and certainty in their trade relations. In the meantime, hidden impediments to trade should also be made more transparent, such as in agriculture, by converting them into tariffs—tariffication. One can add that the spirit of the WTO is to do away with tariffs altogether.

[5]Sungjoon Cho and Jürgen Kurtz, 'Convergence and Divergence in International Economic Law and Politics', *EJIL*, 29 (2018) 1, pp. 169–203; 172.

[6]Ibid., p. 187.

[7]https://www.wto.org/english/thewto_e/whatis_e/tif_e/fact2_e.htm accessed 27 August 2020.

The complex range of instruments on which countries have converged leading up to and from Marrakesh consists of some 60 agreements and other documents with a general agreement establishing the WTO and agreements in relation to three main areas on goods, services and intellectual property, dispute settlement and trade policy review.[8] The main WTO agreements are seen in the Box below.

Box 6.1 WTO Agreements (Particularly Those Resulting from the Uruguay Round of Negotiations Culminating in Marrakesh 1994) '

- Marrakesh Declaration of 15 April 1994
- Final Act
- Agreement Establishing the World Trade Organization

Annex 1

Annex 1A Multilateral Agreements on Trade in Goods

- GATT 1994
  - Must be read with GATT 1947
  - Other duties and charges (GATT Article II:l(b)), Understanding
  - State trading enterprises (GATT Article XVII), Understanding
  - Balance-of-payments, Understanding
  - Regional trade agreements (GATT Article XXIV)
  - Waivers of Obligations, Understanding
  - Concession withdrawal (GATT Article XXVIII), Understanding
  - Marrakesh Protocol to the GATT 1994
- Agriculture
- Sanitary and Phytosanitary Measures
- Textiles and Clothing (NB: this Agreement was terminated on 1 January 2005)
- Technical Barriers to Trade
- Trade-Related Investment Measures (TRIMs)
- Anti-dumping (Article VI of GATT 1994)
- Customs valuation (Article VII of GATT 1994)
- Preshipment Inspection
- Rules of Origin
- Import Licensing
- Subsidies and Countervailing Measures
- Safeguards
- Trade facilitation

[8] https://www.wto.org/english/thewto_e/whatis_e/tif_e/agrm1_e.htm accessed 27 August 2020.

Annex 1B General Agreement on Trade in Services (GATS)

Annex 1C Trade-Related Aspects of Intellectual Property Rights (TRIPS) (unamended version)

TRIPS Agreement (as amended on 23 January 2017) Annex 2

- Annex 2 Dispute Settlement Understanding

Annex 3

- Annex 3 Trade Policy Review Mechanism

Annex 4 Plurilateral Trade Agreements

- Annex 4(a) Agreement on Trade in Civil Aircraft
- Annex 4(b) Agreement on Government Procurement
  - Government Procurement Agreement (GPA) 1994
  - Revised GPA
- Annex 4(c) International Dairy Agreement
- (NB: this Agreement was terminated end 1997)
- Annex 4(d) International Bovine Meat Agreement
- (NB: this Agreement was terminated end 1997) '

Source: Derived from https://www.wto.org/english/docs_e/legal_e/legal_e.htm.

(b) Rules-based Open Multilateralism

There has been much Asian participation in formulating the rules, setting up and growing with the WTO, and building the International Law regime underpinned by those rules and institutional progression. Today, a large number of countries from the region are parties to WTO treaties and participate at the periodic Ministerial meetings where key decisions are adopted. There have also been innovative ways of involving some parts of the Asian region in that participation without being inhibited by the fact that they might not be recognized or recognized fully as States under International Law and relations. Classic situations include Chinese Taipei, Hong Kong/China and Macao/China which are parties to the WTO system in their capacity as customs areas. However, some key Asian countries are not yet parties to the WTO, for instance, Iran and Iraq. When China joined, it was ready to abide by more exigent conditions of entry which were not reciprocal, indicating the importance of trade liberalization through the WTO to the applicant.[9]

[9] 'How China swallowed the WTO'. https://www.wsj.com/articles/how-china-swallowed-the-wto-1509551308 accessed 27 August 2020; S. Mehdi Shafaeddin, 'Some implications of accession to WTO for China's economy', *Int. J. Dev. Issues*, 1 (2002) 2, pp. 93–128.

In regard to the decades of trade negotiations, Asian countries participated well, while admittedly having different positions on some issues, such as agriculture, in the 9 Rounds, most recently with the Doha Round-Doha Development Agenda. This boded well for multilateralism, even though the future is less certain and there is likely to be a shift to a less ambitious framework such as through plurilateral arrangements with fewer participants. *En passant*, there is a difference between multilateral agreements which are negotiated and adopted on the basis that they cover all the member countries of the WTO and plurilateral agreements which cover only the (select) countries that choose to interconnect with them.

(c) Flexibilities

From the GATT to the WTO, the rules stipulated already admit various exceptions which attest to a measure of flexibility which is integrated into the whole system. Most directly, there are the exceptions stated in Articles XX of the GATT, such as possible restrictions to help protect under proviso (a) on 'Public morals", provision (b) on "human, animal or plant life or health" and on proviso g) on the environment {"exhaustible natural resources"}.[10] Many cases on this Article have appeared before the Dispute Settlement Body (DSB) of the WTO, and some are discussed later. Article XIV of GATT also admits various exceptions to the principle of non-discrimination, for instance, where the application of exceptions gives rise the benefits which outweigh the injury incurred. The issue of flexibility is now exemplified by the TRIPS agreement. For instance, there is a provision enabling flexible relations with least developed countries, per its Article 66.[11] In reality, there is a whole range of flexibilities[12] inherent to the TRIPS ranging from standards of protection to enforcement.[13]

The most famous is the flexibility justifying compulsory licensing which enables countries to use a patent, even without the consent of the patent owner, to produce drugs to respond to a pandemic. This was advanced to cover other situations of extreme urgency (not simply emergencies) by the Doha Declaration on the TRIPS Agreement and public health 2001, per its Article 5, the most obvious cases for coverage being "public health crises, including those relating to HIV/AIDS, tuberculosis, malaria and other epidemics".[14] There is the TRIPS Council which helps to oversee the issue.[15] Initially, the provision on this issue in the TRIPS allowed compulsory licensing to produce for local consumption, but this has now been extended by a Protocol to enable export to other countries in need.[16]

---

[10] https://www.wto.org/english/res_e/booksp_e/gatt_ai_e/art20_e.pdf.

[11] https://www.wto.org/english/res_e/publications_e/ai17_e/trips_art66_oth.pdf.

[12] Carlos M Correa, 'Flexibilities provided by the Agreement on Trade-Related Aspects of Intellectual Property Rights', *Bull. World Health Organ.*, 96 (2018) 3, pp. 148–148A.

[13] https://www.wipo.int/ip-development/en/policy/flexibilities.html.

[14] https://www.wto.org/english/thewto_e/minist_e/min01_e/mindecl_trips_e.htm. http://www.cptech.org/ip/wto/doha/overview.html accessed 27 August 2020.

[15] https://www.wto.org/english/tratop_e/trips_e/tripsfacsheet_e.htm.

[16] https://www.wto.org/english/news_e/news17_e/trip_23jan17_e.htm accessed 25 July 2020.

Asiancountries have been favourable to flexibilities for and concessions to developing countries on intellectual property, particularly on medicines/drugs. Thailand and India have led the way by applying TRIPS flexibilities to make generic medicines/drugs more accessible and less expensive, particularly in regard to the HIV/AIDS epidemic, through compulsory licensing.[17] While the possibility of this measure is part of the TRIPS agreement, initially, there was hesitation to use such flexibility for fear of countermeasures from the developing countries housing those companies which own the original patents to the relevant drugs. Yet, progressively countries in Asia became more daring in their approach to use such licensing, while developed countries housing those patents became more accommodating to respect those flexibilities as a reality, without resorting to countermeasures.[18]

To be fair, there are conditions attached before use without consent of the patent owner is allowed by the TRIPS. The party seeking to use the compulsory licence should make an effort to contact the patent owner to get authorization before resorting to the licence. The licence is only for temporary use, and it is non-exclusive. Moreover, the user under the compulsory licence is bound to pay the owner for its economic value per Article 31 of the TRIPS.[19]

In addition, the Doha Declaration opened the door for the "TRIPS waiver" to enable countries, through compulsory licensing, to export to countries in times of need generic pharmaceutical products made under compulsory licences, with an arrangement in 2003.[20] The export–import-related concession was later formalized into a treaty in the form of the Protocol to the TRIPS agreement, and this was motivated in large part by the use of compulsory licensing by Asian countries such as Thailand and India, together with some other key players such as South Africa and Brazil. There remains the issue of extension of the TRIPS moratorium. The latter has been a way of avoiding/suspending application of one of the rules of the WTO which may disadvantage developing and other countries, namely the possibility of using a "non violation complaint".[21] This complaint can take place against a country even where there is no breach of an agreement. It is premised on the trigger reasoning 'where a WTO member believes that the actions of another member deprived it of an expected benefit'.[22]

---

[17]https://www.wto.org/english/tratop_e/trips_e/amendment_e.htm.

[18]Re Compulsory licensing: Keith E. Markus, 'Trade Related Intellectual Property Rights', in *The Oxford Handbook on the WTO*, *supra* note 1, pp. 394–419; 404–405.

[19]For text, see: https://www.wto.org/english/docs_e/legal_e/27-trips_01_e.htm; https://www.wto.org/english/docs_e/legal_e/27-trips.pdf.

[20]For text see: https://www.wto.org/english/tratop_e/trips_e/factsheet_pharm02_e.htm#art31). See further: Markus, *supra* note 18, p. 406.

[21]https://www.wto.org/english/tratop_e/trips_e/nonviolation_background_e.htm accessed 27 August 2020.

[22]https://www.wto.org/english/thewto_e/minist_e/mc11_e/briefing_notes_e/bftrips_e.htm accessed 27 August 2020.

(d) **Special and Differential treatment**

Many Asian countries are developing countries, and they are favourable to concessions to developing countries to help them adjust to WTO treaties and measures. Thus, WTO Agreements integrate the notion of special and differential treatment to help them adapt though a variety of ways and means.[23] An important aspect of special and differential treatment is in the form of tariff reductions and other allowances (especially for industrial goods and agricultural goods) under the Generalized System of Preferences (GSP) by which developed countries provide unilateral (non-reciprocal) concessions to developing countries. This is attributed to the GATT/WTO's "enabling clause" based on a Decision in 1979 which has been used extensively by developed countries and regional organizations, such as the EU, to liberalize market access to various products from developing countries.[24]

(e) **Developing Countries: SDGs and Aid for Trade**

The WTO has opened up more to developing countries through the SDGs and Aid for Trade.

– **SDGS**

The SDGs consist of 17 Goals to be implemented from 2015 till 2020, and Asian countries have been favourable to them.[25] Some of them touch upon trade issues directly, for instance, SDG 17.12 which advocates duty-free and quota-free market access on a lasting basis for all least developed countries, with WTO rules and liberalization of rules of origin as part of the trade preferences.[26] They offer new grounds to the WTO to broaden its work and access to sustainable development. This is an opportunity which should not be downplayed at a time when the more rules based dispute settlement role of the Organization is in difficulties. It also provides a softer edge to the role of trade, not as an end in itself but as vehicle to foster sustainable development whose centrality must be the well-being of humans and respect for nature.

With regard to the most recent Ministerial meeting In Buenos Aires, there was more emphasis on women's participation, development measures linked with SDGs and an opening to address and overcome fisheries subsidies.[27] The understanding since the Nairobi Ministerial meeting, discussed below, preceding that of Buenos Aires and concluding with a successful start to address the issue of elimination of export subsidies on agriculture (while encompassing other key issues such as food security), has been that the Doha Round of negotiations anchored in multilateralism and multilateral agreements is perhaps moribund, and there might be a move

[23] https://www.wto.org/english/tratop_e/devel_e/dev_special_differential_provisions_e.htm.

[24] https://www.wto.org/english/tratop_e/devel_e/dev_special_differential_provisions_e.htm#:~:text=The%20mandate,them%20more%20effective%20and%20operational.

[25] https://www.un.org/sustainabledevelopment/sustainable-development-goals/ accessed 27 August 2020.

[26] https://www.un.org/sustainabledevelopment/sustainable-development-goals/.

[27] https://www.wto.org/english/tratop_e/rulesneg_e/fish_e/fish_e.htm accessed 27 August 2020.

towards other interrelationships.[28] These issues will be followed up at the Kazakhstan Ministerial Meeting projected for 2020, now postponed because of the COVID-19 pandemic.

– AID for TRADE

This measure is a way of channelling aid to poorer countries to stimulate trade, and it is also supported by Asian countries. It has key implications for micro-, small- and medium-scale industries particularly on the supply side and offers an avenue for more gender-sensitive commitments. It is a part of SDG Goal 8 mentioned earlier. The notion of Aid for Trade does not establish commitments as such, but it acts as a means for fostering trade.

This observation is of note: 'Aid for Trade helps developing countries, and particularly least developed countries, trade. Many developing countries face a range of supply-side and trade-related infrastructure obstacles which constrains their ability to engage in international trade.'[29]

There is a natural link in terms of how aid can encourage trade, especially for developing countries, with the entry point being small- and medium-scale industries, aiming for more diversification and an inclusive approach.[30] All this is now tempered by the advent of and devastation caused by COVID-19.

(f) Trade facilitation

One Agreement which has enjoyed much support from Asian countries (and others) is the Agreement on Trade Facilitation which, in essence, helps to reduce bureaucratic red tape and ease the passage of goods through customs.[31] Interestingly, this Agreement also has a provision on special and differential treatment for developing and least developed countries.[32] While the above is a convergent instrument for Asian countries when it was adopted at the Bali Ministerial meeting, it should be noted that India had its own position which was not part of the consensus. Its preoccupation with food security was better reflected in the later Ministerial Meeting in Nairobi.[33]

(g) Trade policy review (TPR)

This is a Review process/mechanism of a country's record among peers and is motivated by the quest for transparency.[34] Interestingly, the TPR can cover even some

---

[28]https://www.ft.com/content/9cb1ab9e-a7e2-11e5-955c-1e1d6de94879; https://www.wto.org/english/res_e/booksp_e/historywto_12_e.pdf accessed 27 August 2020.

[29]https://www.wto.org/english/tratop_e/devel_e/a4t_e/aid4trade_e.htm accessed 27 August 2020.

[30]Ibid.

[31]https://www.wto.org/english/tratop_e/tradfa_e/tradfa_e.htm accessed 27 August 2020.

[32]https://www.wto.org/english/tratop_e/tradfa_e/tradfatheagreement_e.htm.

[33]https://www.wto.org/english/thewto_e/minist_e/mc10_e/briefing_notes_e/brief_agriculture_e.htm accessed 27 August 2020.

[34]https://www.wto.org/english/thewto_e/whatis_e/tif_e/fact2_e.htm accessed 19 January 2020. See further: https://www.wto.org/english/tratop_e/tpr_e/tprm30_e.htm.

areas not covered by WTO treaties, e.g. competitionpolicy. It is based on encouragement rather than critique and offers a platform where national highlights can be shared at the multilateral level.

A recent review of Bangladesh's record exemplifies and illustrates the functioning of the review system which in addition to recognizing the strong economic growth of the country also raised issues of 'climate change vulnerability, efforts at improving workers' safety, diversification of the economy, policies to encourage privatization, expansion of special economic zones, power generation capacity, transport infrastructure development, regulatory guidelines for pharmaceuticals and medical devices, support to the textiles sector, development of the Information, Communications and Technology (ICT) sector, liberalization of trade in services and challenges to the banking sector'.[35]

Ambivalence

Where have Asian countries converged less, thus making trade liberalization more challenging, with inhibitions regrettably protruding? The following entry points deserve note:

(a) **Intellectual Property (IP) and its enforcement**

While some Asian countries have been strict in enforcing IP law and rights, a number of countries have been faced with a struggle to enforce the law based on the TRIPS. Implementation through effective national laws and measures is an inevitable expectation and part of international pressure for accountability. This has led to the adoption of new laws and measures by many Asian countries to afford more protection to intellectual property rights. Where they fail to do so, there is the possibility of resort to the WTO DSB and there have been key decisions from the Panel and the Appellate Body calling for effective coverage of intellectual property in accordance with international standards. The later section on dispute resolution indicates some of the trends.

(b) **Transparency**

The transparency test interrelates with a host of issues linked with trade: (hidden State enterprise) subsidies, Government/public procurement, competition, investment, national treatment, bilateral/regional Free Trade Area (FTA) which might be weak on equity.[36]

[35]CONCLUDING REMARKS BY THE CHAIRPERSON. WT/TPR/M/385 (29 May 2019) (Bangladesh 2019). https://docs.wto.org/dol2fe/Pages/FE_Search/FE_S_S006.aspx?DataSource=Cat&Query=@MeetingId=159129&Language=English&Context=ScriptedSearches&languageUIChanged=true.

[36]ILO, *Social Dimensions of Free Trade Agreements* (Geneva: ILO, 2013). https://www.ilo.org/wcmsp5/groups/public/---dgreports/---inst/documents/publication/wcms_228965.pdf accessed 27 August 2020.

Cases concerning State enterprises have proved difficult under the WTO, and discontent with the situation may have more than economic consequences in terms of a backlash. On government procurement, there is a WTO plurilateral agreement attempting to render the situation more transparent.[37] However, key Asian countries have not joined the agreement.

There are other issues which are not yet covered by WTO rules and which are linked with the question of transparency, e.g. competition. It may be added that while the GATT/WTO opened the door to regional FTAs on the basis of Article XXIV whereby they are supposed to provide a value added, there has only been limited vetting by the WTO on whether they comply with WTO rules and prove that they provide benefits for the concerned regions without discriminating against non-members.

(c) **Agriculture**

This is an issue where there is no common or homogeneous position from the Asianregion. It has been one of the most difficult areas of negotiation.[38] There is differentiation between some of the more developed Asian countries, on the one hand, and developing Asian countries, on the other hand, in regard to agriculture and the issue of subsidies. Especially if they are not agricultural communities, the former are likely to be more interested in the liberalization of services and technological sector (now e-commerce), and they are less entangled with the question of developing countries' dependence on agriculture. The latter—developing countries from Asia—are open to maintaining subsidies for their own produce but are concerned about subsidies in developed countries which might lead to excessive imports affecting negatively local produce and markets. In recent years, they have also been more vocal on safeguarding food security which might be linked with subsidizing local produce.

In terms of evolution, the agricultural lobby has mutated from the Cairns Group of the 1990s involving some key developed countries from beyond Asia and some developing countries from Asia, advocating liberalization in regard to the trade in agricultural products, to realignments in more recent years under the G 20 (20 plus countries mixing between some developed countries, large countries from Central and South America, and sizeable Asian countries such as India, Indonesia and China) and G 33 (group of developing and least developed countries (LDCs)—more than 33 in real terms involving some of those sizeable Asian countries and a number of developing Asian countries).[39]

---

[37] https://www.wto.org/english/thewto_e/minist_e/min99_e/english/about_e/17proc_e.htm.

[38] https://www.wto.org/english/tratop_e/agric_e/negoti_e.htm.

[39] These explanations are pertinent: 'Cairns: Coalition of agricultural exporting nations lobbying for agricultural trade liberalization.

WTO members (19): Argentina, Australia, Brazil, Canada, Chile, Colombia, Costa Rica, Guatemala, Indonesia, Malaysia, New Zealand, Pakistan, Paraguay, Peru, Philippines, South Africa, Thailand, Uruguay, Viet Nam.': https://www.wto.org/english/tratop_e/agric_e/negoti_groups_e.htm accessed 27 August 2020.

The G20 wish to see reduction of subsidies in developed countries and a fairer international trade system, while the G33 wish to see not only reduction of subsidies as mentioned but also food security in developing countries and other concessions and flexibilities to help developing countries. There is the impression that the Cairns group remains intact, while the G 20 has become less cohesive. While the former seeks further liberalization and reform of the agricultural sector, G33 members are more open to extra policy space for developing countries to adopt measures which are more trade restrictive (or more trade distortive) as a part of that space.

It should not be forgotten, however, that even at the time of the Marrakesh Accords, the issue of agriculture was dealt with convergently to an extent, with the multilateral package leading to the Agreement on Agriculture. A major thrust was to convert protectionist measures into tariffs—tariffication to ensure transparency. Underlying the agreement, there were pervasive issues concerning the establishment of disciplines and limits for domestic support, and action on export subsidies to minimize distortions in the agricultural trade. These sensitive areas would need step-by-step negotiation to iron out the differences not only between developing and developed countries, but also the divide within each group—whose voices were not then nor now homogeneous. This is seen in regard to the Cairns Group and the other groups mentioned.

There would also be tariff reductions in regard to the areas listed in the agreed schedules while excluding those which are not listed thereunder. A key concern is agricultural subsidies which, on the one hand, might lead to trade distortions, but which, on the other hand, might have a social purpose, such as to safeguard food security.[40]

Even though there is no single position from Asian countries on the above, there is evidently convergence on some key areas also. This was witnessed at recent WTO Ministerial Meetings with the adoption of a multilateral package, particularly at the

---

'G 20: Coalition of developing countries pressing for ambitious reforms of agriculture in developed countries with some flexibility for developing countries (not to be confused with the G-20 group of finance ministers and central bank governors and its recent summit meetings)

WTO members (23): Argentina, Bolivia, Plurinational State of, Brazil, Chile, China, Cuba, Ecuador, Egypt, Guatemala, India, Indonesia, Mexico, Nigeria, Pakistan, Paraguay, Peru, Philippines, South Africa, Tanzania, Thailand, Uruguay, Venezuela, Bolivarian Republic of, Zimbabwe': https://www.wto.org/english/tratop_e/agric_e/negoti_groups_e.htm accessed 27 August 2020.

' G 33: Also called "Friends of Special Products" in agriculture. Coalition of developing countries pressing for flexibility for developing countries to undertake limited market opening in agriculture

WTO members (47): Antigua and Barbuda, Barbados, Belize, Benin, Bolivia, Plurinational State of, Botswana, China, Congo, Côte d'Ivoire, Cuba, Dominica, Dominican Republic, Ecuador, El Salvador, Grenada, Guatemala, Guyana, Haiti, Honduras, India, Indonesia, Jamaica, Kenya, Korea, Republic of, Madagascar, Mauritius, Mongolia, Mozambique, Nicaragua, Nigeria, Pakistan, Panama, Philippines, Saint Kitts and Nevis, Saint Lucia, Saint Vincent and the Grenadines, Senegal, Sri Lanka, Suriname, Chinese Taipei, Tanzania, Trinidad and Tobago, Turkey, Uganda, Venezuela, Bolivarian Republic of, Zambia, Zimbabwe': https://www.wto.org/english/tratop_e/agric_e/negoti_groups_e.htm accessed 27 August 2020.

[40] https://www.wto.org/english/thewto_e/whatis_e/tif_e/agrm3_e.htm accessed 27 August 2020. See further: Simon Lester, 'Is the Doha Round Over?', *Free Trade Bulletin*, 64 (February 11, 2016), pp.-1–4; 2.

Bali Ministerial Conference on adoption of the Trade Facilitation Agreement; Asian countries signed up to that instrument *en masse*. Later at the Nairobi session, there was also commitment to phase out export subsidies on agriculture while providing for food security and safeguard measures to help developing countries. The Nairobi Package offered Ministerial Decisions on agriculture, cotton and issues related to least developed countries, with a commitment to abolish export subsidies for farm exports, coupled with public provisioning for food security and preferential treatment for least developed countries in relation to services.[41]

(d) FTA and WTO plus

Thereremains a query concerning whether FTAs from the Asian region and other Pacts which include provisions going beyond WTO commitments, such as on protection of intellectual property for an even longer period than under the TRIPs ("evergreen" agreements), comply with Article XXIV of WTO which permits regional trade agreements (RTAs) such as FTAs if they offer a value added.[42] The complex relationship is linked partly to the level of transparency of these arrangements, including whether they cover substantially all trade and whether they are a hindrance to imports from third parties.[43]

It is worth stating further that some Asian countries are involved with bilateral and other arrangements on the basis of WTO Plus (going beyond the WTO-related concessions). While this can be seen as going further in liberalizing trade, other factors come into play which might lead to disadvantages for developing countries, since the negotiating power of the various sides is uneven and is not necessarily cushioned to the same extent that the multilateral checks and balances from an entity such as the WTO would provide. The issues which are certainly seen as problematic by civil society from developing countries are addressed in the later chapter on regionalism, including excessive IP protection, on the one hand, and deficient human rights and environmental protection, on the other.[44]

Aptly, one can now turn to dispute settlement in regard to some of these issues to see how Asian countries have fared. This should not underestimate, however, the disruption caused anew by COVID-19 and the fact that there will be marked recession for most countries in the next phase due to the pandemic as an unforeseen inhibition.

---

[41] The Nairobi package with its **Nairobi Ministerial Declaration** covered the following issues: Agriculture; Special Safeguard Mechanism for Developing Country Members; Public Stockholding for Food Security Purposes; Export Competition; Cotton; and Least Developed Country issues, in particular Preferential Rules of Origin for Least Developed Countries, and implementation of Preferential Treatment in Favour of Services and Service Suppliers of Least Developed Countries and Increasing LDC Participation in Services Trade. See further: https://www.wto.org/english/news_e/news15_e/mc10_19dec15_e.htm; https://www.wto.org/english/thewto_e/minist_e/mc10_e/nairobipackage_e.htm.

[42] https://www.wto.org/english/tratop_e/region_e/region_art24_e.htm accessed 27 August 2020.

[43] Brock R. Williams, *Bilateral and Regional Trade Agreements: Issues for Congress* (Washington: Congressional Research Service, 2018), p. 8.

[44] See further: Masahiro Kawai and Ganeshan Wignaraja, *Asian FTAs: Trends, Prospects, and Challenges*, Asian Development Bank (ADB) Economics Working Paper Series No. 226 (Manila: ADB, 2010); *The Oxford Handbook on the WTO*, *supra* note 1.

This may impact negatively also on the quest to keep markets open, unless there is a genuine commitment to partner well " to recover better, together".[45]

Dispute Settlement

The issue of dispute settlement illustrates through a myriad of cases both the element of engagement and ambivalence interlinked with Asiancountries. There have been seminal cases in a variety of areas as seen below. However, some rulings in this regard have resulted directly or indirectly in negative reaction which has also led to blockages in the world trading system, illustrated by the contretemps between the US and China. At the time of the drafting of this book, there was intransigence concerning appointments of new members of the Dispute Settlement Body (DSB), thus impeding its operationalization.

Asian countries have generally been and are willing to be part and parcel of and to utilize the system under the WTO, especially the DSB. The DSB is under the General Council of the WTO, and it involves all the members of the WTO; for dispute resolution, it establishes panels to deliberate between contending parties.[46] In reality, there are two tiers: the dispute settlement Panel (the first instance/tier) and the Appellate Body. A series of procedures are stipulated to enable the mechanisms to inquire into claims from the complainant country versus the respondent country. Third parties can also intervene. Appeal is possible from the Panel's decision/ruling and the Appellate Body can overrule or confirm parts or the whole of the initial decision. It is the DSB which supervises the enforcement process. Where there is failure to comply with a ruling, the DSB can sanction a countermeasure or "retaliation", such as the imposition of duties, on the non-compliant State.

Many of the cases involving Asian countries discussed below have provided opportunities to hammer out the implications of those WTO agreements and rules through peaceful dispute settlement. Both in quantity and quality, the involvement of such countries in a large number of cases contributes to the building of an international Rule of Law in this regard. The participation by Asian countries was less in the GATT:

'During GATT period, formal trade dispute settlements were not frequently utilized by East Asian countries except for Japan'[47]

Most cases under the GATT concerned Japan, European Community, US:

---

[45] Phrase used by the UN Secretary General in addressing the COVID-19 pandemic. See further: https://www.un.org/en/coronavirus/recoverbetter#:~:text=Recover%20Better%20Together%20Action%20Forum%20(26%20June%202020)&text=The%20Fund%20has%20helped%20expand,in%20countries%20around%20the%20world.

[46] https://www.wto.org/english/tratop_e/dispu_e/disp_settlement_cbt_e/c3s1p1_e.htm accessed 25 March 20. See further: Peter van den Bossche, *The Law and Policy of the World Trade Organisation*, 4th Edition (Cambridge: Cambridge University Press, 2017).

[47] Dukgeun Ahn, 'WTO Dispute Settlement in East Asia', in Takatoshi Ito and Andrew K. Re (eds.), *International Trade in East Asia* (Chicago: University of Chicago Press, 2005), pp. 287–327; 291.

'Among 28 cases brought against Japan in the GATT, only 6 cases ended with a substantive report by the panel. Only 2 out of the 12 cases Japan brought to the GATT dispute settlement system concluded with panel decisions.'[48]

While there has been much more participation by Asian countries under the WTO, this is unfinished business and there are still major impediments to be addressed multilaterally, being open also to other levels of discourse, as seen in the more politically sensitive cases below.

Disputesettlement on this front can be dealt with through these entry points:

(1) **Panorama**

The main issue in the 2019–21 period was the blockage concerning appointments to the Appellate Body of the DSB.[49] This should not obscure the fact that in 2018, there was a high number of disputes with a willingness to resort to the DSB with nearly 40 new consultation requests.[50] The drama should not overlook the panorama below which points to elements of the positive.

Looking back, since the introduction of the DSB in the mid-1990s, Asiancountries countries have been actively participating in the system. The biggest number of cases have involved China, India, Japan and Republic of Korea, respectively, with China being the biggest numerically. On the other side of the world, it is the US which has been involved with the largest number of cases in total. It is true that East Asia has been more active than South Asia:

'While East Asia is highly active in global trade, South Asia is far less present.'[51]

This observation is also of interest:

'Brazil and India led the emerging economics in the use of the Dispute Settlement Body, a test that includes Argentina and Thailand........'[52]

' by 2013: 13 Disputes Thailand, 21 India, 17 Japan, 15 Korea'.[53]

A recent compilation signals the participation of and by Asian countries as in the Table below. Table 6.1 shows the involvement of China, Chinese Taipei, Indonesia, India, Japan, Republic of Korea and Thailand with the most number of cases (e.g. with Japan, India and China numbering over two hundred each, to date). If Russia

---

[48] Ibid., p. 293.

[49] WTO, *Annual Report 2019* (Geneva: WTO, 2019), p. 123.

[50] Ibid., p. 116.

[51] Jean-Pierre Lehmann,' Asian Approaches to the International Trade System', in *International Trade in East Asia, supra* note 47, pp. 55–60; 56.

See further: Chulsu Kim, 'East Asia in the World Trade Organisation Dispute Settlement Mechanism', in Yasuhei Taniguchi, Alan Yanovich and Jan Bohanes (eds.), *The World Trade Organization in the twenty-first Century: Dispute Settlement, Negotiations and Regionalism in Asia* (Cambridge: CUP, 2007), pp. 261–266; Ma Xinmin, 'China's Mechanism and Practice of Treaty Dispute Settlement', *Chinese JIL*, 11 (2012) 3, pp. 387–392; Shin-yi Peng, 'The WTO Legalistic Approach and East Asia: From the Legal Culture Perspective', *APLPJ*, 1 (2000) 2, pp. 13–35.

[52] Biswajit Dhar, *The Future of the WTO*, ADBI Working Paper Series No. 444 (Tokyo: ADB Institute, Tokyo, 2013), p. 16.

[53] Ibid., p. 17. See also Davis Evans and Gregory C. Shaffer, 'Introduction', in Gregory C. Shaffer and Ricardo Melendez-Ortiz (eds.), *Dispute Settlement at the WTO: The Developing Country Experience* (Cambridge: CUP, 2010), pp. 1–10.

Table 6.1 Asian WTO members in dispute settlement[54]

Member	As complainant	As respondent	As third party	Nationals as panelist	Nationals as appellate body members (ABM)
Afghanistan			3		
Armenia		2			
Bahrain		1	14	1	
Bangladesh	1		1	1	
Brunei					
Cambodia					
China	21	44	179	1	2
Cyprus					
Georgia					
Hong Kong/China	1		22	6	
India	24	32	162	7	2
Indonesia	11	15	42	1	
Israel			11	4	
Japan	26	16	212	8	3
Jordan					
Kazakhstan		1	35		
Korea, Republic of	21	18	127	4	2
Kuwait			1		
Kyrgyzstan		1			
Lao Democratic People's Republic (Laos)					
Macao/China					
Malaysia	1	1	24	2	
Maldives					
Mongolia					
Myanmar					
Nepal					
Oman			13		
Pakistan	5	4	10	5	

(continued)

Table 6.1 (continued)

Member	As complainant	As respondent	As third party	Nationals as panelist	Nationals as appellate body members (ABM)
Philippines	5	6	18	7	2
Russian Federation	8	9	79		
Qatar	4	1	13		
Saudi Arabia		2	49		
Singapore	1		57	6	
Sri Lanka	1		4		
Chinese Taipei	7		124	1	
Tajikistan					
Thailand	14	4	96	4	
Turkey	5	12	96		
United Arab Emirates	2	1	12		
Vietnam	5		33		
Yemen			2		

Source Information provided by WTO in letter to the author: 6 December 2019.[55] (WTO permission granted to publish)

and Turkey are counted as Asian, they have also be involved in a large number of cases. There have been few cases involving Central Asia, while the Gulf States have participated in a moderate number of cases.

(2) Lessons

From the range of cases appearing before the DSB, Asian-related cases have been fertile ground for lessons learned in regard to not only substantive law but also procedural law. Moreover, there are implementation and interpretation questions in regard to not only principles and rules but also exceptions and exemptions as illustrated below.

What are some of the seminal case examples pertaining to key issues?

(i) Non-discrimination: MFN and national treatment

Anumber of cases concerned with Asian countries underline the principle of non-discrimination, clarifying the criteria behind the principle, through the MFN and national treatment which are the bedrock of trade liberalization. The first case on

[54] See further: WTO webpage: https://www.wto.org/english/tratop_e/dispu_e/dispu_by_country_e.htm and WTO secretariat's own compilation of data, sent to this author at the end of 2019. The data are until 2019.

[55] The author has left the list of countries as received from the WTO, as it is a very useful list, even though some of the countries mentioned are non-Asian.

the issue involving Asia was: **Japan—Alcoholic Beverages II**: **Canada, Euro-pean**Union **Union (EU), United States (US) v Japan**: **DisputeSettlement (DS) 8, 10, 11 (1996).**[56] It concerned GATT: Article (Article) III:2: national treatment. The key question was the validity of a liquor tax imposed by Japan on foreign alcoholic products, such as vodka, while local products, particularly shochu, were exempted. For identifying the discrimination between the range of products, it was necessary to assess the nature of "like products" and " directly competitive or substitutable products".[57] The Appellate Body upheld the finding of the Panel that there was discrimination in the differentiation of tax in regard to the products with those characteristics. A range of cases involving Asian countries then followed: **Japan—Film**: **US v Japan**: **DS 44 (1998)**[58]**; Korea**: **Alcoholic Beverages**: **EU/US v Korea**: **DS 75, 84 (1999)**[59]; **Korea**: **Beef**: **Australia/US v Korea**: **DS 161, 169 (2001)**[60]; **India—Autos**: **US, European Community/European Union (EC) v India**: **DS 146, 175(2002)**[61]; **China—Auto-Parts**: **US, EC, Canada v China**: **DS 339, 340, 342 (2009)**[62]; **China—Electronic Payment Services**: **US v China**: **DS 413(2012)**[63]; **Indonesia—Iron or Steel Products**: **Chinese Taipei, Vietnam v Indonesia**: **DS 490, 496 (2018)**[64]

A key case which still awaits resolution is: **Thailand—Cigarettes (Philippines)**: **Philippines v Thailand**: **DS 371(2011)**[65] which concerns the Customs Valuation Agreement (CVA) Articles 1, 16; GATT Articles III.2, III 4 and X. In the early phase, there was a claim by the Philippines against Thailand which was upheld by the Panel and Appellate Body. The issue was Thailand's imposition of customs duty/tax on resellers of cigarettes imported from the former, while resellers of like domestic cigarettes were exempted. This led to the finding that Thailand was inconsistent with the requirement of national treatment. There was less favourable treatment of the foreign cigarettes in breach of the national treatment principle per Article III:4; ' when imported and like products are subject to a single regulatory regime with only difference being that imported products must comply with additional requirements, this would provide a significant indication that imported products are treated less favourably.'[66]

---

[56]WTO, *WTO Dispute Settlement One-Page Case Summaries 1995–2018*(Geneva: WTO, 2019), p. 10. For those looking for more details, full references in regard to the cases cited here are provided at the end of this WTO publication. The author has economised by citing summaries as illustrations, and it is not intended to provide lengthy analysis of the cases cited.

[57]Ibid.

[58]Ibid., p. 22.

[59]Ibid., p. 36.

[60]Ibid., p. 67.

[61]Ibid, p. 62.

[62]Ibid., p. 143.

[63]Ibid., p. 175.

[64]Ibid., p. 213.

[65]Ibid., p. 154.

[66]Ibid.

The case has not yet ended as there is pending before the DSB. The issue of compliance pursuant to the earlier decision is now affected by the impasse concerning appointment of DSB members to deal with the issue. There has also been an intermingling of politics and economics at the national level where prosecutions were initiated against the multinational company involved with the imports for various alleged wrongdoings in Thailand.[67]

(ii) **Prohibition on Quantitative Restrictions: Textiles**

This is another area where a case involving Asian countries has helped to develop WTO jurisprudence to eliminate quantitative restrictions and comply with the need for transparency. At times, there is a balancing act whereby a country before the adjudicating bodies might lose on some grounds but win on other grounds. A case in point was **Turkey-Textiles: India v Turkey: DS 34 (1999)**[68] which concerned GATT XI, XIII, XXIV, ATC 2.6. This case illustrated well the liberalization of trade and commerce via the WTO through the prohibition of quantitative restrictions such as quotas. India took action against Turkey in the case of such restrictions on textile exports from India to Turkey. The Panel found that the restrictions were not consistent with the GATT rules and the Agreement on Textiles and Clothing (ATC). Turkey's measures were also new restrictions which came into being after the enforcement of the ATC which prohibited such restrictions. As for Turkey's claim that the measures were necessary for it to form a customs union under Article XXIV of the GATT, both the Panel and Appellate Body reasoned that those measures were not justified.[69]

(iii) **LIberalization of Agriculture**

A sensitive issue throughout the years has been how to liberalize the agricultural sector in regard to cross border flows, bearing in mind the Agreement on Agriculture with its thrust to convert hidden measures into tariffs—tariffication—and subsequent negotiations to open up the sector and eliminate (export) subsidies. Two cases illustrate the sensibilities concerned. The case of **India (Balance of Payment (BOP)): US v India: DS 90 (1999)**[70] concerned GATT Articles XI and XVIII; AA Article 4.2. It stands astride the aspiration to make agriculture related restrictions more transparent through tariffication under the Agreement on Agriculture (AA), the prohibition of quantitative restrictions and the balance with national interest such as balance of payment considerations. India imposed import restrictions claiming that they were necessary for the country's BOP. The Panel found against import restrictions holding that they were inconsistent with Article XI:1 and rejected the BOP claim on the basis that the country's monetary measures were adequate per Article XVIII. On the AA, the domestic measure was in breach of the 'obligation under Article 4.2 not to maintain measures of the kind required to be converted into ordinary customs duties

[67] Vitit Muntarbhorn, 'Thailand', in Simon Chesterman, Hiroshi Owada and Ben Saul, *The Oxford Handbook of International Law in Asia and the Pacific* (Oxford: OUP, 2019), pp. 363–385; 382.

[68] *WTO Dispute Settlement One-Page Case Summaries 1995–2018*, *supra* note 56, p. 21.

[69] Ibid.

[70] Ibid., p. 40.

and they could not be justified under Footnote(FN)16 to Article 4.2 either since the measures were not measures maintained under BOP provisions.'[71]

Furthermore, there was the case of **Korea: Beef: Australia/US v Korea: DS 161, 169 (2001)**[72] concerning GATT Articles III.4, XX, XI:1, XVII:1 AA Articles 3, 4, 6 and 7. (The case indicated a balancing act whereby a country before the DSB might lose on some grounds but win on other grounds.) In this regard, while finding against Korea in relation to the discrimination from the dual retail system obliging imported beef to be sold in different stores from local beef, the Appellate Body 'reversed the Panel's ultimate finding that Korea acted inconsistently with Article 3.2 of the AA (domestic support) by exceeding its commitment levels for total support for 1997 and 1998 as the Panel had also relied on improper methods for its own calculation.'[73]

(iv) **TRIPS: IP Protection**

Cases from the Asian region exemplify the weakness of several Asian countries concerning intellectual property protection and the need to have effective domestic laws and related implementation to protect intellectual propertyrights in keeping with the TRIPS and the International Law on the subject. The DSB will also examine the state of national law and implementation to the extent of ensuring compliance with the obligations under the treaty. On the other hand, flexibilities enabling resort to compulsory licensing have been used innovatively by some Asian countries faced with the HIV/AIDS pandemic, and this has led to the lowering of prices for essential medicines to help persons in need. One might prospect whether a similar issue will arise in regard to a possible anti-COVID-19 vaccine.

Seminal cases include: **India-Patents (US): US v India: DS 50 (1998)**[74] which concerned TRIPs Articles 70.8 and 70.9. It related to the US complaint in regard to patent applications for pharmaceutical and agricultural chemical products and India's Patents Act 1970, particularly whether that law fulfilled the TRIPS obligations. The Appellate Body and the Panel found against India on the issue of the system for filing patent application: ' The system did not provide the "means" by which applications for patents for such invention could be securely filed within the meaning of Article 7, 8(a), because, in theory, a patent application filed under the administrative instruction could be rejected by the Court under the contradictory mandatory provisions of the existing Indian Law: Patents Act 1970.'[75] On another issue per TRIPS Agreement Article 70.9 (exclusive marketing rights): ' The Appellate Body agreed with the Panel that there was no mechanism in place in India for the grant of exclusive marketing rights for the products covered by Article 70.8(a), and thus, Article 70.9 was violated.'[76] There followed another case: **India—Patents: European Community/European Union (EC) v India: DS 79 (1998).**[77]

---

[71]Ibid.

[72]Ibid., p. 67.

[73]Ibid.

[74]Ibid., p. 26.

[75]Ibid.

[76]Ibid.

[77]Ibid., p. 38.

The conflict between the US and China was then illustrated in the case of **China—IP: US v China: DS 362(2009)**[78] which concerned TRIPS Articles 9, 41, 46, 59, 61 and the Berne Convention (Berne Convention for the Protection of Literary and Artistic Works). The US took action against China in relation to the Chinese Copyright Law which did not afford protection to work that had not been authorized for publication in China. The Panel found against China's reasoning in relation to Article 9.1 of the TRIPS which incorporated the Berne Convention as part of the obligation under the TRIPS treaty and Article 4.1 on enforcement on the ground that while China could prohibit the circulation of works as per Article 17 of the Berne Convention, this 'does not justify the denial of all copyright protection in any work.'[79] Thus, the failure to protect copyright of a prohibited work was inconsistent with the treaty, as the copyright in those prohibited works could not be enforced.

(v) **Trade-Related Investment Measures**

The WTO's Trade-Related Investment Measures (TRIMS) Agreement is not about the promotion or regulation of foreign investment. It has the more modest objective of applying the principle of non-discrimination to imports and exports linked with the trade in goods, and from that angle, with implications for investment. A key instance is where ' a local content requirement imposed in a non-discriminatory manner on domestic and foreign enterprises is inconsistent with the TRIMs Agreement because it involves discriminatory treatment of imported products in favour of domestic products.'[80] The earliest case on this front Asian countrieswas **Indonesia—Autos: EC, Japan, US v Indonesia: DS 54, 55, 59, 64 (1998).**[81] It concerned TRIMS Article 2.1; GATT Articles I:1, III:2 and the Agreement on Subsidies and Countervailing Measures (ASCM) Articles 5(c), 6, 27.9 and 28. A key issue was the 1993 Programme of Indonesia 'that provided import duty reductions or exemptions on imports of automotive parts based on the local content per cent…'.[82] The Panel found a violation in relation to Article 21 of the TRIMS Agreement because '(1) the measure was a trade-related investment measure and (2) the measure, as a local content requirement, fell within para 1 of the illustrative list of TRIMS in the Annex to the TRIMS Agreement, which sets out trade-related investment measures that are inconsistent with national treatment obligation under GATT Article III:4.'[83]

Inter alia, the Panel found that various tax benefits from Indonesia on imports of automotive parts were a trade-related investment measure and that this was inconsistent with the national treatment obligation. Various tax exemptions also violated the MFN principle.

[78]Ibid., p. 150.

[79]Ibid.

[80]'The term "trade-related investment measures" ("TRIMs") is not defined in the Agreement. However, the Agreement contains in an annex an Illustrative List of measures that are inconsistent with GATT Article III:4 or Article XI:1 of GATT 1994.':

https://www.wto.org/english/tratop_e/invest_e/invest_info_e.htm accessed 28 August 2020.

[81]*WTO Dispute Settlement One-Page Case Summaries 1995–2018, supra* note 56, p. 27.

[82]Ibid.

[83]Ibid.

With regard to the issue of safeguards, under ASCM Article (c), it found that the 'duty and sales tax exemptions under the 1996 National Car Programme were "specific subsidies" which had caused "serious prejudice" through significant prices undercutting under Article 6.3(c) to like imports of EU (but not US) imports under Article 5(c).'[84]

(vi) **Anti-dumping**

There have been a large number of anti-dumping cases involving Asian countries, and they illustrate the criteria and evidence needed to legitimize anti-dumping measures. Dumping can be explained simply as the situation 'of international price discrimination, where the price of a product when sold in the importing country is less than the price of that product in the market of the exporting country.'[85]

Anti-dumping measures, such as anti-dumping duties, are only justifiable if it is proved that '(a) that dumping is occurring, (b) that the domestic industry producing the like product in the importing country is suffering material injury, and (c) that there is a causal link between the two.'[86]

Many of the cases before the DSB are complex, as illustrated by several actions on the part of the importing country—known as "zeroing" which results in miscalculation of the dumping margin and which then leads to distorted anti-dumping duties: 'replacing the actual amount of dumping calculated for model or sales comparisons that yield negative dumping margins (i.e. models or export transactions for which the export price exceeds the calculated normal value) with a value of zero prior to the final calculation of a weighted average margin of dumping for the product under investigation. Zeroing, thus, has the effect of overstating dumping margins by denying the full impact of non-dumped or negatively dumped models/export sales on the dumping margin for the product as a whole.'[87]

[84] Ibid.

The case also concerns Safeguards. The issue of Safeguards, dealt with in a later section of this chapter, is covered by the Agreement on Safeguards ("SG Agreement" or "SA"), in regard Article XIX of GATT 1994. 'Safeguard measures are defined as "emergency" actions with respect to increased imports of particular products, where such imports have caused or threaten to cause serious injury to the importing Member's domestic industry. Such measures, which in broad terms take the form of suspension of concessions or obligations, can consist of quantitative import restrictions or of duty increases to higher than bound rates.

Major guiding principles of the Agreement with respect to safeguard measures are that such measures must be temporary; that they may be imposed only when imports are found to cause or threaten serious injury to a competing domestic industry; that they be applied on a non-selective (i.e. most favoured nation" or "MFN") basis; that they be progressively liberalized while in effect; and that the Member imposing them must pay compensation to the Members whose trade is affected':

https://www.wto.org/english/tratop_e/safeg_e/safeint.htm accessed 28 August 2020.

[85] Obviously, the importing country might be disadvantaged by the flooding of goods with a distorted price reaping benefit for the exporting country. The details are found in the Anti-Dumping Agreement or "The Agreement on Implementation of Article VI of GATT 1994". https://www.wto.org/english/tratop_e/adp_e/adp_info_e.htm accessed 24 January 20.

[86] Ibid.

[87] Edwin Vermulst and Daniel Ikenson, 'Zeroing Under the WTO Anti-Dumping Agreement: Where Do We Stand?', *Glob. Trade Cust. J.*, 2 (2007) 6, pp. 231–242; 231.

The first case involving an Asian country on the issue was **US—DRAMS: Korea v US: DS 99 (1999)**[88] which concerned the Anti-Dumping Agreement (ADA) Articles 11, 2.2, 6.6 and 58. In this case, the DSB ruled partly in favour of Korea while the US won concerning other parts of the decision. The US had imposed anti-dumping duties on products from Korea (DRAMS linked with Hyundai and LG Semicon). The Panel found that the US had not fulfilled the standard required in ADA Article 11.2 (Review of anti-dumping duties—the likely standard): 'the "not likely" standard in US regulation is inconsistent with Article 11.2 ("likely" standard) because a failure to find that an exporter is "not likely" to dump does not necessarily lead to the conclusion that the exporter is "likely" to dump.'[89] However, the Panel found against Korea in regard to its claim that the US authorities had accepted unverified data. In another case, the DSB laid down the rules for calculating the dumping margin and determination of the injury: **Thailand—H-BEAMS: Poland v Thailand: DS 122 (2001).**[90] Here, in regard to the issue of injury determination under ADA Article 3.1, the Appellate Body overturned the Panel's interpretation that 'Article 3.1 requires an anti-dumping authority to base its determination only upon evidence that was disclosed to interested parties during the investigation' which had led to a finding by the Panel against Thailand.[91]

The issue of zeroing was then illustrated in **EC—Bed Linen: India v EC: DS 141 (2001)**[92] involving ADA Articles 2, 3, 5, 12, 15; DSU Article 6.2. The case concerned anti-dumping duties imposed by the EC on import of Indian bed linen. How was the dumping to be determined? Both the panel and the Appellate Body found against the EC in relation to its method of calculation—namely, "zeroing" the negative dumping margins: per Article 2.4.2: by "zeroing" the "negative dumping margins", the EC failed to take fully into account the entirety of prices of some export transactions.[93] As a result, the EC did not establish ' "the existence of margins of dumping" for cotton-type bed linen on the basis of comparison of the weighted average normal value with the weighted average of prices of all transactions involving all models or types of cotton type bed linen.'[94]

With regard to ADA Article 3.4 concerning determination of the injury, the Panel found (and was confirmed) that the EC had failed to fulfil Article 3.4. by not considering "all" injury factors listed in Article 3.4. It also ' found that the EC could consider under Article 3 information related to companies outside the sample, where such information was drawn from the "domestic end"'.[95] However, the EC was inconsistent with Article 3.4 to the extent that it had relied on information on producers

---

See also https://www.wto.org/english/tratop_e/adp_e/adp_info_e.htm.

[88] *WTO Dispute Settlement: One-Page Case Summaries*, *supra* note 56, p. 42.

[89] Ibid.

[90] Ibid., p. 51.

[91] Ibid.

[92] Ibid., p. 60.

[93] Ibid.

[94] Ibid.

[95] Ibid.

not part of the "domestic industry". Interestingly, in regard to the special and differential treatment provision to help developing countries per Article 15, it was held that there was a breach by the EC which had not explored "constructive remedies", such as 'imposition of anti-dumping duties in less than full amount and price undertakings, before applying definitive anti-dumping duties to export from a developing country.'[96]

There followed a host of other cases including: **EC v Bed Linen (Article 21.5): India v EC: DS 141(2003)**[97]; **US-Steel Plate: India v US: DS 206 (2002)**[98]; **US—Corrosive Resistant Steel Sunset Review: Japan v US: DS 244 (2004)**[99]; **Korea—Certain Paper: Indonesia v Korea: DS 312 (2005)**[100]; **Korea—Certain Paper: Indonesia v Korea: DS 312(2007)**[101]; **US—Zeroing (Japan): Japan v US: DS 322 (2007)**[102]; **US—Zeroing (Japan): Japan v US (Article 21.5—J) DS 322 (2009)**[103]; **US—Anti-dumping Measures on PET Bag: DS 383(2010): Thailand v US**[104]; **US—Zeroing (Korea): Korea v US: DS 402 (2011)**[105]; **US—Shrimp and Sawblades (China): China v US: DS 422(2012)**[106]; **US-Shrimp (Vietnam): Vietnam v US: DS 429 (2015)**[107]; **China—Autos (US): US v China: DS 440(2014)**[108]; **US—Anti-dumping Methodology (China): China v US: DS 471 (2017)**[109]; **US—OCTG (Korea): Korea v US: DS 488 (2018)**[110]

(vii) **Sanitary and Phytosanitary Measures**

The Agreement on Sanitary and Phytosanitary Measures (SPS) advances GATT rules on these matters, respectful of a State's choices in regard to measures but with conditions against arbitrary action. The end purpose has to be food, plant and animal health and safety, based on scientific data and targeted to harmonization of standards (even though the WTO does not specify them). Cases from the region pinpoint the need for such data and evidence based assessments.[111] The initial case was **Japan—Agricultural Products II: US v Japan: DS 76 (1999)**[112] which concerned the Agreement

[96]Ibid.

[97]Ibid., p. 61.

[98]Ibid., p. 82.

[99]Ibid., p. 98.

[100]Ibid., p. 129.

[101]Ibid.

[102]Ibid., p. 135.

[103]Ibid., p. 136.

[104]Ibid., p. 160.

[105]Ibid., p. 170.

[106]Ibid., p. 179.

[107]Ibid., p. 183.

[108]Ibid., p. 189.

[109]Ibid., p. 200.

[110]Ibid., p. 212.

[111]https://www.wto.org/english/tratop_e/sps_e/spsund_e.htm accessed 25 January 2020.

[112]*WTO Dispute Settlement One-Page Case Summaries 1995–2018, supra* note 56, p. 37.

on the Application of Sanitary and Phytosanitary Measures (SPS) Articles 2.2, 5.7, 5.6, 5.1. Under the SPS, there is a need for sufficient scientific evidence. In this case, both bodies found that Japan's blockage of plant imports from the US was not justified since there was no sufficient scientific evidence. There then followed: **Japan Apples: US v Japan: DS 245 (2003)**[113]; **Japan—Apples (Article 21.5—US)1: (DS245)**[114]; **India: Agricultural Products: US v India: DS 430(2015)**[115]; **Korea—Radionuclides (Japan): DS 495 (2019).**[116]

(viii) **General Exceptions: Article XX GATT**

Asia-related cases have tested importantly the meaning and scope of this famous Article. At times, there is a delicate balance between multilateralism and unilateralism, and between objective standards posited by International Law and subjective claims based on the national interest. Of particular interest are exceptions (a), (b) and (g) (on protection of public morals, protection of human and other life, and conservation of exhaustible natural resources, respectively) which have been the crux of key cases between countries. It is also important not to focus only on such provisions but also to test them from compliance with the overarching "chapeau" of the Article which counters discrimination and arbitrariness.[117]

The first case of its kind was **US—Shrimp**: **India, Malaysia, Pakistan, Thailand v US: DS 58 (1998)**[118] involving GATT Articles XI and XX. The case concerned the ban by the US against import of shrimp products from various countries claiming that the latter had not used a type of net to catch shrimps. The US understood that its measures violated GATT Article XI. However, the key issue was whether the US could invoke the general exception concerning protection of exhaustible natural resources under XX(g) to validate its action. The Appellate Body reversed partly the decision of the Panel on the sequencing of criteria; it held that the US measure was covered by Article XX(g) exception, but failed to satisfy the chapeau of the provision since the ban constituted "arbitrary" and "unjustifiable" discrimination. 'The measure was "unjustifiably" discriminatory because of its intended and actual coercive effect on the specific policy decisions made by foreign governments that were member(s) of the WTO. They were also "arbitrary" because of the rigidity and inflexibility in its application, and the lack of transparency and procedural fairness in the administration of trade regulations.'[119] With various adjustments, the US was then vindicated in **US—Shrimp (Article 21.5—Malaysia)**: **Malaysia v US:**

[113]Ibid., p. 99.

[114]Ibid., p. 100.

[115]Ibid., p. 184.

[116]https://www.wto.org/english/tratop_e/dispu_e/cases_e/ds495_e.htm accessed 26 July 2020.

[117]https://www.wto.org/english/tratop_e/envir_e/envt_rules_exceptions_e.htm accessed 25 January 2020.

[118]*WTO Dispute Settlement One-Page Case Summaries 1995–2018*, *supra* note 56, p. 29.

[119]Ibid.

DS 58 (2001).[120] There followed: **US—Shrimp (Thailand), US—Customs Board Directive: Thailand/India v US: DS 343, 345 (2008).**[121]

The fact that the rubric of public morals should not be invoked too easily was also seen in **China—Public and Audio-visual Products: US v China: DS 363 (2010)**[122] concerning GATT Articles III:4, and XX(a) and GATS Articles XVI and XVII; and China's Accession Protocol and Working Report. The case concerned various measures taken by China to regulate the import of various publications and products. The issue was further related to whether the country could invoke the protection of public morals to restrict such materials as part of the exceptions to restrict circulation as permitted by GATT Article XX(a). Both the Appellate Body and the Panel found that 'provisions in China's measures that either limit to wholly State-owned enterprises importation rights regarding or prohibiting foreign-invested enterprises in China from importing reading materials, recordings' were inconsistent with China's obligation under its Accession Protocol.[123] While the Appellate Body differed from the Panel on some of the reasoning for its findings in regard to Article XX(a), it agreed with the latter that China had not shown that the various measures were "necessary to protect public morals".[124] It also agreed with the Panel that there was a breach of the national treatment obligation.

This was followed by **China—Rare Earths: US, EU, Japan v China: DS 431, 432, 433 (2013)**[125] involving Accession Protocol, Working Party Report and Marrakesh Agreement, GATT Articles XI and XX. A key issue was China's export quota concerning those raw materials and whether it could invoke Article XX(g) GATT exception in regard to protection of exhaustible natural resources. The Appellate Body confirmed the Panel's finding that the invocation of that exception was unjustified. 'It should focus on the measures' design and structure rather than on their effects in the market place.'[126] Moreover, in **Indonesia—Chicken: Brazil v Indonesia: DS 484 (2017)**[127] concerning GATT Articles XI, III:4, XX; AA Articles. 4.2, invocation of Article XX(d) (claiming the need to ensure compliance with a national law as a valid basis for imposing a trade barrier) was rejected as not satisfying its criterion.

(ix) **Safeguard Measures**

The issue of safeguards was referred to earlier in the context of another issue. Herewith are some cases more directly on the application and validity of safeguard measures, involving Asian countries. A key criterion to justify the invocation of these measures is the threat of serious injury to the industry of the importing country

---

[120] Ibid, p. 30.

[121] Ibid., p. 145.

[122] Ibid, p. 151.

[123] Ibid., p. 151.

[124] Ibid.

[125] Ibid., p. 185.

[126] Ibid.

[127] Ibid., p. 208.

due to the product coming in from another country.[128] In the seminal case, **Korea Dairy**: **EU v Korea**: **DS 98 (2000)**[129] involving SA Articles. 2.1, 4.2, 5.1, 12 and GATT Article XIX.1, various safeguards had been adopted by Korea concerning import of skimmed milk powder from the EU. A key issue was whether there was a threat of serious injury to the local industry. Both the Panel and the Appellate body found against Korea on this issue:

' (Korea) did not adequately examine *all* serious injury factors listed in Article 4.2 (e.g. import increases, market share, sale, production, productivity, etc.) and neither did it provide sufficient reasoning in its explanations of how certain factors support, or detract from, a finding of serious injury.'[130]

Moreover, the Appellate Body agreed with the Panel that Article 5.1 first sentence 'imposes obligation on Members applying a safeguard measure to ensure that the measure applied is not more restrictive than necessary to prevent or remedy serious injury or facilitate adjustment'.[131] It overturned the Panel's decision that Article 5.1 imposes ' an obligation on a member applying a safeguard measure to explain that the measure is necessary to remedy serious remedy and to facilitate adjustment.'[132] The Appellate Body considered that the clear justification requirement under the second sentence of Article 5.1 applies only to a 'quantitative restriction that reduces the quantity of imports below the average of imports in the last three representative years for which statistics are available.'[133] There followed **US—Line Pipe**: **Korea v US**: **DS 202 (2002)**[134] where the Appellate body found against the US in regard to safeguards which were not sufficiently backed by explanation concerning the injury caused the domestic industry.

(x) Subsidies and Countervailing Measures

TheWTO Agreement on Subsidies and Countervailing Measures regulates the use of subsidies. The country adversely affected is entitled to adopt countervailing measures.[135] A difficult issue is to what extent State enterprises should be considered as public bodies linked with subsidies, implying unfair trade/competition, and

---

[128]' A WTO member may take a "safeguard" action (i.e. restrict imports of a product temporarily) to protect a specific domestic industry from an increase in imports of any product which is causing, or which is threatening to cause, serious injury to the industry.

Safeguard measures were always available under the GATT (Article XIX). However, they were infrequently used, and some governments preferred to protect their industries through "grey area" measures ("voluntary" export restraint arrangements on products such as cars, steel and semiconductors).

The WTO Safeguards Agreement broke new ground in prohibiting "grey area" measures and setting time limits ("sunset clause") on all safeguard actions.':

https://www.wto.org/english/tratop_e/safeg_e/safeg_e.htm accessed 25/1/20.

[129]*WTO Dispute Settlement One-Page Case Summaries 1995–2018*, *supra* note 56, p. 41.

[130]Ibid.

[131]Ibid.

[132]Ibid.

[133]Ibid.

[134]Ibid., p. 80.

[135]See further: https://www.wto.org/english/tratop_e/scm_e/scm_e.htm.

whether they are to be subjected to countermeasures by the State importing goods produced by those enterprises. This is in essence a transparency issue facing the Asian (or another) setting which is not easily resolved, due to the political-economy complexity behind such enterprises. In **Korea—Commercial Vessels: EC v Korea: DS 273 (2005)**[136] concerning ASCM Articles 3.1(a), 3.2, 4.7, 5(c) and 8.3(a), the Panel found against export subsidies to the country's shipbuilding industry. There then followed **Japan—DRAMS (Korea): Korea v Japan: DS 336 (2007).**[137]

Some of the most thorny cases have involved the US and China particularly in regard to transparency of State enterprises, and these have had an impact on US-China trade relations as a whole. In **US—Anti-Dumping and Countervailing Duties: China v US: DS 379(2011)**[138] concerning ASCM Articles 1.1, 2.1, 2.2., 10, 12, 14, 19.3, 19.4, 32 and GATT Article 1, VI:3, the issue was US action against China; US measures were based on the belief that the import of steel products was linked with subsidies from public bodies. Inter alia, the Appellate Body found against the US which had claimed that certain State-owned enterprises of China constituted public bodies. The Body reversed the ruling of the Panel which had found those enterprises to be public bodies. Rather, per ASCM Article 1.1(a)(1), a public entity 'is an entity that possesses, exercises or is vested with governmental authority'.[139]

There then followed: **US—Countervailing Measures (China): China v US: DS 437(2017)**[140]concerning GATT Article VI; SCM Articles 1.1., 5.1(a)(1), 1.1(b), 2, 10. 11, 12.7 and 32.1 DSU Articles 6.2 and 11. There was a similar finding in this case against the US which had claimed that certain State-owned enterprises were public bodies ' based solely on the grounds that they were majority owned by the Government of China'.[141] The most recent case is this area is **US—Coated Paper (Indonesia): Indonesia v US: DS 491 (2018).**[142]

(xi) Technical Barriers to Trade (TBT)

The TBT Agreement deals with technical regulations and standards to ensure that they do not give rise to discrimination and inhibit trade. However, there are concessions for health and environment issues. Notifications to the WTO are encouraged to promote transparency.[143] The Asia-related case below provides components of what to bear in mind in testing whether the TBT are discriminatory in comparing imports and home products, e.g. 'physical characteristics, end use, consumer tastes and habits and tariff classification'.[144]

---

136 *WTO Dispute Settlement One-Page Case Summaries 1995–2018, supra* note 56, p 113.

137 Ibid, p. 141.

138 Ibid., p. 156.

139 Ibid.

140 Ibid., p. 187.

141 Ibid.

142 Ibid., p. 214.

143 Transparency is an imperative in this agreement, and it calls for three actions: notifications; establishment of enquiry points; publication requirements. https://www.wto.org/english/tratop_e/tbt_e/tbt_e.htm accessed 26 August 2020.

144 *WTO Dispute Settlement One-Page Case Summaries 1995-2018, supra* note 56, p. 173.

A key case was **US—Clove Cigarettes: Indonesia v US: DS 406 (2012)**[145] which concerned the Agreement on Technical Barriers to Trade (TBT) Articles 2.1 and 2.12; Doha Ministerial Decision on Implementation. The issue was closely linked with the principle of non-discrimination and the "no less favourable treatment" principle integrated into the TBT. The DSB favoured Indonesia's claim of discrimination against import of its clove cigarettes by comparison with treatment of menthol cigarettes produced in the US. ' The Appellate Body upheld, although for different reasons, the Panel's finding that clove cigarettes imported from Indonesia and menthol cigarettes produced in the US were "like products" within the meaning of Article 2.1. The Appellate Body disagreed with the Panel that the concept of "like products" in Article 2.1. should be interpreted based on the regulatory purpose of the technical regulation at issue. Instead the Appellate Body considered that the determination of whether products are "like" within the meaning of Article 2.1. is a determination about the competitive relationship between the products, based on an analysis of the traditional "likeness" criteria of physical characteristics, end use, consumer tastes and habits and tariff classification'.[146]

Hindsight

In retrospect, there have been many inputs from cases concerning Asia for the jurisprudence on trade and commercial issues under the WTO. A key challenge emanating from dispute resolution through some of the cases above is that the domestic background enjoyed by the Parties interlinks importantly with their capacity to trade and their fairness in trade. Democratic countries have more checks and balances and are subject to transparency and scrutiny which make them difficult to distort trade, e.g. in relation to subsidies, government procurement and competition. Other States, with fewer checks and balances, and less transparency and accountability backdrop, tend to have more leeway to employ less open methods giving them possibly advantages in trade relations. The classic test case is to what extent State enterprises should be considered as Governmental entities subject to stricter rules of conduct than ordinary companies are, especially if the former benefit from incentivization from the authorities. Put it another way, how fair is the context where a State can intervene and control the trade set-up, when compared with a system based on laissez faire, namely, where the State does not intervene too much and should let market dynamics follow their natural course?

Added to this is the competition for techno superiority and the issue of IP—protection, registration and remediation. Today, this is rendered more complex by advantages through contract research and spread of influence through Big data and intellectual institutions and systems with a competitive edge.

---

[145] Ibid.

[146] Ibid.

On the other hand, unilateralism in addressing the above gives rise to fragmentation, subjectivity and politicization, jeopardizing an open rules based system and a sense of convergence between the multiplicity of States. Ironically, discussions which should be in a multilateral setting are circumvented and the discourse becomes limited to a few parties outside the bigger circle, with centrifugal and fractious implications. As for multilateralism, it is also changing or having to change. The rules based system may have to adjust or be adjusted to address more concretely the non-transparent set-up which gives rise to unfair advantages, no less in regard to procurement and competition matters. Multilateralism is still key in that adjusted sense. Meanwhile, other discourses are inevitable—such as more plurilateral arrangements. Regional FTAs are also emerging as bigger blocks, economically/politically as checks and balances, and needing checks and balances. They too need to be viewed from the vantage point of transparency and value added—fair play. This can be explored further in the next chapter on Regionalism.

On the salutary side, generally Asiancountries are still committed to multilateralism; this orientation may help to sustain the international trade-and-commerce system, albeit with the need to evolve with the times and to leverage well in regard to those other undercurrents. There is then the vision that trade and free trade should be a means and not an end in themselves. Asia (and elsewhere) should not neglect the human face of equity and fair distribution. This is now faced with the ravages of COVID-19 and the ensuing socio-economic and commercial traumas, haunted by recession, bankruptcies and massive unemployment in many countries. If there is omission on this front, cynicism might arise and reduce the argument for rules based multilateralism, especially when faced with more populistic and nationalistic policies which claim the ground of legitimacy by responding more equitably to the needs and entitlements of the local population. Indeed, the multilateral system of trade liberalization built on the shoulders of universal rules has to prove that it empathizes more deeply with local plights and expectations. It has to strive towards a preferred balance between globalization and localization, grounded on not only freer trade but also fairer trade with a more inclusive approach and agenda.[147] What space is there then for regionalism and what should be its end goals? The next chapter turns to that conundrum.

---

[147]With foresight, see message on WTO at 25 from the WTO itself through its Director General Azevedo: noting political engagement to resolve the dispute settlement issue. With the new administration of the UN in 2021 under the new Presidency of Mr. Biden, there are signs of return to multilateralism which should also open doors to settling question of appointments in the WTO, as well as a constructive approach to reform.

https://www.wto.org/english/news_e/news20_e/dgra_01jan20_e.htm accessed 25 January 2020.

Chapter 7
Regionalism and Eclecticism

The purpose of this final Chapter is twofold. First, it aims to take stock of some regional/subregional developments, their strengths and weaknesses. Second, it targets various issues linked with multilateralism and a forward-looking agenda for discussion under the heading "eclecticism". It covers human inputs in the form of peacekeepers and volunteers, reflections concerning UN reforms, and then emerging challenges such COVID-19, digitalization and Artificial Intelligence (AI). In a way, these dimensions also correspond to different scale of activities: micro, mezzo and macro.

Regionalism?

One of the key developments in the Asian region is how countries have been grouping up in regional arrangements and organizations (of different shapes and sizes) since the end of the Second World War. This path of regionalism is one with a diversity of forms. What the Chapter seeks to avoid is to do a listing of the various groups and groupings found in the region.[1]

[1]If the reader would like a list, an available list notes about 10 Asian regional organizations (https://www.auswaertiges-amt.de/en/aussenpolitik/regionaleschwerpunkte/asien/-/231346): ASEAN, ASEAN + 3(namely, China, Japan and Republic of Korea), East Asia Summit, Asia-Europe Meeting (ASEM), ASEAN Regional Forum, SAARC, Pacific Islands Forum (PIF), SCO, and Asia-Pacific Economic Cooperation. That list, however, includes groupings which are not quite "organizations" with an international legal personality and omits developments in Central Asia and West Asia, such as the Gulf Cooperation Council. It does not include various cooperative groupings such as the Greater Mekong Sub-region, Bay of Bengal Multi sectoral Technical and Economic Cooperation (BIMSTEC) and the Asia Cooperation Dialogue (ACD), some of which are more active than others. On another front, there is now the emerging Regional Comprehensive Economic Partnership (RCEP) linking Southeast, Northeast Asia and the Pacific. If India chooses to join, there will also be a link with South Asia.

V. Muntarbhorn, *Challenges of International Law in the Asian Region*,
https://doi.org/10.1007/978-981-16-2047-8_7

Rather, it addresses two issues. First, to what extent are there regional intergovernmental organizations which address key themes or subject-matters of human existence and wellbeing, namely peace and cooperation, democracy and human rights, sustainable development and environment, and multifaceted security (not simply regional or national security but also human security), and how do they fare? The rationale behind this *optique* is to underline that regional (or other) organizations are means and not ends. Those ends should be much to do with human existence and wellbeing. Second, the Chapter will single out some economic landmarks of the day in terms of regionalism, replete with political underpinnings—call this "Economic Plus" cooperation: regional trade agreements (RTAs), and "Asia and Beyond" cooperation in the form of the Belt and Road Initiative (BRI). They deserve to be assessed from the angle of their value-added and concomitant challenges.

(A) Subject Matters

(i) Peace and Cooperation

The archetypal regional organization responding to this call must be the Association of Southeast Asian Nations (ASEAN), even though today, this organization tends to be seen from a politico-economic angle of expanding Free Trade Area in the region and acting as the key enabler of other projects such as the East Asia Summit (EAS) and the Regional Comprehensive Economic Partnership (RCEP).[2] ASEAN now consists of 10 countries, several of which were previously enemies. It should be remembered that when the organization was set up in 1967 by the Bangkok Declaration consisting of five countries, namely Indonesia, Malaysia, Thailand, Singapore and the Philippines, later to be joined by Brunei, with the decades that followed till the 1990s, there was an international war ravaging the Southeast Asian region—involving Cambodia, Laos and Vietnam which were antithetical to the other five, but which would later join the ASEAN. Burma/Myanmar was out on a limb, being a semi-closed country under military rule until it gradually opened up by joining ASEAN, together with the other three, in the 1990s. Membership of ASEAN meant/means peace among and between neighbours. Disputes between them, such as Philippine claims to Sabah, [3] now a part of Malaysia, or the old Confrontasi (or confrontational) tension between Indonesia and Malaysia[4,5] are dealt with peacefully under a process of accommodation.

---

[2] https://asean.org/; https://www.aseansec.org/.

[3] S. Jayakumar, 'The Philippine Claim to Sabah and International Law', *Mal LR*, 10(1968)2, pp. 306–335.

[4] *Marsita Omar*, 'Indonesia–Malaysia Confrontation'. https://eresources.nlb.gov.sg/infopedia/articles/SIP_1072_2010-03-25.html. Accessed 29 August 2020.

[5] https://asean.org/treaty-amity-cooperation-southeast-asia-indonesia-24-february-1976/. Accessed 29 August 2020.

Map 7.1 ASEAN. *Source* Map drawn by author's team

This door was bolstered by the ASEAN Treaty of Amity and Cooperation (TAC) 1976 which is now open to signature to countries from beyond the ASEAN region.[6] At the heart of the TAC is the promise of peace and support for the basic precepts of the UN Charter. Interestingly, the TAC also provides a political mechanism for dispute resolution in the form of a High Council, but it has never been used. In several (mostly peaceful) contretemps between neighbours, the disputants have preferred to use multilateral dispute settlement mechanisms, such as the ICJ, ITLOS and or the WTO DSB seen in the previous Chapters, rather than ASEAN's homegrown mechanism.

To its credit, the group has also propelled the **Southeast Asia Nuclear Weapon-Free Zone (SEANWFZ)** in the region, but the nuclear powers have shunned joining in, even though there is a Protocol open to membership by the latter. Part of the problem is that the non-nuclear Zone covers various maritime zones —territorial sea, continental shelf, exclusive economic zone, where there are issues of freedom of navigation, including for warships which might be nuclearized. For that reason,

[6]https://asean.org/?static_post=treaty-on-the-southeast-asia-nuclear-weapon-free-zone. Accessed 29 August 2020.

the Powers prefer to retain their discretion rather than be part of the promise to denuclearize in all those zones.

In another corner of Asia, Central Asia has seen various initiatives by governments to congregate in a forum of peace in that region. Four countries—Kazakhstan, Kyrgyzstan, Tajikistan and Uzbekistan- helped to establish the Central Asian Cooperation Organization (CACO), sometimes called Central Asian Union and *Central Asian Economic Community*, converging loosely from the 1990s.[7] However, the formation was without much structure. The heads of Government of Kazakhstan, Kyrgyzstan, Tajikistan, Uzbekistan and Turkmenistan meet for a summit every two years and the latest was in Tashkent in 2019. In 2006, those five countries helped to establish Nuclear Weapon-Free Zone in Central Asia.[8] In 2005, there was a merger of CACO with the Eurasian Economic Community, thus linking with Russia and Belarus. That organization was superseded by the Eurasian Economic Union (The Eurasian Economic Community ceased to exist from 2015 due to the establishment of the Eurasian Economic Union, referred to below in relation to regional free trade areas).

While the above organizations are salient examples of a commitment to peace as the value added, all the other regional organizations below also promote peace and cooperation among the members, to a lesser or greater extent, since this is an inevitable motivation of grouping up. There may also be other emphases as will be evident.

ii. Democracy/Human Rights

Interestingly, there is no regional intergovernmental organization in Asia dedicated to the promotion and protection of democracy. The irony is that the region is home to many non-democracies ranging from the Gulf region through Central Asia to parts of Southeast and Northeast Asia. However, Asia is also home to a number of the biggest democracies—e.g. India, Indonesia. The verbiage of democracy seeps or creeps into many organizations and policies in the region—rather as a perfunctory exercise, given that there is much lip service. By contrast, there are many members of civil society working on democracy and it is they who are at times persecuted as dissidents.

There is also no intergovernmental organization at the Asian level for the promotion and protection of human rights. The presence of subregional human rights mechanisms was already covered in an earlier Chapter. As already discussed, they suffer from either a weak protection mandate (such as AICHR) or critiques in regard to their credibility (particularly the Arab Human Rights Court). Some other subregional organizations may have potential to explore a human rights mechanism. For instance, there is the South Asian Association for Regional Cooperation (SAARC) which comprises eight Member States: Afghanistan, Bangladesh, Bhutan, India,

[7]https://www.cacianalyst.org/publications/analytical-articles/item/13547-regional-cooperation-in-central-asia-relevance-of-world-models.html. Accessed 29 August 2020.

[8]https://www.nti.org/learn/treaties-and-regimes/central-asia-nuclear-weapon-free-zone-canwz/. Accessed 29 July 2020.

Maldives, Nepal, Pakistan and Sri Lanka, established in 1985.[9] It already has various specific treaties dealing with human rights related issues, particular conventions against human trafficking and on child welfare arrangements.[10] There is also the SAARC Social Charter which commits to poverty eradication.[11] It would be a good candidate to explore a human rights mechanism, but the persistent conflict between two major members—India and Pakistan—has impeded progress.

Where there is a void, UN presence may well be needed. Two inputs are timely. First, the UN now has a Democracy Fund which opens the door to assisting both governmental and civil society groups, including those from Asia.[12] Nor does the UN advocate that there is a unique, single model of democracy.[13] Second, the OHCHR has regional and national presences which help on human rights protection, especially where national systems are weak on this front. Appearing after the turn of the millennium, the OHCHR established regional presences in Bangkok, Beirut and Fiji.[14] In the Republic of Korea, an office has also been opened to collect information in regard to violations in the nearby North (as part of follow up to the seminal UN Commission of Inquiry on the North Korea/Democratic People's Republic of Korea - DPRK).[15]There are also national presences such as the OHCHR stand-alone office in Cambodia.[16]

iii. Sustainable Development/Environment

Sustainable development, especially with the impetus of SDGs, has enjoyed "good-buy" in from Asian States. Regional and subregional organizations, such as ASEAN, are inevitably covering aspects of SDGs as part of their natural mandate. Yet, transparent implementation is key, and the best monitoring is provided not necessarily by a (sub)regional organization from the region but by the regional office of the UN in the form of the Regional Commission for Asia and the Pacific (ESCAP) situated in Bangkok.[17]In West Asia, there is also the UN Economic and Social Commission for West Asia(ESCWA) seated in Beirut. [18]

Environmental issues are now also covered to a lesser or greater extent by all regional organizations, at least in terms of verbal commitment, and there has been good participation of Asian countries in many environmental treaties. ASEAN has adopted an agreement to tackle transboundary haze,[19] but the fact that such haze

---

[9]https://www.nti.org/learn/treaties-and-regimes/south-asian-association-regional-cooperation-saarc/. Accessed 29 August 2020.

[10]https://saarc-sec.org/about-saarc.

[11]Ibid.

[12]https://www.un.org/democracyfund/. Accessed 29 August 2020.

[13]https://www.un.org/en/sections/issues-depth/democracy/. Accessed 29 August 2020.

[14]https://www.ohchr.org/EN/Countries/Pages/RegionalOfficesIndex.aspx.

[15]https://www.ohchr.org/EN/NewsEvents/Pages/UNHRChiefopensnewofficeinSeoul.aspx.

[16]https://cambodia.ohchr.org/.

[17]https://www.unescap.org/.

[18]https://www.unescwa.org/.

[19]https://haze.asean.org/?wpfb_dl=32.

blankets parts of ASEAN each year indicates the gap between law and practice. SAARC has a treaty on environmental protection.[20] In Asia, the two key countries with major carbon footprints are, of course, China and India and the fact that they have committed to the Paris Agreement to tackle Climate Change is welcome.[21] Here again the challenge is not so much law or policy but practice, particularly to end the use of fossil fuels and to adapt to renewable sources of energy. The regional presence of UN development arm —UN Development Programme (UNDP), and UN environment arm—UN Environment Programme (UNEP) helps to provide stimulus.

Leading up to 2020, through UN ESCAP monitoring of SDG implementation, key issues included underperformance or regression on SDG 10, 16, 8 and 12, and pervasively SDG 13 on climate change.[22]

iv. Multifaceted Security

With the presence of many States advocating broad notions of national security, that mindset also pervades regional cooperation with a strong emphasis on regional security and the oft-excessive flagging of the non-interference principle. One does not have to look far for examples. In reality, there is a profusion of security-related organizations and actions from the region.

ASEAN is an organization dealing consciously with regional security. It is comprised of 3 communities: ASEAN Political Security Community, ASEAN Economic Community and ASEAN Sociocultural Community.[23] It covers traditional security, such as issues of peace and disarmament (see TAC and SEANWFZ above), and opens the door to non-traditional security such as issues of human trafficking and drugs trafficking. It has a broader security-based umbrella in the form of the ASEAN Regional Forum which provides the sole forum in Asia where ASEAN countries and many other partners, including the Superpowers, congregate to deal with issues of international/regional peace and security.[24] On a connected front, military personnel cooperate through the meetings of Defence Ministers and carry out joint military-related exercises periodically. Yet, the notion of Human Security has been much less voiced, even though it was concept espoused by the 2005 World Outcome Document and a more recent UN GA resolution.[25] This may be due to the fear that it might open the door to external pressures or intervention, even though the concept itself has distanced itself from such interpretation.

There is also the ASEAN Convention against Terrorism which places counterterrorism high on the ASEAN agenda and which requires good monitoring to ensure that counterterrorism is well balanced with protection of human rights and human

---

[20] https://www.nyulawglobal.org/globalex/SAARC1.html.

[21] Joyeeta Gupta,' The Paris Climate Change Agreement: China and India', Clim. Law, 6(2016) 1–2, pp. 171–81.

[22] https://www.un.org/sustainabledevelopment/sustainable-development-goals/.

[23] https://asean.org/storage/2012/05/7.-Fact-Sheet-on-ASEAN-Community.pdf. Accessed 29 August 2020.

[24] https://aseanregionalforum.asean.org/.

[25] General Assembly resolution 66/290 of 10 September 2012.

security.[26] SAARCalso has a counterterrorism Convention[27]: This is now supplemented by a Protocol which targets financing of terrorism[28]: However, at one point, relations between India and Pakistan became very fragile due to a terrorist attack on Bombay which was allegedly linked with support from the latter.

Bridging Central Asia and East Asia, another key organization with much emphasis on security is the Shanghai Cooperation Group (SCO).[29] It is comprised of 8 member states: India, Kazakhstan, China, Kyrgyzstan, Pakistan, Russian, Tajikistan, and Uzbekistan, originally established in Shanghai in 2001. It is now closely linked with China's Belt and Road Initiative and Russia's Eurasian Economic Union.[30] On the security front, there is the Convention of the Shanghai Cooperation Organization on Combating Extremism 2017[31]: Its latest summit adopted the Bishkek Declaration countering terrorism and extremism, while underlining the non-interference principle.[32]

Interestingly, there is no Northeast Asian regional organization dealing with security issues, partly because of the difficult relationship between to two Koreas, as well as with US, Japan and China. On the North Korean denuclearization issue, there have been several talks involving six countries—Russia, China, Japan, USA, North Korea and South Korea, but they have been discontinued.

(B) "Economic Plus" Cooperation

There is a plethora of economic-cum-political groupings, arrangements and organizations in the Asian region. The best known are the Free Trade Areas (FTAs) which come in various shapes and sizes, at times bilateral, at times subregional, at times regional and at times regional with extra-regional links. However, there are other entry points. Two landmarks will be singled out for consideration: Regional Trade Agreements (RTAs) such as FTAs and Regional Comprehensive Economic Partnership (RCEP), and the China propelled Belt and Road Initiative (BRI).

(1) **RTAs**

There is a variety of regional trade arrangements/agreements in the Asian region and in view of their scope which may extend beyond the free trade issue, it might be better to describe them as instruments of regional "economic plus" cooperation. The best known are the FTAs which come in various shapes and sizes, at times bilateral,

[26] https://asean.org/wp-content/uploads/2012/05/ACCT.pdf

[27] https://www.saarclaw.org/saarc-agreements-and-conventions.php. Accessed 6 April 2020.

[28] Ibid.

[29] https://eng.sectsco.org/. Accessed 29 August 2020.

[30] https://www.cfr.org/backgrounder/shanghai-cooperation-organization. Accessed 13 February 2020. See also Eleanor Albert, 'The Shanghai Cooperation Organization: A Vehicle for Cooperation or Competition?', 21 June 2019. https://thediplomat.com/2019/06/the-shanghai-cooperation-organization-a-vehicle-for-cooperation-or-competition/. Accessed 13 February 2020.

[31] https://rusemb.org.uk/fnapr/6271. Accessed 6 March 2020.

[32] Mutlaq Al-Qahtani, 'The Shanghai Cooperation Organization and the Law of International Organizations', *Chinese JIL*, 5(2006)1, pp. 129–47.

at times subregional, at times (almost) regional and at times regional with extra-regional links.[33] While the value added is naturally the liberalization of trade, there remains the question whether that wealth is then shared well among the population. Moreover, while they tend to liberalize in regard to the flow of goods and services, the least covered angle is freedom of movement of workers. New arrangements such as RCEP invite new scrutiny, particularly in regard to intellectual property, environmental, labour and human rights issues. Should trade be so divorced from those concerns?

ASEAN again provides the archetype and it has also been a driver of other groupings, recently RCEP. The ASEAN FTA was formulated in 1992 and starting with elimination of tariffs for goods, the scope of liberalization expanding to cover services and investment. The main agreements are ASEAN Agreement on Trade in Goods (ATIGA), ASEAN Framework Agreement on Services (AFAS) and ASEAN Comprehensive Investment Agreement (ACIA). The many channels of cooperation extend far beyond trade and commerce since the latter are part of one out of three communities which form the ASEAN backbone. While there is no common currency, there is joint cooperation on some aspects of capital such as currency supports in case of emergency known as SWAP ("Chiangmai initiative").[34] There are also new aspects such as communications and e commerce-related cooperation.[35] However, despite a couple of declarations on migrant workers, the movement of migrant workers tends to be regulated between two countries in a bilateral setting, such as Thailand's MOU with each of its neighbours, rather than in a regional agreement on the flow of migrant workers.[36] With the advent of COVID-19, the region has also come together to set up a support fund to deal with the pandemic, an interesting development to address regional health issues.[37] The flow of migrant workers has been blocked due to the pandemic.

---

[33]Masahiro Kawai and Ganeshan Wignaraja, 'Policy Challenges posed by Asian FTAs: A Review of the Evidence', in Richard Baldwin, Masahiro Kawai and Ganeshan Wignaraja (eds), *A WTOfor the 21st Century The Asian Perspective*, Asian Development Bank Institute (Cheltenham: Glos/Northampton: Edward Elgar Publishers, 2014), pp. 182–238.

Also: in the Foreword, ibid, p. X: 'The number of ratified FTAs grew from 36 in 2002 to 113 in the beginning of 2014. As tariffs are generally not a significant barrier anymore, these agreements have increasingly focused on non-tariff trade facilitation measures…Coexistence between FTAs and the multilateral trading system is likely to continue for the foreseeable future. The key is how best to pursue coherence between them. In light of the growing supply chains as the basis for deepening Asia's regional and global integration, there is a need for a path toward gradual multilateralization: the extension of existing arrangements in a non-discriminatory manner to additional parties.' It is noted that Singapore has the greatest number of FTAs in the Southeast Asian region.

[34]https://aric.adb.org/initiative/chiang-mai-initiative. Accessed 29 August 2020.

[35]https://etradeforall.org/asean-e-commerce-set-to-dominate-the-region-in-2019/. Accessed 29 August 2020.

[36]https://www.mfa.go.th/main/en/news3/6886/95148-Thailand-uses-MOU-system-to-recruit. Accessed 29 August 2020.

[37]ASEAN COVID-19 fund. https://www.mfa.go.th/main/en/news3/6885/119180-Prime-Minister-Attended-the-36th-ASEAN-Summit-and.html. Accessed 29 August 2020.

The popularity of economic cooperation, especially via FTAs, means that they appear in many corners of the Asian region. For instance, in West-South Asia there is the Economic Cooperation Organization or ECO; it is an Asian political and economic intergovernmental organization which was founded in 1985 in Tehran by the leaders of Iran, Pakistan, and Turkey. It provides a platform to discuss ways to improve development and promote trade and investment opportunities.[38] The aim is to establish a single market for goods and services, along the lines of the European Union.

The Central Asian Cooperation Organization was already mentioned earlier (initially created under the name of Central Asian Union in 1994, by Kazakhstan, Kyrgyzstan and Uzbekistan, later joined by Tajikistan). It then tried to find a model for trade liberalization and was merged into another body, now linked with the Eurasian Economic Union.[39] Further, South, SAARC also has an FTA but it has not gained much traction due to too many exceptions as part of the sensitive list which countries can set up to exempt themselves from FTA obligations, and there are also hidden barriers to trade, such as "para tariffs".[40] Nearby there is the Bay of Bengal Initiative for Multi-Sectoral Technical and Economic Cooperation (BIMSTEC); it is an international organization of seven nations of South Asia and South East Asia—Ban gladesh, India, Myanmar, Sri Lanka, Thailand, Nepal and Bhutan housing some 1.5 billion people and having an approximate GDP of some three trillion USD.[41]

Interlinking between Europe and Asia, there is the Eurasian Economic Union (EAEU) 2015,with the participation of Belarus, Kazakhstan, Russia, Armenia and Kyrgyzstan. It targets free flow of goods and services, with common areas of cooperation for a market of some 180 million people. The institutional set-up is as follows:

> As a union, the EAEU comprises several governing bodies with equal representation of members. These are the Supreme Council—consisting of the heads of state, the Intergovernmental Council—consisting of heads of government, and a two-tier Eurasian Economic Commission. The upper body, the Eurasian Economic Commission (EEC) Council, includes deputy heads of government, and the lower body, the EEC Collegium, comprises ministers nominated by member states. All bodies make decisions by consensus, except the EEC Collegium, which adopts acts with a two-thirds majority.'[42] There is also a judicial organ—the Court of the EAEU. To date, a key benefit has been reduction of non-tariff barriers. However, it has a more political orientation in Russia's own leverage and outreach to the region covered.

[38] https://www.eco.int/. Accessed 29 August 2020.

[39] https://www.eaeunion.org/?lang=en.

[40] Sanjay Kathuria and Nadeem Rizwan, 'How South Asia can become a free trade area', 14 February 2019. https://blogs.worldbank.org/endpovertyinsouthasia/how-south-asia-can-become-free-trade-area. Accessed 6 April 2020.

[41] https://www.eurasiareview.com/27062020-sri-lanka-to-host-bimstec-summit-in-2020-analysis/#:~:text=The%20region%20has%20a%20combined,than%20other%20areas%20of%20cooperation. Accessed 29 August 2020.

[42] https://www.evnreport.com/understanding-the-region/fact-sheet-what-is-the-eurasian-economic-union. Accessed 15 August 2020.

Perhaps the most ambitious regionalization process today under the guise of economic cooperation is the lead up to establish RCEP, paralleling also the shift from the now defunct Trans Pacific Partnership Cooperation (TPPC) and the emergence of Comprehensive and Progressive Agreement for Trans-Pacific Partnership (CPTPP).[43]

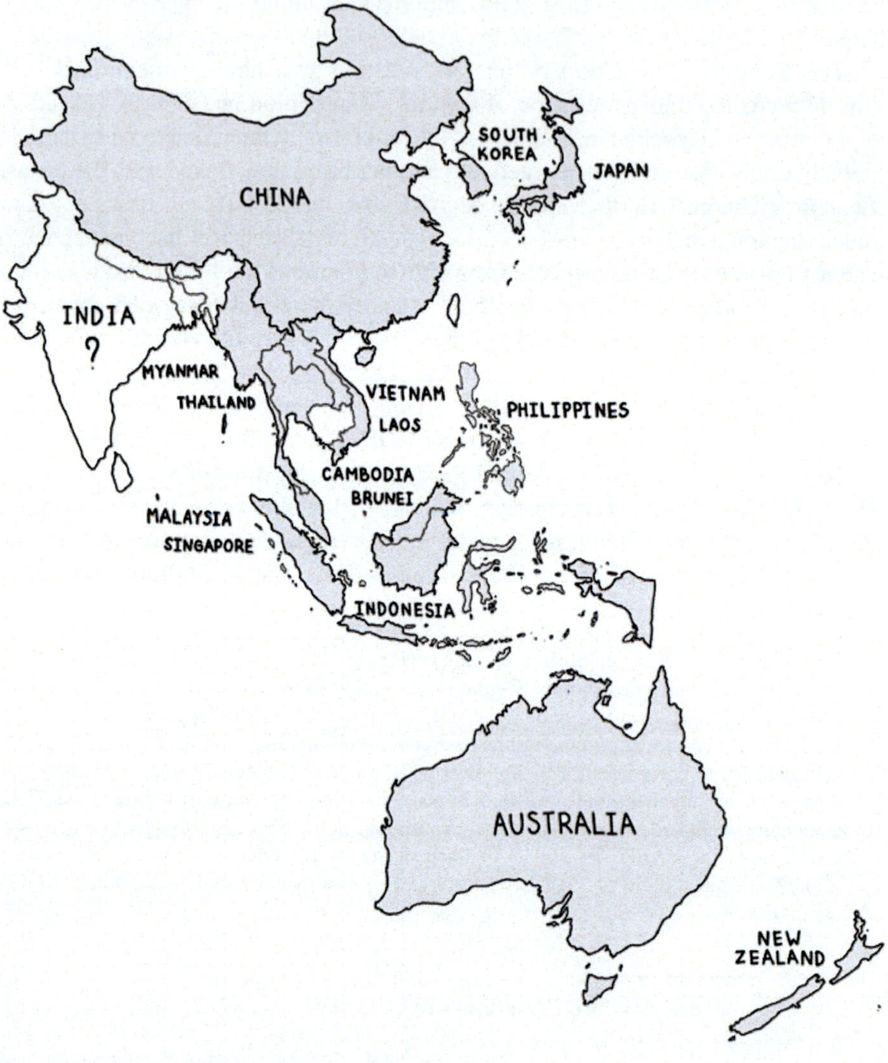

Map 7.2 RCEP. *Source* Map drawn by author's team

43https://www.mfat.govt.nz/en/trade/free-trade-agreements/free-trade-agreements-in-force/cptpp/. Accessed 29 August 2020.

As a RTA, the RCEP now covers about 30% of the world's population but has the potential of covering over half the world's population if India joins. Its membership was initially projected for 16 members—the 10 ASEAN countries, China, India, Japan, Republic of Korea, Australia and New Zealand, but India's membership is on hold for the moment.[44] By comparison with another regional group nearly—Comprehensive and Progressive Agreement for Trans-Pacific Partnership (CPTPP)—it is much less ambitious and concentrates on liberalization of trade while not touching upon environmental and labour rights issues. As it is much propelled by the ASEAN group, it also helps to interlink between that long established subregional organization and other parts of the Asia-Pacific region.[45]RCEP is based on an agreement of 20 Chapters and the directions were laid down at the latest Summit on 4 November 2019, in Bangkok per this statement:

> Chapters on: '1) Initial Provisions and General Definitions; 2) Trade in Goods; 3) Rules of Origin, including Annex on Product Specific Rules; 4) Customs Procedures and Trade Facilitation; 5) Sanitary and Phytosanitary Measures; 6) Standards, Technical Regulations and Conformity Assessment Procedures; 7) Trade Remedies; 8) Trade in Services, including Annexes on Financial Services, Telecommunication Services, and Professional Services; 9) Movement of Natural Persons; 10) Investment; 11) Intellectual Property; 12) Electronic Commerce; 13) Competition; 14) Small and Medium Enterprises; 15) Economic and Technical Cooperation; 16) Government Procurement; 17) General Provisions and Exceptions; 18) Institutional Provisions; 19) Dispute Settlement; and 20) Final Provisions.'[46]

COVID-19 did not disrupt the signing of membership of RCEP in late 2020. One of the most contentious areas has been the breath of coverage of intellectual property rights. The agreement follows WTO rules, in particular the Doha Declaration referred to earlier in the Chapter on Trade Liberalization and Inhibition, to an extent as follows, especially on the protection of pharmaceuticals:

> Article 11.8: The TRIPS Agreement and Public Health
>
> 1. The Parties reaffirm the Doha Declaration on the TRIPS Agreement and Public Health adopted on 14 November 2001. In particular, the Parties have reached the following understandings regarding this Chapter:
>
> (a) the Parties affirm the right to fully use the flexibilities as duly recognised in the Doha Declaration on the TRIPS Agreement and Public Health;
>
> (b) the Parties agree that this Chapter does not and should not prevent a Party from taking measures to protect public health; and

---

[44] https://asia.nikkei.com/Economy/Trade/India-s-absence-looms-over-progress-on-RCEP-Asian-trade-deal. Accessed 29 August 2020.

[45] Kaewkamol Pitakdumrongkit, 'ASEAN's RCEP and sustainability challenges and achievements'. *East Asia Forum*. 24 January 2020. file:///C:/Users/Admin/Documents/RCEP%20and%20sustainability%20challenges%20and%20achievements%20_%20East%20Asia%20Forum.html. Accessed 29 August 2020.

[46] Joint Leaders' Statement on the REGIONAL COMPREHENSIVE ECONOMIC PARTNERSHIP (RCEP).

4 November 2019, Bangkok, Thailand. See also: https://www.business-standard.com/about/what-is-rcep.

(c) the Parties affirm that this Chapter can and should be interpreted and implemented in a manner supportive of each Party's right to protect public health and, in particular, to promote access to medicines for all.

2. In recognition of the Parties' commitment to access to medicines and public health, this Chapter does not and should not prevent the effective utilisation of Article 31bis of the TRIPS Agreement, and the Annex and Appendix to the Annex to the TRIPS Agreement.

3. The Parties recognise the importance of contributing to the international efforts to implement Article 31bis of the TRIPS Agreement, and the Annex and Appendix to the Annex to the TRIPS Agreement.'[47]

However, there is the issue whether the RCEP will go beyond WTO rules to benefit the business sector to the detriment of the general public. The civil society community has been vigilant with regard to those intellectual property rights which could impose more conditions than the WTO's requirements, for instance to extend protection by another five years beyond the 20-year threshold. This may be an impediment to the production of pharmaceuticals in the region from the angle of affordability and accessibility.[48] The issue revisits the problem of intellectual property rights and flexibilities which gave rise to much contestation in the WTO such as on compulsory licensing of Anti-AIDS drugs mentioned in the earlier Chapter on trade matters in this book.

(2) Belt and Road Initiative (BRI)

The BRI was initiated by China in 2013 as an economic cooperation project with vast outreach to/through Asia and other parts of the world, by land and sea.

In China's own policy planning, projected under the BRI are 7 pillars of cooperation ranging from infrastructure to economic and trade; production capacity and investment; financial cooperation, environmental cooperation; maritime cooperation and socio cultural cooperation.[49] *En route*, there are enormous sums involved—with costs estimated between over 500 billion usd to 800 billion usd.[50] In a sense, given the country's rapid economic growth, it is understandable that China would now seek to use its economic weight in this way. There are opportunities for marketing Chinese goods and technology, as well as increasing the influence of Chinese expertise and

---

[47] https://rcepsec.org/legal-text/ accessed 25 January 2021.

[48] **Shailly Gupta, Don't shut down the pharmacy of the developing world.** https://www.expresspharma.in/management-pharma/dont-shut-down-the-pharmacy-of-the-developing-world/382878/. Accessed 30 August 2020.

[49] Ibid., pp. 18–42. There are five routes which encircle Asia and Europe with possible offshoots to Africa and beyond: Office of the Leading Group for the Belt and Road Initiative, *Building the Belt and Road: Concept, Practice and China's Contribution*, May 2017, pp. 9–11. https://www.beltroad-initiative.com/documents/; https://www.pacificjournal.com.cn/EN/news/news281.shtml. Accessed 29 August 2020.

[50] See further: http://economictimes.indiatimes.com/articleshow/71102781.cms?utm_source=contentofinterest&utm_medium=text&utm_campaign=cppst; Somik V. Lall and Mathilde Lebrand, *Who Wins, Who Loses? Understanding the Spatially Differentiated Effects of the Belt and Road Initiative*, Policy Research Working Paper (Washington: World Bank, 2019), p. 2. https://siteresources.worldbank.org/INTEAPREGTOPINTECOTRA/Resources/chapter+1.pdf. Accessed 29 August 2020.

personnel. This is evidently a testament to China's recent economic mega-success, not only exporting its excess capacity but also transforming itself from producer of goods to provisioner of higher technology and graduating to become prime driver of econ-techno standard setting and operationalization with global reach. To date, some 80 States have signed some form of agreement with China.[51]

Yet, there are key questions of great sensibility such as: Is it really an economic cooperative platform? Is it a geo-strategic scaffolding anchored in massive infrastructural investment to build regional and world influence? Could this be the Pax Sinica brought by China's economic weight with transnational political clout? The enigma behind all this is that there is most probably a grain of truth touching upon all the disciplines—economic, political, social, cultural and legal. The panorama backed by vast sums of money is geared to loans and lending rather than gifts to the State partnering with the initiative, and the expansionist implications of the BRI have to be addressed with a call for check and balances, as well as transparency.[52] The Xinjiang region is directly relevant and a sensitive area, part of the China–Pakistan Economic Corridor, which links Kashgar in Xinjiang with the Port of Gwadar.[53]

There are some other considerations along the way. First, the urban hubs along the BRI are more likely to benefit than rural areas.[54] There is then the fear of debt.[55] For instance, there has been rethinking by Malaysia and Pakistan of the commitments to the BRI. A lesson learned was also the incident in Sri Lanka: 'With Sri Lanka unwilling to service a 8 billion usd loan at 6% interest that was used to finance the construction of Hambantota Port, China agreed in July 2017 to a debt for equity swap accompanied by a 99 years least for managing the port'.[56]

It would also be wise to take stock of some of the politico-economic tensions which might accompany the huge initiative.[57] Nor should the impact on human rights be underestimated along the way. The BRI also has to be seen now in the

---

[51] *China and the World Trade Organization*, The State Council Information Office of the People's Republic of China, Beijing, June 2018. See also: https://www.cfr.org/backgrounder/chinas-massive-belt-and-road-initiative.

[52] Peter Cai, *Understanding China's Belt and Road Initiative* (Sydney: Lowy Institute, 2017), pp. 5–6. https://www.lowyinstitute.org/publications/understanding-belt-and-road-initiative. Accessed 29 August 2020.

[53] Ibid., p. 7.

[54] Somik V. Lall and Mathilde Lebrand, *supra* note 50, pp. 4–5.

[55] John Hurley, Scott Morris, and Gailyn Portelance, *Examining the Debt Implications of the Belt and Road Initiativefrom a Policy Perspective,* Centre for Global Development (CGD) Policy Paper 121 (Washington: GDC, 2018), p. 2.

[56] Mauro Boffa, *Trade Linkages Between the Belt and Road Economies. Macroeconomics, Trade and Investment Global Practice.* Policy Research Working Paper No 8423 (Washington: World Bank, 2018), p. 20. https://openknowledge.worldbank.org/handle/10986/29768. Accessed 29 August 2020.

[57] See further: Keith Bradsher, 'China Renews its Belt and Road Push for Global Sway'.
https://www.nytimes.com/2020/01/15/business/china-belt-and-road.html;
Andrew Chatsky and James McBride, 'China's Massive Belt and Road Initiative'.
Council of Foreign Relations. https://www.cfr.org/backgrounder/chinas-massive-belt-and-road-initiative.

light of the challenges posed by COVID-19 to the network of countries linked with the BRI, impeded by global recession, mounting debt, and uncertain prospects for regeneration.

(3) Demarches

Looking back at all these developments in terms of regionalism, the positive side of the power of cooperation is that the various initiatives from the regional, to the regional plus links, can contribute much to the development and progression of the Asian region. This is accompanied by the caveat that those demarches are not alternatives to nor substitutes for the need for transparent, equitable and accountable nation building in each country of the region together with the variegated and eclectic spaces for regionalism. Rather, they should enable progressively an effective response to those basics of common humanity which cannot be measured by the quantum of economic growth and liberalization alone but which must also be assessed from the quality of people-focused inclusion and benefit-sharing.

Ironically, in this decade, the fact that COVID-19 started in Asia is both ominous, portentous and perhaps propitious. It is ominous because the future of this region will have to deal more with the threat of pandemics and other disasters, especially presaged by global warming. It is portentous because like other regions, the Asian region has, to date, been (over)fixated on economic and commercial liberalization in recent decades, without adequate distribution policies to reach vulnerable groups. It is the inevitable sign of the times that the focus has to shift much more to development-cum-environmental issues which will be the cutting edge for human survival. Yet, good cooperation between different partners in the region and beyond would, could provide opportunities for a propitious future which can help to achieve much more that one country can do alone. And there is a bottom line; regionalism has to be tried and tested to assess how it responds substantively and effectively to the quadruple nexus between peace, human rights, democracy and sustainable development which are at the heart of humanity and our shared potential. Aptly, these trails lead to various paths below.

Eclecticism?

There are perhaps three dimensions under this heading leading to the conclusion of this study. First, how have Asians contributed to multilateral activities at the grounded, human level and is this a field to be fostered? Second, what are the prospects for reform of multilateral institutions, especially the UN? And third, how has COVID-19 reshaped multilateral relations and what are some of the accompanying International Law challenges for which we should be prepared?

While the Asian region is a crucible of many egregious violations, it also provides space for commitment to International Law through human/humane actions. At least two contributions at the international level from the Asian region can be singled out: the involvement of Asians in international peace-keeping and the participation of Asians in *pro bono* international/national work such as community volunteers.[58] How Asians at the human level can contribute to the international community as part of a cooperative spirit is a linchpin of the operationalization of International Law today. Having said that, this is certainly not a solo Asian phenomenon - we will find good people everywhere, on any continent, despite the presence of the not-so-good steeped in abuse of power, also an ubiquitous challenge.

It is salutary to note that to date, it is Asians, such as Indians, Pakistanis, Bangladeshis, Indonesians and Nepalis, who have contributed the largest numbers to international peacekeeping forces.[59] At the turn of the millennium, as an anecdote witnessed by this author, it was the Thais and Malaysians who helped with UN peacekeeping in Timor Leste at the time of its independence, and the military hospital was run by doctors from the Thai military—next to the local Thai restaurant in Dili. China is also playing an increasing role in contributing personnel and other resources to international peace-keeping, despite initial hesitation.[60]

It is instructive that with several peacekeeping missions, there are human rights units which accompany them. These units should not be watered down nor undermined but strengthened. Indeed, peacekeepers should be seen as adhering to the universality of International Law, shunning instrumentalization by a particular Power to advance its expansive agenda. Moreover, while traditionally, they brought on board the interests of the general population nearby, today there is an additional issue concerning the behavioural responsiveness and accountability of the peacekeepers themselves in serving the local population in their role as an interposition force based on UN mandate.[61]

While regional organizations, particularly ASEAN, might be called upon as a group to undertake more peacekeeping, to date this has been difficult due to their attachment to the sovereignty and non-interference principle. Where countries, such

---

[58]WPS Sidhu, 'What drives South Asians to peacekeeping?', 11 January 2016. https://peaceoperationsreview.org/article/what-drives-south-asians-to-peacekeeping/; https://www.unv.org/Success-stories/Volunteering-forefront-peace-operations; https://www.babseacle.org/articles/collaborative-pro-bono-asia/; https://www.volunteerworld.com/en/volunteer-abroad/asia. Accessed 30 August 2020.

[59]The Nation, 'Which Asian country provides the most troops for the UN peacekeeping mission?', 7 December 2017. https://www.nationthailand.com/asean-plus/30333379. Accessed 30 August 2020.

See further: Sebastian von Einsiedel and Anthony Yazaki, 'East Asian perceptions of the UN and its role in peace and security', UN University, 1 June 2016. https://cpr.unu.edu/east-asian-perceptions-of-the-un-and-its-role-in-peace-and-security.html. Accessed 30 August 2020; Chiyuki Aoi and Yee-Kuang Heng (eds.), Asia Pacific Nations in*International Peace Support and Stability Operations* (New York: Palgrave Macmillan, 2014); Brendan Howe and Boris Kondoch (eds.), *Peacekeeping and the Asia–Pacific*, (New York: Brill/Nijhoff, 2016).

[60]ICG, *China's Growing Role in UN Peacekeeping*, **Report 166, 17 April 2009**.https://www.crisisgroup.org/asia/north-east-asia/china/china-s-growing-role-un-peacekeeping. Accessed 30 August 2020; Christoph Zuercher, 'China's peacekeepers—new resources, new values; Democratic nations should resist Beijing's attempts to downgrade human rights', *Nikkei Asian Review*, 12 FEBRUARY 2019. https://asia.nikkei.com/Opinion/China-s-peacekeepers-new-resources-new-values. Accessed 8 April 2020.

[61]https://www.un.org/preventing-sexual-exploitation-and-abuse/. Accessed 20 August 2020.

as Indonesia, Thailand and Malaysia, contribute, they do so in an individual capacity rather than as representing the (sub)regional organization. To their credit, these countries have acted as a hub for training on peacekeeping: Vietnam, Cambodia, Indonesia and Thailand. Given the vagaries of budgets and political will (or lack of it), it is likely that there will be smaller peacekeeping activities in future, but this should not downplay the importance of peacekeeping for international peace and security.

As for peacebuilding, there is a UN organ—the Peacebuilding Commission—through which Asians can contribute. There is also a peacebuilding fund. To date, however, most of the peacebuilding operations have been in Africa. Some Asian countries, such as Sri Lanka and Afghanistan, are beginning to enjoy some coverage. Activities include building of justice system, security system and transitional justice such as through truth and reconciliation commissions. Till recently, this was too much of an *ex post* situation which did not address the issue of prevention of conflicts, particularly by tackling root causes. However, with the UN's more recent reshaping of the peace concept to cover "sustainable peace"[62], there are opportunities for more *ex ante* action. In Africa, this has opened the door also for pairing with world financial bodies, such as the World Bank, and regional organizations, and perhaps this predicates some possibilities in the Asian region.

On another front, we can welcome more Asian participation in people to people activities such as in the UN Volunteers and other volunteer groups, including through Asian (sub)regional organizations. This is also a gateway for South–South cooperation, and links between Asians and between Asians and other parts of the world, such as Africa, are to be lauded; the transcontinental and transcultural collaboration should be maximized. SDGs also offer channels of cooperation through its various goals which require multi-stakeholder inputs and partnerships. There is also the Asia Youth Volunteer Exchange Programme.[63] Meanwhile, ASEAN has also indicated its commitment to build what could be called ASEAN Peace Corps, basically a gathering of youth volunteers to help communities in ASEAN and possibly elsewhere. As a background stimulus, there is also the ASEAN Declaration on Young Entrepreneurs adopted in Brunei, highlighting the role of young entrepreneurs in helping to develop the region.[64] There is this projection of activities under Youth Plan 2015-20 which offers youth volunteerism from educational activities to field oriented work[65].

With regard to UN reform, one quandary concerns what to do with the UN which is the backbone of multilateralism on which the global community still relies but

---

[62]https://www.un.org/pga/71/wp-content/uploads/sites/40/2016/12/Sustainable-Peace-and-2030-Agenda_Concept-note_FINAL.pdf; https://reliefweb.int/report/world/un-s-new-sustaining-peace-agenda-policy-breakthrough-making. Accessed 30 August 2020.

[63]See further: https://www.unv.org/tags/asia-youth-volunteer-exchange-programme; https://www.cn.undp.org/content/china/en/home/about-us/united-nations-volunteers/un-youth-university-volunteers.html; https://www.unv.org/tags/asia-youth-volunteer-exchange-programme.

[64]Bandar Seri Begawan Declaration on Youth Entrepreneurship and Employment, 2013. https://asean.org/storage/2012/05/2013_BSB-Declaration-on-Youth-Entrepreneurship-and-Employment_23rd-Summit.pdf. Accessed 30 August 2020.

[65]https://asean.org/storage/2018/02/ASEAN-Work-Plan-on-Youth-2016-2020_Post-Mid-Term-Review.pdf. Accessed 13 February 2020.

from which more should be expected, and how the Asian region might help. The last round of major reforms was in 2005 with the World Outcome Document which did away with the no longer needed Trusteeship Council and the much critiqued Commission on Human Rights, replacing it with the UN Human Rights Council. It established the Peace-building Commission and introduced the Democracy Fund. It left the UNSC and GA almost untouched—apart from the consecration or (impugned) legitimization of the R2P concept which was discussed earlier. 2020 was supposed to be a year of reflection on newer reform.

The UN 2020 Initiative basically advocated a key role for the UN SG; prevention and sustaining peace; a people-centred UN; One UN; regionalism; adequate funding; and continuing space for UN reform.[66] However, this has been delayed by the advent of COVID-19, and the only major news at the beginning of 2021 was that the current UNSG is now to seek a second term of office.[67] In that setting, the UNSC is still top heavy and often dysfunctional with the Superpowers' overuse of the veto, while the general UN budget is still skewed. Ironically, the allocation for human rights is around 3.7% of the official budget and much of the UN activities on human rights depends on extra-budgetary contributions which might be earmarked or unearmarked.[68]

Another anomaly is that despite all the talk about "We the Peoples" as the very first words of the UN Charter (and hopefully its raison d'etre), inherently necessitating people's participation and stakeholdership, the UN is still basically an intergovernmental organization consisting of mainly representatives from the Executive branch of Government sitting on its various main organs. Is it not about time that we had a UN People's Assembly or Parliament as a counterweight to the domination by the Executive branch?[69] As an inanimate body, the UN could benefit from humanization and democratization with more spaces for civil society and other members of national communities. A soft entry point for this might be to set up a People's Assembly with at least the power to be consulted by the UNSC and UNGA when there are key issues of peace, human rights, democracy and sustainable development. Modalities will have to be worked out on the selection or election process, and it could draw some experience from existing interparliamentary (non-UN) organizations, such as the Interparliamentary Union.

Finally, there is the reality of COVID-19 and its gargantuan consequences. In early 2021 when the last part of this book was being redrafted, Coronavirus or COVID-19 was wreaking havoc in the Asian region and beyond. Nearly one hundred million had been infected worldwide and a huge number of deaths was piling up in many

---

66 https://un2020.org/a-progressive-reform-agenda-for-the-united-nations/.

67 https://www.thenationalnews.com/world/antonio-guterres-seeks-second-term-as-un-secretary-general-1.1144319. Accessed 26 January 2021.

68 https://www.ohchr.org/EN/AboutUs/Pages/FundingBudget.aspx#:~:text=Human%20rights%20gets%20a%20tiny,UN%20regular%20budget%3A%20only%203.7%25&text=While%20approximately%20half%20of%20all,the%20total%20UN%20regular%20budget. Accessed 30 August 2020.

69 https://www.internationaldemocracywatch.org/index.php/campaign-for-a-more-democratic-united-nations. Accessed 30 August 2020.

parts of the world.[70] Tens of millions were out of work due to the pandemic, and its impact on the economy globally and locally was more than harrowing, with grave recession looming ominously around the corner. Many governments were adopting a lockdown asking or compelling people to stay home to stem the tide of the virus, while others went further to use emergency directives or laws to close off regions and countries from the outer world, even to the extent of imposing a curfew or the equivalent, preventing people from travelling internally/externally and or from being outside their homes during certain periods of the day. Yet, with wise strategy and effective action, various countries were starting to contain the virus and the number of victims was reaching a plateau in some regions of the world, pending the wait for arrival of a vaccine.

If this was the most intractable test for the world community there and then, what message might it have for International Law and the Asian region (or vice versa) with a sense of immediacy—especially from the angle of how the one might inform the other to act/react humanely in the most dire circumstances? On the one hand, it can be submitted that in such situation, International Law definitely contributes to the Asian region by underlining three dichotomies with the need for checks and balances against misuse of power and or overzealous policies which might be misguided or misdirected resulting in injustices. This balance of power is also useful for disease control and eradication.

First, Objectivity and Subjectivity. International Law cannot leave States to take action without some objective criteria. This is a key premise of International Law which, while respecting much in terms of State action and State discretion, cannot yield to the claim of unfettered discretion as part of the State's subjectivity. The parameters of State action must be tested by how it complements rather than undermines International Law, and those international standards are aplenty, embodying objectivity, as found in many of the sources and discourses of International Law, such as treaties and State practice.

Second, Individuality and Collectivity. Clearly there is a balance to be struck between individuals and the community. In the COVID-19 situation, it is understandable, for example, that many rights and liberties usually associated with the individual can be and should be constrained to help to protect the collectivity—within reason. Here again, International Law offers tools to balance between the two; for instance, if freedom of expression and freedom of movement are to be limited in times of emergency, constraints still need to offer convincing explanations of why—and there are tests of legality, necessity, proportionality, legitimacy, universality and equality which come into play already mentioned in the earlier Chapter of this book on plights and human rights.[71]

Third, Responsibility and Solidarity. Obviously in times of crisis, the issue of responsibility emerges strongly. On the one hand, State responsibility. On the other hand, individual and or group responsibility to help control and overcome the disease.

---

[70] https://www.worldometers.info/coronavirus/. Accessed 25 January 2021.

[71] Adina Ponta, 'Human Rights in the time of Coronavirus', *ASIL*, 24(2020)5. https://www.asil.org/insights/volume/24/issue/5/human-rights-law-time-coronavirus. Accessed 30 August 2020.

Yet, there is a bridge for shared responsibility to tackle health and other crises. And that mutuality is one which opens the door to both national and international solidarity in terms of partnering for support and cooperation.

Those considerations are all at the heart of international relations and International Law, and concomitantly the international system in which they are anchored.

Conversely, what lessons might the Asian region in its response to COVID-19 have for International Law underlining some priority issues which might have a broader outreach?

Interestingly, effective action against COVID-19 (so far and not yet finished) has been based upon at least three T's[72]: Trace, meaning trace those who might be infected including the asymptomatic carriers; Test, meaning use medical tests ("swabs") to find out whether a person is a carrier and extend such tests to as many people as possible to identity the group which could have a multiplier effect; and Treat, meaning that once a person is discovered to be a carrier, appropriate treatment should be adopted—including self quarantine or in more serious cases, hospitalization (bearing in mind that there is a wait for access to vaccines and there is also the fear of disparity between the rich and the poor which will condition access thereto).

Those three T's can also be summed up nicely as highlighting the call for accessibility (Trace), transparency (Test) and accountability/remedy (Treat) which are also highly relevant to International Law and how it interplays with the Asian region, its States and peoples.[73] Those three musketeers might also do well as proponents of the kind of International Law which should progress—it should be well grounded and reach out with relevancy and credibility to the common humanity that awaits its wisdom.[74]

Thus, a time of crisis may also be a time of contribution and reflection, if not an opportunity. A forward-looking agenda concerning the Asian region might be tempted to address particularly these emerging issues. COVID-19 has accentuated the advent of the three A's: Automation, Artificial Intelligence (AI), and Algorithms

---

[72]Nazihah Muhamad Noor and Jomo Kwame Sundaram, 'East Asian Lessons for Controlling Covid-19'. https://www.ipsnews.net/2020/03/east-asian-lessons-controlling-covid-19/. Accessed 8 April 2020.

[73]See further: Binaifer Nowrojee,' It's not too late for Europe and the US to learn lessons from Asia to fight COVID-19'. https://www.euronews.com/2020/03/25/it-s-not-too-late-for-europe-and-the-us-to-learn-lessons-from-asia-to-fight-covid-19-view. Accessed 8 April 2020.

[74]https://www.un.org/sg/en/content/sg/statement/2020-06-25/secretary-generals-full-transcript-of-his-press-conference-the-launch-of-the-un-comprehensive-response-covid-19-delivered. Accessed 25 June 2020. The message from the UN Secretary General in mid 2020 sounded the following note on our desired future:

'More than 230,000 people in 193 Member States and observer states engaged in our (UN) forward-looking UN75 survey.

The responses paint a clear picture of priorities in the time of COVID-19 and beyond:
Number one: universal access to healthcare.
Number two: strengthen solidarity between people and nations.
Number three: rethink the global economy against inequality.'

linked with digitalization which can either be disruptive or transformative.[75] The ILO at its Centenary already warned through its Global Commission on the World of Work that there is a need for preparedness and to adapt and reskill.[76] There are two prongs of sensibility. First, how to evolve some rules (hard or soft) to prepare for (preempt?) the 3 A's, especially the fact that AI may one day act contrary to the human order. Second, how to ensure that the 3 A's serve humanity and can be ultimately directed by human command.

The advent of new technology, including digital technology and AI, is already here and requires responsiveness for now and for the future. It has been accelerated and necessitated also by the menace of COVID-19 and other pandemics. Asian countries are an inevitable cog in this wheel of futurism which is also a test for human capacity and survival. In fairness, there is no gainsaying that some areas in Asia, as elsewhere, can naturally benefit from the three A's, especially AI. For instance, there is huge potential for robots to help in the medical field on surgical tasks which demand precision and repetition. Some Asian countries with good medical health system can prospect to expand the medical services field linked with AI as part of its future development not only for its nationals but also for non-nationals, as part of its future economy. Interestingly also, China now supersedes the US in being the No1 applicant for patents and we know that there is also competition between the Superpowers for 5G technology and all the implications of comparative advantage foreshadow a changing world order, replete with the presence of more inanimate actors.[77]

What rules, if any, should one evolve to enjoy the value added of new technology while preventing it from becoming an insidious threat to humanity and the natural order? Also why not encourage Asia to become more of a sentinel in the forefront of humanizing the process—at least starting with a substantive alliance between democratic and open-minded countries from this region?[78]

More specifically on AI, globally Governments in 2019 already started to propose some principles to deal with AI, in particular the following: "inclusive growth, sustainable development and well-being", "human-centered values and fairness", "transparency and explainability", "robustness, security and safety" and "accountability".[79]

European catalysts have provided elements of future deliberation, possibly with a Code of Ethics as the starting point to regulate AI. The elements of concern include: ethics, safety, transparency, comprehensibility, monitorability and accountability, privacy, norms, standards and infrastructure, impact on work, employment, working conditions and social systems, education and skills, accessibility, social

---

[75] ILO, *Negotiating the Algorithm: Automation, Artificial Intelligence and Labour Protection*, Employment Working Paper No. 246 (Geneva: ILO, 2018).

[76] Global Commission on the World of Work, *Work for a Brighter Future* (ILO: Geneva 2019).

[77] See further: Nicol Turner Lee, *Navigating the US-China 5GCompetition* (Washington: Brookings Institute, 2020). https://www.brookings.edu/research/navigating-the-us-china-5g-competition/.

[78] Marcelo Corrales, Mark Fenwick & Nikolaus Forgó (eds), *Robotics, AI and the Future of Law* (Singapore: Springer, 2018).

[79] G20 Ministerial Statement on Trade and Digital Economy. 8–9 June 2019. https://www.oecd.org/going-digital/ai/principles/. Accessed 30 August 2020.

(in)equality, inclusiveness and distribution, law and regulation, governance and democracy, warfare and superintelligence. There is a predominant message that AI should be for the benefit of humanity.[80] A related idea calls for the banning of autonomous weapons which is discussed below. The UNI Global Union[81] an international Union movement, identifies various key principles concerning the ethics of AI, inviting serious contemplation, including the need for AI transparency; the call for AI to have an ethical black box to contain relevant data; genderless AI; and the need to share the benefits of AI and to ensure that it serves humanity.[82]

Much soul-searching and reflection have been witnessed by the European region, inviting the Asian region to be more cognizant of the following issues:

- Human agency and oversight,
- Technical robustness and safety,
- Privacy and data governance,
- Transparency,
- Diversity, non-discrimination and fairness,
- Societal and environmental wellbeing, and
- Accountability.[83]

In the nexus between International Law and the Asian region, there are at least two major windows of opportunities for action:

1. On human rights, especially privacy, data protection and non-discrimination.

The advent of AI and the use of algorithms which interlink with how data are accumulated, collated and analyzed may have positive results in facilitating services on some fronts, but they may also impinge on privacy, data handling and usage with impact on how people are profiled and treated. Given that the Asian region has quite a few non-democracies present, a crucial challenge is data utilization and surveillance for so-called national security (which is often not much more than self-preservation of the elite). Beware of authoritarianism turning into totalitarianism! The more enlightened partners in progress should help to devise ways and means of using data and technology to counter surveillance systems where they undermine peace, human rights, democracy and sustainable development.

---

[80] *Opinion of the European Economic and Social Committee on 'Artificial Intelligence—The consequences of artificial intelligence on the (digital) single market, production, consumption, employment and society' (own-initiative opinion) (2017/C 288/01) Rapporteur: Catelijne MULLER.* https://eur-lex.europa.eu/legal-content/EN/TXT/PDF/?uri=CELEX:52016IE5369&from=EN. Accessed 30 August 2020.

[81] See further: https://www.uniglobalunion.org/news/uni-global-union-joins-partnership-ai#:~:text=UNI%20Global%20Union%20this%20week,the%20future%20world%20of%20work.

[82] https://www.oecd-forum.org/users/75928-dr-christina-j-colclough/posts/29527-10-principles-for-ethical-artificial-intelligence.

[83] Brussels, 19.2.2020 COM (2020) 65 final WHITE PAPER On Artificial Intelligence—A European approach to excellence and trust, p.9. https://ec.europa.eu/info/sites/info/files/commission-white-paper-artificial-intelligence-feb2020_en.pdf. Accessed 30 August 2020.

2. On safety and effective functioning of AI.

This may range from the dangers from various AI-linked machines, such as weapons which may cause deadly, incalculable harm, to more simple AI instruments such as self-driving cars. Beware of artificial responsibility (or lack of responsibility!).

Preparedness and preventive action are perhaps the answer to those puzzles, while not forgetting to protect people's rights and remediation for wrongs. They range from the possibility of an international agreement to outlaw some forms of AI to other interventions more related to training/education, data control and monitoring, as well as post facto, curative measures.

With regard to the space for an international agreement, perhaps the most immediate stepping stone is to work towards an international agreement to prohibit or at least control autonomous weapons, such as killer robots. Thus there have been discussions in recent years to expand the reach of existing treaties or conventions on weapons control and disarmament. The most natural entry point is to extend the reach of the Convention concerning Conventional Weapons (CCW)[84] which already has various Protocols to regulate or prohibit use of various weapons, such as blinding laser weapons and explosive remnants of war. Possibly another Protocol could be agreed upon to outlaw killer robots. How to extend the scope of the CCW via a new Protocol or opt for a totally new treaty? There is a certain logic to how such an additional Protocol or new treaty would be structured: it should address and include provisions on these elements:

- Underlying rationale: to ban or regulate?
- Definition of autonomous weapons: noting that there is currently no agreed definition, although an ICRC meeting in 2014 referred to them as: 'weapons that can independently select and attack targets. These are weapons systems with autonomy in the "critical functions" of acquiring, tracking, selecting and attacking targets.'[85]
- Issues of prohibition or regulation of production, possession, transfer, use and related elimination
- Agency and attribution: if accountability is to be attributed to the human hand behind the robot, what element of control needs to be proved—overall control, effective control or some other control test[86], with varying degrees of strictness in regard to attribution to humans?
- Complicity

[84]Convention on Prohibitions or Restrictions on the Use of Certain Conventional Weapons which may be deemed to be Excessively Injurious or to have Indiscriminate Effects 1980. https://treaties.un.org/pages/ViewDetails.aspx?src=TREATY&mtdsg_no=XXVI-2&chapter=26&lang=en https://www.icrc.org/en/doc/assets/files/other/icrc_002_0811.pdf. Accessed 30 August 2020.

[85]ICRC, *Autonomous Weapon Systems: Technical, Military, Legal and Humanitarian Aspects. Expert Meeting: Geneva, Switzerland: 26–28 March 2014* (Geneva: ICRC 2014), p. 5.

[86]For example: Djemila Carron, 'When is a conflict international? Time for new control tests in IHL ', *IRRC*, 98(2016)3, pp. 1019–041.

- Responsibility, including in regard to non-State actor, such as the techno-AI businesses
- Verification and monitoring
- Remedy and assistance for victims
- Education and awareness raising
- Reporting and Review of the Protocol or treaty
- Link with UN system, possibly with the UNGA and the UNSC for possible leveraging
- Resources and commitments.

However, ratification of the CCW by Asian countries has been limited to date, and there should be more stimulus to encourage Asian countries, as well as regional organizations, to be involved in this spectrum.[87]

With regard to the other question interwoven with human rights, privacy and oversight, and bearing in mind the important role of the private sector, options to forestall harm include softer measures (such as Codes of Conduct pertaining to industries linked with the AI) and or harder oversight (such as national laws and International treaties imposing supervision and responsibility), as well as a variety of actions to check and balance for transparency, prevention of abuse, protection of rights, responses to vulnerabilities, and remedies cum accountability/responsibility.

Comprehensive action inevitably depends upon: training data[88]; data and record-keeping[89]; information to be provided[90]; robustness and accuracy[91]; human oversight; and specific requirements for remote biometric identification.[92]

Especially on human oversight,[93] measures of a preventive nature as well as remedial kind are both required, identifying possibly cooperation and operationalization in a practical manner, at least with measures to ensure that humans are able to review the AI system; monitoring with checks to deactivate when needed; and automatic constraints to stop the system from proceeding in some situations (e.g. a driverless car must stop under certain weather conditions with poor visibility).[94]

AI is on the cusp of being omnipresent in the Asian region, as elsewhere.[95] Asian countries and regional organizations need to be ready to harness its positive side while preventing and remedying its negative implications, including abuses for surveillance and undemocratic purposes. Collateral to this, civil society and enlightened nations

[87] About 30 Asian countries are parties to the CCW: https://treaties.un.org/pages/ViewDetails.aspx?src=TREATY&mtdsg_no=XXVI-2&chapter=26&lang=en. Accessed 2 September 2020.

[88] *Brussels, 19.2.2020 COM(2020) 65 final WHITE PAPER On Artificial Intelligence—A European approach to excellence and trust, supra* note 83.

[89] Ibid.

[90] Ibid.

[91] Ibid.

[92] Ibid.

[93] Ibid. p.21.

[94] Ibid.

[95] See further: https://www.fintechnews.org/adoption-of-artificial-intelligence-on-the-rise-in-asean/. Accessed 2 September 2020.

need to be ever vigilant and advocate for precautions against insidious acts and inhumane actions.

Underpinning those orientations is the ***human-in-command*** approach to AI which, in an earlier reference, was described as 'including the precondition that the development of AI be responsible, safe and useful, where machines remain machines and people retain control over these machines at all times.'[96]

That precept is linked with at least two prospective actions. First, in the development of AI, humans must have the power to control the inanimate actor. "It" would be switched off indubitably on human command. This also implies human accountability behind all the AI. Second, autonomous AI and machines need to be well regulated and or prohibited, as discussed above starting with killer robots. This interlinks closely with International Law, IHL, human rights and disarmament in an expanded panorama.

The invitation to the Asian region, possibly as a sentinel of the humanizing process, is thus to explore, interlink and share well with its many stakeholders on that path-finding journey. This is anchored in the platitude that ultimately it is the human face/fate which should shape the preferred future, especially when and where inanimate actors appear as a potential existential challenge.

Harking to and heartened by a people-based approach, there lingers then the question: faced with those novel challenges of International Law, will the Asian region be well prepared, persistent and prescient?

Source: Author's Team.

[96]*Opinion of the European Economic and Social Committee on 'Artificial Intelligence—The consequences of artificial intelligence on the (digital) single market, production, consumption, employment and society' (own-initiative opinion)(2017/C 288/01)*, *supra* note 80, p. 2; para. 1.6.

Appendix A

Vitit Muntarbhorn, 'International Law and Asia: A New Era ... Miracle or Mirage?' (conference paper 2011) (This paper by Vitit Muntarbhorn was for the Asian Society of International Law Conference in Beijing, August 2011. All views expressed are personal. The author conveys his warmest thanks to Paisit Pusittrakul for help in providing documentation for the paper.).

The relationship between International Law and Asia was fully on display recently in 2011 when the International Court of Justice (ICJ) ordered provisional measures in regard to a conflict between Thailandand Cambodia over an age-old dispute concerning an ancient Temple located near their border. Basically, the court ordered the troops of both parties to leave the area in which the Temple is found and created a provisional demilitarized zone in the process. The dispute between the two countries dates back to 1962 when in an earlier case, the Court adjudged that the temple itself was in territory under Cambodian sovereignty. The current dispute concerns the surrounding area and the military conflict which erupted in recent times. While there can, of course, be a debate concerning the impact of those provisional measures and the extent to which either party is fully satisfied with the Court's order, what is welcome is the peaceful settlement of the dispute by international judicial means. Hence, the relevancy and value added of International Law in all its immediacy.

On scrutiny, the dispute is also a microcosm of various key issues of International Law which are pertinent to Asia's relationship with International Law as a whole. For example, in the Court's judgment in 1962, it had to deliberate on treaties and a map drawn up in the early part of the twentieth century linked with the colonial period in Southeast Asia. Thus there were—and are—questions concerning the impact of colonization on the formation of International Law and its nexus with those countries affected thereby. In the 1962 case, the Court applied the principle of estoppel, a principle found in many national jurisdictions which has also become a principle of International Law. Thus there was—and is—an umbilical relationship between national law/jurisprudence, State practice and the sources of International Law. As a consequence of the 1962 judgement, Thailand also withdrew its troops from the Temple and returned artefacts previously taken from it. Thus this provided a lesson

V. Muntarbhorn, *Challenges of International Law in the Asian Region*,
https://doi.org/10.1007/978-981-16-2047-8

concerning the compliance with and enforcement of International Law, which is still a key question concerning other parts of the world today.

While the vestiges of colonization still inflict negative impact on the Asian region in various settings, it should be noted that Asian countries, including those casting off the colonial yoke, have largely embraced International Law including the rules that were formulated during colonial times, such as those concerning the acquisition of territories. This approach can perhaps be explained by the fact that those rules provide a degree of certainty, stability and security in the conduct of international relations. However, at times those rules may also be seen as giving rise to a "fait accompli" which is not always acceptable today. It is thus not surprising that some Asian countries have put forward their approaches to aspects of International Law seeking more space for evolving such law, some examples of which can be seen in the discussion below.

On another front, in recent years, the performance of several Asian countries in economic terms has been nothing short of stellar, thereby being described as an economic "miracle". Can that miracle be translated into a new era also for International Law and its linkage with Asia? In a sense, the twenty-first century offers the region a host of opportunities to help shape the contemporary setting of International Law. If the nineteenth century was (arguably) the European century and the twentieth century was (arguably) the American century, will the twenty-first century be the Asian century? Can the region rise credibly and assuredly to such an epoch-making challenge?

The answer to that conundrum may well depend upon how the Asian region is able to respond to a series of key challenges encapsulated below. Asia's own development and engagement with the world is now raising issues that move beyond colonial times to embrace the more modernistic challenges of Statehood and its relationship with other catalysts, both nationally and internationally in terms of peace, security, development and participation. For instance, the premise that International Law is very much at the service of the State (or rather the Government) is being impugned increasingly in a world of multi-polarity and a plurality of actors beyond the State itself. Indeed, it may be posited that while International Law is a set of norms, that normativity is now enmeshed in a pool of other considerations in terms of how it mirrors the needs of the globe and its eclectic mix of States, international organizations, communities, individuals, other non State entities and Nature itself with inter-generational implications.

The challenges at Asia's doorsteps include the following:

1. Sovereignty-cum-security

Although the notion of sovereignty itself developed with the rise of the nation State and the Westphalian concretization of that entity in the seventeenth century, thus laying the groundwork for European States to expand their scope of influence in other parts of the world, it has been embraced by the countries of the Asian region as a whole. National sovereignty is a concept and catchphrase that predominates in the practice of AsianStates.

The most frequent manifestation of such practice is perhaps in regard to the advocacy of the principle of non-interference in the internal affairs of a State. Several Asian Governments espouse this principle almost in extremis when it comes to the issue of how they treat the people under their jurisdiction. When the international community raises the concern of human rights in this regard, there is almost a kneejerk reaction on the part of less-than-democratic countries (and sometimes democratic countries!) to claim the non-interference principle based on national sovereignty to rebut the international claim.

Today, however, it can be argued that sovereignty is not absolute, is no longer State/Government-centric and is measured by the duty and obligation on the part of the State/Government to respond to the expectations of the population, including their protection. This mirrors a more human face to sovereignty. A clear development on this front at the international level is the notion of the Responsibilityto Protect(RtoP/R2P), implying that the State (or rather the Government) is obliged to protect its population from serious violations, namely genocide, crimes against humanity, war crimesand ethnic cleansing, failing which the international community has the right to offer assistance to that State to fulfill that function. If that pillar of support fails to work, then the international community can resort through the United Nations(UN) to other measures, including enforcement measures under Chapter VII of the UN Charter. While the principle has been particularly applied through UN Security Council resolutions on protection of civilians, and in regard to various African States, such as Libya, the message therefrom should not be lost on those Asian countries which indulge in repression and oppression.

Another manifestation of sovereignty is its linkage with the issue of security, especially national security. While the latter is particularly relevant today in a world where new threats, such as terrorism, have been spreading, it also needs to be balanced with the demands of democracy. In several Asian countries (and elsewhere), national security is often used and abused to confer broad discretion on the authorities to curb the activities of their population who are seeking more space and participation in the country. Thus, the rise of human security as a notion internationally which can help to humanize the former preoccupation with national security.

2. Equitable Development

Development is both a material and non-material issue, and it has both individual and collective aspects and national and international dimensions. In historical terms, one of the most egregious impediments to human development was slavery and colonization. In more recent times, the issue of development has progressed to become one where there is an inevitable interface between developed and developing countries and between developed and developing communities (some of which may be internal—within a country—rather than external).

International Law classically did not reflect these concerns adequately and it was incumbent upon developing countries, including Asian countries, to advocate a more balanced approach internationally. Thus the rise of the "right to development" propounded by a UN General Assembly Resolution which is celebrating its 25th anniversary this year. The right itself calls for a more equitable international system and a national system that is a gateway to overcoming poverty, promoting social justice and fulfilling the needs of groups requiring special attention, such as women and children.

One key test case today is to reach out to heavily indebted countries, and there is a host of actions which help to implement that right. For instance, in addition to debt relief for least developed countries, international aid is also being given to stimulate small scale commercial activities so that the local population can be more involved in trade—"aid for trade". At the national level, there is the crucial test of how national development planning can be more attuned to satisfying the basic needs of the population. Increasingly, the issue of transparency and equitable allocations is raised. In real terms, this implies measures to overcome corruption, to ensure more sharing of land, other resources, and national budget in a pro-poor (people) framework, as well as to shift military expenditure to the social development sector.

From the angle of measures to deal with poverty, while some Asian countries have fared well in their response, as seen in their fulfillment of the global MillenniumDevelopment Goals (MDGs), others lag behind, at times aggravated by hermetic political situations which hamper people's basic needs.

3. Protection of Rights

The rise of human rights in the post Second World War period complements, and is complemented by, the rise of the nation State in Asia as part of liberation from colonization. It can be noted that the right to self-determination has been espoused and enjoyed by many peoples seeking to free themselves from colonial fetters here in Asia and elsewhere.

Beyond that scenario, the picture is intriguing, particularly from the angle of the relationship between the State and the rights of the individual and/or community. For instance, apropos the 9 core international human rights treaties stipulating standards for protecting those rights, there is a paucity of ratifications from Asian countrieson several fronts. Only the Convention on the Rights of the Child has been ratified by all Asian countries, attesting to the broad political will from the region in a specific area. However, increasingly more Asian countries are becoming parties to the Covenant on Civil and Political Rights, the Covenant on Economic, Social and Cultural Rights and the Convention on the Elimination of All Forms of Racial Discrimination. A while ago, China signed the Covenant on Civil and Political Rights, and its ratification is awaited with much anticipation.

In regard to situations concerning warfare or armed conflicts, international humanitarian law comes into play. Flashpoints in Asia include the Middle East, Iraqand Afghanistan. It is salutary that all Asian countries are parties to the four Geneva Conventions of 1949 in this respect. However, a number have still not acceded to the 1977 Protocols which build upon those four Conventions. From the angle of protection of civilians from the impact of various armaments, the picture is also varied. For example, while most Asian countries are parties to the Convention to prohibit stockpile and use of anti-personnel mines, some key Asian countries (including some big ones) have kept their distance from the Convention and still produce and deploy such mines against the international tide. Nuclear weapons also come into play in regard to how Asian countries participate in key treaties on this front. Particularly with respect to the Nuclear Non-proliferation treaty, India, Pakistanand Israel are not yet parties thereto. The more recent Comprehensive Nuclear Test Ban treaty also deserves universal ratification and implementation.

The mere fact that a country ratifies a treaty, of course, does not necessarily mean that it will be well implemented. Conversely, non-ratification does not necessarily imply non-respect of rights. Yet, that umbrella of international treaties has a value added which invites ratification because it provides a degree of certainty as to what the rights are and how they should be implemented and interpreted—objectively (with international monitoring) rather than subjectively (based on State discretion). It should also not be forgotten that those international standards merely stipulate basic minimum standards, not basic maximum. If and where AsianStates wish to perform better than international standards, all the better, but they should not undermine those standards. That is the preferred value in the spirit of International Law which posits the uniformity of rights while respecting the diversity of peoples.

Aptly this leads to the now rather "clichéd" question of "Asian values" and their relationship with human rights and their universality. There is a tendency on the part of some Asian Governments to claim that various practices—"particularities"—found in this region need to be highlighted and where there is conflict with international standards, those particularities should prevail. As claimed, the particularities include Asian diligence and respect for authority. At the heart of the issue is that some Asian Governments are uncomfortable with civil and political rights, such as freedom of expression and association which are at the heart of democracy, even though they are ready to espouse economic, social and cultural rights, such as the right to food, with enthusiasm. From an international human rights perspective, while values that enrich universal standards are welcome, those which are sub-par need to be reformed and brought up to the basic minimum international standards. Indeed, Asian countries should be proud of the fact that the country with biggest democracy (numerically) is in Asia and the world's biggest Islamic population in a democracy is also in Asia. Non-violence imbued with the Gandhian spirit is also a positive value that Asia proffers to the world. Yet, some of the world's key non-democracies, including the most totalitarian and violent, are visibly in Asia.

The wisdom of the man, woman and child on the street or in a distant village as part of a value from the Asian region to enrich International Law could perhaps be tendered as follows. The right to food and the right to comment on the quality of the food are equally important and indivisible—without which Asian (or any other) stomachs may be inflicted with (political) indigestion.

4. Territorial Ambiguities

Territoriality is at the heart of the rise of the nation State in this region and elsewhere. It is also a common feature that ambiguities are present on the frontiers of many States and their neighbours. Interestingly, some International Law principles in regard to the intangibility of frontiers and how to deal with disputes deriving from colonial times, may at times offer both benefits (e.g. certainty in regard to frontiers inherited from a former colonial master) and disadvantages (e.g. injustices caused by colonization and unequal bargaining power). For instance, while the ICJ has sometimes resorted to the principle of "uti possidetis" (linked with the intangibility issue) which has its origins in colonization, it has also acknowledged the ambivalent nature of colonial maps by intimating that the maps are not necessarily conclusive (as in the court case between Burkina Faso and Mali).

Given that territorial disputes affect many Asian countries, it should be recognized that at times, their quest for judicial settlement has also led to the development of International Law in a constructive manner. For instance, in the two cases concerning maritime disputesbetween Malaysiaand Indonesia and between Singaporeand Malaysia, before the ICJ, the Court underlined the importance of proof of effective activities by the parties in the disputed area—"effectivites"—to help reach a judgement concerning territorial delimitation.

At another level, the ambiguities may pertain to land, sea and/or air. Some have been settled through diplomatic negotiations, while others have reached out to judicial settlement. Others, such as the dispute over the Spratly islands and other islands in the South China sea, remain hotspots. One situation of possible convergence is a shared approach, such as through joint development areas between various countries concerning overlapping maritime resources. It would be salutary if all Asian countries could also become parties to the UN Convention on the Law of the Sea, so as to have a rules-based approach for negotiations within an international framework.

5. Eco-sensibility and Disaster Response

It should not passed unnoticed that one of the key treaties which addressed global warming and the issue of capping carbon emissions was formalized in Asia in the form of the Kyoto Protocol which helps to implement the international framework Convention on Climate Change. Its focused approach concretises fixed targets for reducing carbon emissions while allowing a degree of flexibility for developing countries to follow that path. In this regard, the convergence of Asian countries with other countries is welcome.

The challenge now is to move beyond the Kyoto targets which end in 2012, and current negotiations, most recently in Cancun, provide for key incentives to move towards the next phase, possibly with a new facility to help developing countries invest in activities that limit climate change. The issues of what target for which countries—in a spirit of common but differentiated targeting—and what monitoring are still open to debate, but the sense of urgency awaiting a possible agreement should not be lost in the diplomacy: the world needs to cap the rise in global temperature at no more than 2 degrees celsius in the next phase. Failure to act on this front may portend a doomsday scenario for Asia and the globe.

On a related front, it can be recognized that despite the tragedy of natural disasters, including the recent Tsunami disaster inflicted on Japan, this is an area which lends itself relatively easily to constructive cooperation between countries. The picture of the leaders of China, Republic of Koreaand Japan coming together to sympathise with the victims of the Tsunami in Japan this year was a testament to the spirit of cooperation which transcended boundaries and politics. En passant, looking back to the progression of international disaster response, what started several decades ago as the International Decade on disaster response, was followed up with a "soft law" global plan of action under the title the Yokohama Plan of Action, to which the Hyogo Plan of Action succeeded, to guide the world in disaster response and cooperation. Disaster preparedness, disaster prevention, disaster management and disaster mitigation invite cooperative actions on which Asian countries can converge well not only between themselves but also with other countries. Perhaps the region could also help open the door to a possible multilateral treaty on this matter which facilitates channels of cooperation, aid and assistance in such area, bearing in mind the potential role of international support to complement the key role of local actors and actions to prepare for and mitigate the impact of disasters. These can be complemented by regional initiatives, as witnessed in the Association of Southeast Asian Nations (ASEAN) through its agreement on disaster response and its treaty on transboundary haze.

The issue of man-made disasters should not be forgotten and this is much linked to the armed conflicts which play havoc on people's lives. The rules of international humanitarian law, referred to above, are particularly important in this respect and they need to be followed, implemented and strengthened in their outreach to potential and actual victims.

6. Humane Globalization

The advent of globalization in the form of quicker information, quicker communications and a more integrated global economic and trade regime is closely interlinked with the period of a more dynamic Asia and its impact on the globe. Membership by Asian countries in the World Trade Organization (WTO) has increased with time, and Asian countries have contributed to, benefited from and critically tested that regime in key areas.

A notable case in point is the intellectual property agreement in the WTO framework—the Trade-related Intellectual Property (TRIPs) agreement. Several Asian countries faced with the threat of HIV/AIDS have tested the various flexibilities available under that agreement and subsequent developments, such as the Doha Declaration concerning health, diseases and intellectual property, to produce generic drugs to help those affected by HIV/AIDS so as to enable them to access key drugs at lower cost. While some patent holders in developed countries see this as a dilution of intellectual property protection, many lives have, in fact, been saved by the use of these flexibilities. The Asian input, especially from civil society, has been to mitigate the strictures of the intellectual property regime, balancing between the patent protection based on commercial rationalization, particularly the need to provide incentives to inventors/inventions, and flexible concessions to humanize the gains from intellectual property, particularly to enable the poor and sick to access essential medicines.

The advent of globalization is also tested by the proliferation of free trade areas (FTAs) at the regional and bilateral levels (namely, the spaghetti situation, which might, in Thai-Asian metaphor, be termed the "kuay teow" 'noodles' effect). As with the global regime under the WTO, while the intention to open up markets and liberalise the trading system is laudable at one level, there arises the issue of how those who are unable to compete will also be catered to. The access to medicines issue, for example, repeats itself in a chameleon-like manner when some of these FTAs now try to impose a TRIPs-plus setting whereby more intellectual property guarantees than those recognized under the WTO regime will be introduced between the parties (such as protection for patents for more than 20 years which is the usual period for patent protection). Is this an insidious distortion of globalization, a de-humanizer?

The FTAs tend to open up markets in relation to trade, services and finance while not attending adequately to the question of how the wealth is shared and how people as a whole benefit from the process. A case in point is whether these FTAs open the door to enabling migrant workers to be managed in a humane way. In reality, several FTAs tend to open the door to "white collar workers" rather than "blue collar workers". The issue of migrant workers, legal and illegal ("no collar workers"), deserves attention also. In some countries, there are various objectionable practices which rightly raise eyebrows; these include the caning of migrant workers and the deportation of a migrant worker who has a child with a local resident. Added to that are complications emanating from human smuggling and trafficking which are enmeshed with irregular migration, and the need to treat the victims as victims rather than as "illegals" subjected to punishment—and multiple traumatization.

7. Responsibilities

The issue of responsibilities interplays with both the State level and the individual level. The notion of RtoP/R2P was referred to earlier in this paper in the recent developments at the international level, making at least the State (or Government) more accountable in regard to egregious violations.

At another level, there is the rise of international criminal responsibility in regard to serious crimes committed by individuals. The advent of the International Criminal Court helps to fill in gaps and act against impunity where the national setting is unable or unwilling to act vis a vis individuals who should be responsible for, in particular, genocide, crimes against humanityand war crimes. While a welcome development is that the Republic of Korea exemplifies an Asian country ready to be a member from the start, and that a South Korean judge has reached the topmost position in the Court, the participation deficit on the part of other countries should not be overlooked. Many Asian countries have not become parties to the Statute setting up the Court, even though the work of the international court complements the national setting.

Asia also offers space for experiments of a mixed kind—intermingling between national and international jurisdiction. The Khmer Rouge tribunal in Cambodia is an example of this judicial cocktail, with judges drawn from both the national and international settings. While the number of international judges per bench is smaller than the number of local judges, judgements depend on a double majority rule whereby the mere majority vote from local judges is not adequate for judgements; there is still a need for the vote of some of the international judges to enable a judgement to be reached and rendered.

On another front, the advent of a diversity of actors—and their responsibility —at the national and international levels deserves note. "Non-State actors" is a term that has emerged in the national and international vocabulary. This includes the corporate sector. Interestingly, the notions of corporate responsibility and corporate social responsibility are rather incipient in many Asian countries. However, at a transnational level, several corporate activities in the Asian region have given rise to corporate accountability at times extraterritorially. Perhaps the most famous situation is in regard to the application of the US Alien Tort Claims Act to corporate activities in Southeast Asia, particularly in regard to allegations of violations in Myanmar, which have given rise to lawsuits in the US and which have led to large sums negotiated in dispute settlement.

On a more disconcerting level, Asia is regrettably the crucible of a number of terrorist organizations and activities which wreak havoc both locally and internationally. A number of treaties to counter such practices have been emerged in the region—including the ASEAN Convention to counter terrorism and another convention from the Central Asian region linked with the Shanghai Cooperation group. These are paralleled by some 14 multilateral counter-terrorism treaties and the UN Security Council's own decisions on this front. It can be added that the latter has increasingly voiced that actions to make perpetrators responsible for terrorist acts also need to abide by human rights, without which there can be no genuine rule of law.

Needless to say, while laws and law enforcement are crucial in this regard, the root causes of insecurity, frustration and disaffection which breed the excesses leading to terrorism should not be overlooked here and elsewhere. One should not forget that the endemic troubles of the Middle East are also Asian in origin (at least geographically). There is a multi-dimensional angle to the notion of responsibilities which cannot be satisfied by the adoption of laws alone but which must be complemented by a variety of measures that reach deep into the psyche of violence. Added to that is the challenge raised by the asymmetry of conflicts which target uniformed elements and civilians indiscriminately for political ends, often in a mediatized vortex to generate widespread fear.

8. Pacific Settlement of Disputes

Given the actual and potential conflicts over a range of issues in the Asian region, the question of dispute prevention and settlement is a continuing issue for this region and beyond. The ICJ has witnessed the presence of Asian countries as litigants before the court in just over ten cases, the most recent of which was referred to above. A case is also pending between Australia and Japan in relation to marine resources. Another channel in regard to marine issues is the International Tribunal on the Law of the Sea, and some Asian countries which are parties to the UN Law of the Sea Convention are beginning to use this channel.

The array of modalities on dispute settlement underlined by Chapter VI of the UN Charter offers space for exploration by Asian countries. Arbitration is a key entry point and the ASEANCharter 2007 adverts to arbitration explicitly as a possible dispute settlement mechanism for the region. It is interesting to note, however, that even though regional mechanisms are available on this matter, some countries have preferred to use multilateral mechanisms than regional mechanisms (for example, the maritime cases above between Singapore, Malaysiaand Indonesia all of which are members of ASEAN). Is this a corollary of the so-called non-confrontational approach voiced by some countries in regard to their inter-State relations at the regional level? Or is it a matter of credibility of those regional mechanisms?

Interestingly, the dispute settlement panel of the WTO has flourished with a range of cases concerning Asian countries. India has been the most active litigant in using the panel. One of the most recent cases concerning Asian countries was between Thailandand Philippines over tariffs/taxes imposed on cigarettes from the latter. The appellate panel confirmed the lower panel's decision that various practices adopted by the former, such as higher tariffs for foreign cigarettes than for local cigarettes, were discriminatory and in breach of WTO rules.

However, some regional conflicts do not lend themselves to easy resolution through judicial settlement and invite other modalities of convergence. As indicated above, maritime claims between different countries in regard to overlapping areas are a case in point. The preferred way may be to have joint development and joint sharing of resources, and much will also depend upon political will to reach such compromise. The evolution of a Code of Conduct for the South ChinaSea which helps to create confidence between ASEAN countries and China is thus welcome as a bridge for dialogue and joint action.

With regard to conflicts between the State and individuals/communities, the first entry point for dispute settlement is at the local level, but effectiveness of the judicial system on this matter varies per country. India is often cited as an Asian country with a proactive judiciary, par excellence, that reaches out to the population. However, in several settings in Asia, the judiciary is neither independent or effective. Thus a series of checks and balances has to be built to control the use and abuse of power. This has led to the rise of national human rights institutions, such as National Human Rights Commissions, in over ten countries which may offer a helping hand to settle disputes, such as through mediation, in a more flexible manner than through the judicial process. An active non-governmental sector is also critical for community vigilance which can sound bells against actual or potential violations and violence and thus contribute to both dispute prevention and settlement.

Where there are no national remedies in regard to State-individual conflicts, resort to regional and international mechanisms may be available at times. However, the various human rights treaties which open the door to accepting petitions from individuals have witnessed only a paucity of ratifications from Asian countries. For instance, one of the rare Southeast Asian countries which has become party to the (first) Protocol to the Covenant on Civil and Political Rights, which opens the door to such petitions to the Human RightsCommittee (established under the Covenant) from individuals against the State, is the Philippines. Other countries remain uncommitted and aloof, most probably because of the fear of encroachment on their sovereignty.

9. People-based International System

An underlying thread in this paper is the interface between International Law and the people at large, moving beyond the rather State (Government)-centric origins of International Law. While classically, the individual being was not seen as having international legal personality, increasingly the evidence is shifting the other way—in some situations, as above, the individual is becoming a person with rights and vested with guarantees which no longer treat him/her as merely an object of International Law. The spread of the international human rights mandate indicates this trend. Human rights advocacy—to offer protection to individuals and communities- cannot be seen as interference in the internal affairs of a State, but is very much part of the international mandate—and prerogative of the world today.

Yet, at the national level, Asia is regrettably host to a number of cloistered countries which run counter to the tide of people's participation. At the regional level, while regional organizations have grown in numbers, there is still an absence of genuine space for people at large to be involved in the institutions and processes linked with these organizations. For instance, while ASEAN has set up a range of mechanisms under the ASEANCharter (and opened the door to the establishment of the first regional human rights mechanism of its kind in Southeast Asia), there is still no body that represents the people of ASEAN directly at the regional level. Although the idea of a Peoples' Assembly in the ASEAN structure has been voiced by civil society, that cudgel has not yet been taken up by the countries of that region. Thus the organization is more of an inter-State or inter-Executive (branch) entity rather than an inter-peoples' entity. The same applies to other groupings in the region such as the Gulf Cooperation Council, the South Asian Association for Regional Cooperation and the Shanghai Cooperation Group.

Internationally, the lack of or limited participation by people at large is witnessed no less by the UN structure itself. The organs of the UN are principally inter-governmental. In relation to the Security Council, there should be more room for participation from Asian countries (and other regions), and several, such as Japanand India, are candidates for seats in this regard. However, while the most representative UN organ in a sense is the General Assembly, this forum is not a peoples' forum but an inter-governmental setting. The idea of a Peoples' Assembly should be a key agenda from the more enlightened Asian countries in the next phase of UN reforms, granted that the most recent reforms of 2005 which established new organs such as the UN Human Rights Council and the UN Peace-building Commission have been welcomed by Asian countries. In fairness, it should be recognized that through the recent reforms, a little more space is now available for civil society to voice its concerns in various organs of the UN (e.g. through the Universal Periodic Review in the Human Rights Council and through the UN Security Council setting up an ombudsperson to deal with possible discrepancies in regard to sanctions imposed on individuals listed as terrorists). Yet the challenge of establishing a Peoples' Assembly, or equivalent, with representation from people(s) at large is an immediate test for the new era, without which the UN itself will be emburdened with a democracy deficit.

10. Transcultural/Transfrontier Cooperation

Given the heterogeneous nature of Asia, cooperation between the different countries and communities has emerged as a welcome development in recent decades. Cooperation is evidenced particularly in the spread of bilateral and regional networks and arrangements, at times leading to the establishment of regional organizations. Innovative areas include contribution to peacekeeping, as seen in the stationing of peacekeepers from some Asian countriesin Timor Leste at the time of its birth as a new State.

There is also a shift from the image—and substance—of Asian countriesas developing countries, to middle income countries and graduating to the status of developed countries. It is thus interesting to see the change in UN relationship with a number of Asian countries which is increasingly based on a partnership for development rather than as a recipient of international aid.

The potential of Asian countries assisting other countries in a "South-South" relationship is coming increasingly to the fore. Some heavyweight Asian countries are, for example, reaching out much more to Africa, at times mixing political interests with competition for new energy resources. From a global development perspective, the international goal which invites developed countries to provide at least 0.7% of their Gross Domestic Product to international aid to help developing countries is one which Asian countries should help to implement—by setting examples particularly to reach out to less fortunate communities.

Given the difficulties enmeshed with ethnic and religious conflicts on several fronts, a key entry point locally and globally is trans-cultural or cross-cultural cooperation and understanding from a young age. This has much to do with nurturing an empathetic mindset through education and awareness raising which, while recognizing the diversity of cultures, propels an appreciation of equality and non- discrimination.

This invites the teaching, education and research on International Law also to aim for a more humanistic target which goes beyond the imputed miracles of a material kind. Innovations should include more sharing of educational resources between Asian countries to give greater focus to issues pertaining to Asia, and Asia's inputs for the world "with a human face". Multi-lingualism to enable students to study a variety of Asian languages as part of the educational process, and cross-cultural links though rotation of students between different Asian countries, transfrontier field visits and pro bono work by students to help deprived communities (perhaps, even the formation of an "Asian Voluntary Service Corps" and "Asian Legal Aid/Dissemination Programme"), should be encouraged.

Ultimately, this is a mirror which interfaces with Asia, reflecting, and reflecting on, how and if the region responds adequately to the rights, needs, aspirations and expectations of its plurality of peoples with a "shared and sharing" mindset ... without which the claim of a new era may merely mislead, engendering not-much-more-than-a-mirage.

Appendix B

Table B.1 Recent UN Security Council resolutions on R2P: voting pattern of Asian States

UNSC resolution	UN chapter and situation	Context	Voting by Asian members (out of 15 members)		
			In favour	Against	Abstaining
S/RES/2533 29 June 2020	Chapter VII Mali	"*Reiterates* that the Malian authorities have primary responsibility to protect civilians in Mali, reaffirms its past resolutions on the Protection of civilians in armed conflicts, children and armed conflicts, women, peace and security, and youth, peace and security, calls upon The United Nations multidimensional integrated stabilization mission in Mali (MINUSMA)and all military forces operating in Mali to take them into account and to abide by international humanitarian, human rightsand refugee law, and recalls the importance of training in this regard"	China Indonesia Vietnam **(unanimous vote of 15)**		

(continued)

V. Muntarbhorn, *Challenges of International Law in the Asian Region*,
https://doi.org/10.1007/978-981-16-2047-8

Table B.1 (continued)

UNSC resolution	UN chapter and situation	Context	Voting by Asian members (out of 15 members)		
			In favour	Against	Abstaining
S/RES/2521 29 May 2020	Chapter VII South Sudan	"*Strong condemning* past and ongoing human rights violations and abuses and violations of international humanitarian law, further condemning harassment and targeting of civil society, humanitarian personnel and journalist, emphasizing that those responsible for violation of international humanitarian law and violations and abuses of human rights must be held accountable, and that the Revitalized Transitional Government of National Unity (RTGNU) bears the primary responsibility to protect its population from genocide. war crimes, ethnic cleansing, and crimes against humanity,"	Indonesia Vietnam		China
S/RES/2514 12 March 2020	Chapter VII South Sudan	"South Sudan's government bears the primary responsibility to protect its population from genocide, war crimes, ethnic cleansing, and crimes against humanity, and *expressing concern* that despite the signing of the revitalised agreement, violations including rape and sexual violence continue to occur which may amount to international crimes, including war crimesand crimes against humanity"	China Indonesia Vietnam ***(unanimous vote of 15)***		
S/RES/2502 19 December 2019	Chapter VII Democratic Republic of the Congo (DRC)	"*Recalling* the Government of DRC bears the primary responsibility to protect civilians within its territory and subject to its jurisdiction, including protection from crimes against humanityand war crimes"	China Indonesia Kuwait ***(unanimous vote of 15)***		

(continued)

Table B.1 (continued)

UNSC resolution	UN chapter and situation	Context	Voting by Asian members (out of 15 members)		
			In favour	Against	Abstaining
S/RES/2499 15 November 2019	Chapter VII Central African Republic(CAR)	"*Recalling* the CAR authorities have the primary responsibility to protect all populations in the CAR in particular from genocide, war crimes, ethnic cleansingand crimes against humanity,"	China Indonesia Kuwait ***(unanimous vote of 15)***		
S/RES/2463 29 March 2019	Chapter VIII Democratic Republic of the Congo	"*Recalling* that the Government of DRC bears the primary responsibility to protect civilians within its territory and subject to its jurisdiction, including protection from crimes against humanityand war crimes"	China Indonesia Kuwait ***(unanimous vote of 15)***		
S/RES/2459 15 March 2019	Chapter VII South Sudan	"…*emphasizing* that those responsible for violations of international humanitarian law and violations and abuses of human rights must be held accountable, and that South Sudan's government bears the primary responsibility to protect its populations from genocide, war crimes, ethnic cleansing, and crimes against humanity …"	China Indonesia Kuwait ***(unanimous vote of 15)***		
S/RES/2457 27 February 2019	Chapter VIII Silencing the Guns in Africa	"*Recalling* that the prevention of conflict remains a primary responsibility of States, and further recalling their responsibility to protect Civilians and to respect human rights, as provided for by relevant International Law, and further reaffirming the responsibility of each individual State to protect its populations from genocide, war crimes, ethnic cleansing, and crimes against humanity…"	China Indonesia Kuwait ***(unanimous vote of 15)***		

(continued)

Table B.1 (continued)

UNSC resolution	UN chapter and situation	Context	Voting by Asian members (out of 15 members)		
			In favour	Against	Abstaining
S/RES/2449 13 December 2018	Chapter VII Syria	"*Reaffirming* the primary responsibility of the Syrian authorities to protect the population in Syria and, reiterating the parties to armed conflict must take all feasible steps to protect civilians"	Kazakhstan Kuwait		China
S/RES/2444 14 November 2018	Chapter VII Somalia	"*Recalling* that the Federal Government of Somalia (FGS) has primary responsibility to protect its population, and recognizing the FGS's responsibility, working with the Federal Member States(FMSs), to build the capacity of its own national security forces, as a matter of priority…"	China Indonesia Kuwait ***(unanimous vote of 15)***		
S/RES/2439 30 October 2018	Chapter VII Democratic Republic of the Congo	"*Recalls* that the Government of the DRC bears the primary responsibility to protect civilians within its territory and subject to its jurisdiction, including protection form crimes against humanityand war crimes…"	China Indonesia Kuwait ***(unanimous vote of 15)***		

Source Author's own table (with part of the information derived from web of Global Centre for the Responsibility to Protect)

Appendix C

Table C.1 Asian countries and International Humanitarian Law

Country/convention	GC I–IV		AP I		AP II		AP III	
	S	R	S	R	S	R	S	R
East Asia								
China	10 Dec. 1949	28 Dec. 1956		14 Sep. 1983		14 Sep. 1983		
DPRK		27 Aug. 1957		9 Mar. 1988				
Japan		21 Apr. 1953		31 Aug 2004		31 Aug 2004		
Mongolia		20 Dec. 1958	12 Dec. 1977	6 Dec. 1995	12 Dec. 1977	6 Dec. 1995		
ROK		16 Aug. 1966	7 Dec. 1977	15 Jan. 1982	7 Dec. 1977	15 Jan. 1982	2 Aug. 2006	
Southeast Asia								
Brunei Darussalam		14 Oct. 1991		14 Oct. 1991		14 Oct. 1991		
Cambodia		8 Dec. 1958		14 Jan 1998		14 Jan 1998		
Indonesia		30 Sep. 1958						
Lao PDR		29 Oct. 1956	18 Apr. 1978	18 Nov. 1980	18 Apr. 1978	18 Nov. 1980		
Malaysia		24 Aug. 1962						
Myanmar		25 Aug. 1992						

(continued)

V. Muntarbhorn, *Challenges of International Law in the Asian Region*,
https://doi.org/10.1007/978-981-16-2047-8

Table C.1 (continued)

Country/convention	GC I–IV		AP I		AP II		AP III	
	S	R	S	R	S	R	S	R
Philippines	8 Dec. 1949	6 Oct. 1952	12 Dec. 1977	30 Mar. 2012		11 Dec. 1986	13 Mar. 2006	22 Aug. 2006
Singapore		27 Apr 1973					2 Aug. 2006	7 Jul 2008
Thailand		29 Dec. 1954						
Timor-Leste		8 May 2003		12 Apr. 2005		12 Apr. 2005	8 Dec. 2005	29 Jul. 2011
Viet Nam		28 Jun. 1957	12 Dec. 1977	19 Oct. 1981				
South Asia								
Afghanistan	8 Dec. 1949	26 Sep. 1956		10 Nov. 2009		10 Nov. 2009		
Bangladesh		4 Apr. 1972		8 Sep. 1980		8 Sep. 1980		
Bhutan		10 Jan. 1991						
India	16 Dec. 1949	9 Nov. 1950						
Iran*	8 Dec. 1949	20 Feb. 1957	12 Dec. 1977		12 Dec. 1977			
Maldives		18 Jun. 1991		3 Sep. 1991		3 Sep. 1991		
Nepal		7 Feb. 1964					14 Mar. 2006	
Pakistan	12 Aug. 1949	12 Jun. 1951	12 Dec. 1977		12 Dec. 1977			
Sri Lanka	8 Dec. 1949	28 Feb. 1959						
Central Asia								
Kazakhstan		5 May 1992		5 May 1992		5 May 1992		24 Jun. 2009
Kyrgyzstan		18 Sep. 1992		18 Sep. 1992		18 Sep. 1992		25 Jan. 2019
Tajikistan		13 Jan. 1993		13 Jan. 1993		13 Jan. 1993		
Turkmenistan		10 Apr. 1992		10 Apr. 1992		10 Apr. 1992		
Uzbekistan		8 Oct. 1993		8 Oct. 1993		8 Oct. 1993		

(continued)

Table C.1 (continued)

Country/convention	GC I–IV		AP I		AP II		AP III	
	S	R	S	R	S	R	S	R
West Asia								
Bahrain		30 Nov. 1971		30 Oct. 1986		30 Oct. 1986		
Iraq		14 Feb. 1956		1 Apr. 2010				
Israel	8 Dec. 1949	6 Jul. 1951					8 Dec. 2005	22 Nov. 2007
Jordan		29 May 1951	12 Dec. 1977	1 May 1979	12 Dec. 1977	1 May 1979		
Kuwait		2 Sep. 1967		17 Jan. 1985		17 Jan. 1985		
Lebanon	8 Dec. 1949	10 Apr. 1951		23 Jul 1997		23 Jul 1997		
Oman		31 Jan. 1974		29 Mar. 1984		29 Mar. 1984		
Palestine		2 Apr. 2014		2 Apr. 2014		4 Jan. 2015		4 Jan. 2015
Qatar		15 Oct. 1975		5 Apr. 1988		5 Jan. 2005		
Saudi Arabia		18 May 1963		21 Aug 1987		28 Nov. 2001		
Syria	12 Aug. 1949	2 Nov. 1953		14 Nov. 1983				
United Arab Emirates		10 May 1972		9 Mar. 1983		9 Mar. 1983		
Yemen		10 Jul. 1970	14 Feb. 1978	17 Apr. 1990	14 Feb. 1978	17 Apr. 1990		

Note
GC I–IV Geneva Conventions I–IV. Geneva, 12 August 1949
AP I Additional Protocol to the Geneva Conventions of 12 August 1949, and relating to the Protection of Victims of International Armed Conflicts. Geneva, 8 June 1977
AP II Additional Protocol to the Geneva Conventions of 12 August 1949, and relating to the Protection of Victims of Non-International Armed Conflicts. Geneva, 8 June 1977
AP III Additional Protocol to the Geneva Conventions of 12 August 1949. And relation to the Adoption of an Additional Distinctive Emblem. Geneva, 8 December 2005
S Signature
R Ratification
*Iran fits into South Asia or West Asia. The above classification is flexible for all the Tables
Source Table by author's team derived from https://ihl-databases.icrc.org/ihl, accessed 20 August 2020

Appendix D

Table D.1 Asian countries and the International Criminal Court Statute

Country/convention	Rome Statute of the international criminal court	
	Signature	Ratification
East Asia		
China		
DPRK		
Japan		17 Jul. 2007 (a)
Mongolia	29 Dec. 2000	11 Apr. 2002
ROK	8 Mar. 2000	13 Nov. 2002
Southeast Asia		
Brunei Darussalam		
Cambodia	23 Oct. 2000	11 Apr. 2002
Indonesia		
Lao PDR		
Malaysia		
Myanmar		
Philippines*	[28 Dec. 2000]	[30 Aug. 2011]
Singapore		
Thailand	2 Oct. 2000	
Timor-Leste		6 Sep. 2002 (a)
Viet Nam		
South Asia		
Afghanistan		10 Feb. 2003 (a)
Bangladesh	16 Sep. 1999	23 Mar. 2010
Bhutan		

(continued)

V. Muntarbhorn, *Challenges of International Law in the Asian Region*,
https://doi.org/10.1007/978-981-16-2047-8

Table D.1 (continued)

Country/convention	Rome Statute of the international criminal court	
	Signature	Ratification
India		
Iran	31 Dec. 2000	
Maldives		21 Sep. 2011 (a)
Nepal		
Pakistan		
Sri Lanka		
Central Asia		
Kazakhstan		
Kyrgyzstan	8 Dec. 1998	
Tajikistan	30 Nov. 1998	5 May 2000
Turkmenistan		
Uzbekistan	29 Dec. 2000	
West Asia		
Bahrain	11 Dec. 2000	
Iraq		
Israel	31 Dec. 2000	
Jordan	7 Oct. 1998	11 Apr. 2002
Kuwait	8 Sep. 2000	
Lebanon		
Oman	20 Dec. 2000	
Palestine		2 Jan. 2015 (a)
Qatar		
Saudi Arabia		
Syria	29 Nov. 2000	
United Arab Emirates	27 Nov. 2000	
Yemen	28 Dec. 2000	

Note
(a) means Accession
*Philippines have withdrawn from Rome Statute of the International Criminal Court. Philippines filed the notification on 17 March 2018, and it came to effect on 17 March 2019
Source Table by author's team derived from https://treaties.un.org/pages/ViewDetails.aspx?src=TREATY&mtdsg_no=XVIII-10&chapter=18&clang=_en, accessed 25 August 2020

Appendix E

Table E.1 Asian countries' ratification of the 1951 Refugee Convention and its 1967 Protocol

Country/convention	Convention relating to the status of refugees 1951		Protocol relating to the status of refugees 1967	
	Signature	Ratification	Signature	Ratification
East Asia				
China		24 Sep. 1982 (a)		24 Sep. 1982 (a)
DPRK				
Japan		3 Oct. 1981 (a)		1 Jan. 1982 (a)
Mongolia				
ROK		3 Dec. 1992 (a)		3 Dec. 1992 (a)
Southeast Asia				
Brunei Darussalam				
Cambodia		15 Oct. 1992 (a)		15 Oct. 1992 (a)
Indonesia				
Lao PDR				
Malaysia				
Myanmar				
Philippines		22 Jul. 1981 (a)		22 Jul. 1981 (a)
Singapore				
Thailand				
Timor-Leste		7 May 2003 (a)		7 May 2003 (a)
Viet Nam				
South Asia				
Afghanistan		30 Aug. 2005 (a)		30 Aug. 2005 (a)

(continued)

V. Muntarbhorn, *Challenges of International Law in the Asian Region*,
https://doi.org/10.1007/978-981-16-2047-8

Table E.1 (continued)

Country/convention	Convention relating to the status of refugees 1951		Protocol relating to the status of refugees 1967	
	Signature	Ratification	Signature	Ratification
Bangladesh				
Bhutan				
India				
Iran		28 Jul. 1976 (a)		28 Jul. 1976 (a)
Maldives				
Nepal				
Pakistan				
Sri Lanka				
Central Asia				
Kazakhstan		15 Jan. 1999 (a)		15 Jan. 1999 (a)
Kyrgyzstan		8 Oct. 1996 (a)		8 Oct. 1996 (a)
Tajikistan		7 Dec. 1993 (a)		7 Dec. 1993 (a)
Turkmenistan		2 Mar. 1998 (a)		2 Mar. 1998 (a)
Uzbekistan				
West Asia				
Bahrain				
Iraq				
Israel	1 Aug. 1951	1 Oct. 1954		14 Jun. 1968 (a)
Jordan				
Kuwait				
Lebanon				
Oman				
Palestine				
Qatar				
Saudi Arabia				
Syria				
United Arab Emirates				
Yemen		18 Jan. 1980 (a)		18 Jan. 1980 (a)

Note
(a) means Accession
Source Table by author's team derived from https://treaties.un.org/pages/Treaties.aspx?id=5&subid=A&clang=_en, accessed 25 August 2020

Appendix F

V. Muntarbhorn, *Challenges of International Law in the Asian Region*,
https://doi.org/10.1007/978-981-16-2047-8

Table F.1 Asian countries and human rights conventions: ratifications

Country/convention	S	R	S	R	S	R	S	R	S	R
	ICCPR		ICESCR		CEDAW		CRC		CAT	
East Asia										
China	5 Oct. 1998		27 Oct. 1997	27 Mar. 2001	17 Jul. 1980	4 Nov. 1980	29 Aug. 1990	2 Mar. 1992	12 Dec. 1986	4 Oct. 1988
DPRK		14 Sep. 1981 (a)		14 Sep. 1981 (a)		27 Feb. 2001 (a)	23 Aug. 1990	21 Sep. 1990		
Japan	30 May 1978	21 Jun. 1979	30 May 1978	21 Jun. 1979	17 Jul. 1980	25 Jun. 1985	21 Sep. 1990	22 Apr. 1994		29 Jun. 1999 (a)
Mongolia	5 Jun. 1968	18 Nov. 1974	5 Jun. 1968	18 Nov. 1974	17 Jul. 1980	20 Jul. 1981	26 Jan. 1990	5 Jul. 1990		24 Jan. 2002 (a)
ROK		10 Apr. 1990 (a)		10 Apr. 1990 (a)	25 May 1983	27 Dec. 1984	25 Sep. 1990	20 Nov. 1991		9 Jan. 1995 (a)
Country/convention	CED		CERD		CRPD		CMW			
	S	R	S	R	S	R	S	R		
China				29 Dec. 1981 (a)	30 Mar. 2007	1 Aug. 2008				
DPRK					3 Jul. 2013	6 Dec. 2016				
Japan	6 Feb. 2007	23 Jul. 2009		15 Dec. 1995 (a)	28 Sep. 2007	20 Jan. 2014				
Mongolia	6 Feb. 2007	12 Feb. 2015	3 May 1966	6 Aug. 1969		13 May 2009 (a)				

(continued)

Table F.1 (continued)

Country/convention	S	R	S	R	S	R	S	R	S	R
ROK			8 Aug. 1978	5 Dec. 1978	30 Mar. 2007	11 Dec. 2008				
Southeast Asia										
Brunei Darussalam						24 May 2006 (a)		27 Dec. 1995 (a)	22 Sep. 2015	
Cambodia	17 Oct. 1980	26 May 1992 (a)	17 Oct. 1980	26 May 1992 (a)	17 Oct. 1980	15 Oct. 1992 (a)		15 Oct. 1992 (a)		15 Oct. 1992 (a)
Indonesia		23 Feb. 2006 (a)		23 Feb. 2006 (a)	29 Jul. 1980	13 Sep. 1984	26 Jan. 1990	5 Sep. 1990	23 Oct. 1985	28 Oct. 1988
Lao PDR	7 Dec. 2000	25 Sep. 2009	7 Dec. 2000	13 Feb. 2007	17 Jul. 1980	14 Aug. 1981		8 May 1991 (a)	21 Sep. 2010	26 Sep. 2012
Malaysia						5 Jul. 1995 (a)		17 Feb. 1995 (a)		
Myanmar			16 Jul. 2015	6 Oct. 2017		22 Jul. 1997 (a)		15 Jul. 1991 (a)		
Philippines	19 Dec. 1966	23 Oct. 1986	19 Dec. 1966	7 Jun. 1974	15 Jul. 1980	5 Aug. 1981	26 Jan. 1990	21 Aug. 1990		18 Jun. 1986 (a)
Singapore						5 Oct. 1995 (a)		5 Oct. 1995 (a)		
Thailand		29 Oct. 1996 (a)		5 Sep. 1999 (a)		9 Aug. 1985 (a)		27 Mar. 1992 (a)		2 Oct. 2007 (a)
Timor-Leste		18 Sep. 2003 (a)		16 Apr. 2003 (a)		16 Apr. 2003 (a)		16 Apr. 2003 (a)		16 Apr. 2003 (a)

(continued)

Table F.1 (continued)

Country/convention	S	R	S	R	S	R	S	R	S	R
Viet Nam		24 Sep. 1982 (a)		24 Sep. 1982 (a)	29 Jul. 1980	17 Feb. 1982	26 Jan. 1990	28 Feb. 1990	7 Nov. 2013	5 Feb. 2015
Country/convention	CED		CERD		CRPD		CMW			
Brunei Darussalam					18 Dec. 2007	11 Apr. 2016				
Cambodia		27 Jun. 2013 (a)	12 Apr. 1966	28 Nov. 1983	10 Oct. 2007	20 Dec. 2012	27 Sep. 2004			
Indonesia	27 Sep. 2010			25 Jun. 1999 (a)	30 Mar. 2007	30 Nov. 2011	22 Sep. 2004	31 May 2012		
Lao PDR	29 Sep. 2008			22 Feb. 1974 (a)	15 Jan. 2008	25 Sep. 2009				
Malaysia					8 Apr. 2008	19 Jul. 2010				
Myanmar						7 Dec. 2011 (a)				
Philippines			7 Mar. 1966	15 Sep. 1967	25 Sep. 2007	15 Apr. 2008	15 Nov. 1993	5 Jul. 1995		
Singapore			19 Oct. 2015	27 Nov. 2017	30 Nov. 2012	18 Jul. 2013				
Thailand	9 Jan. 2012			28 Jan. 2003 (a)	30 Mar. 2007	29 Jul. 2008				
Timor-Leste				16 Apr. 2003 (a)				30 Jan. 2004 (a)		
Viet Nam				9 Jun. 1982 (a)	22 Oct. 2007	5 Feb. 2015				

(continued)

Table F.1 (continued)

Country/convention	S	R	S	R	S	R	S	R	S	R
South Asia										
Afghanistan		24 Jan. 1983 (a)		24 Jan. 1983 (a)	14 Aug. 1980	5 Mar. 2003	27 Sep. 1990	28 Mar. 1994	4 Feb. 1985	1 Apr. 1987
Bangladesh		6 Sep. 2000 (a)		5 Oct. 1998 (a)		6 Nov. 1984 (a)	26 Jan. 1990	3 Aug. 1990		5 Oct. 1998 (a)
Bhutan					17 Jul. 1980	31 Aug. 1981	4 Jun. 1990	1 Aug. 1990		
India		10 Apr. 1979 (a)		10 Apr. 1979 (a)	30 Jul. 1980	9 Jul. 1993		11 Dec. 1992 (a)	14 Oct. 1997	
Iran	4 Apr. 1968	24 Jun. 1975	4 Apr. 1968	24 Jun. 1975			5 Sep. 1991	13 Jul. 1994		
Maldives		19 Sep. 2006 (a)		19 Sep. 2006 (a)		1 Jul. 1993 (a)	21 Aug. 1990	11 Feb. 1991		20 Apr. 2004 (a)
Nepal		14 May 1991 (a)		14 May 1991 (a)	5 Feb. 1991	22 Apr. 1991	26 Jan. 1990	14 Sep. 1990		14 May 1991 (a)
Pakistan	17 Apr. 2008	23 Jun. 2010	3 Nov. 2004	17 Apr. 2008		12 Mar. 1996 (a)	20 Sep. 1990	12 Nov. 1990	17 Apr. 2008	23 Jun. 2010
Sri Lanka		11 Jun. 1980 (a)		11 Jun. 1980 (a)	17 Jul. 1980	5 Oct. 1981	26 Jan. 1990	12 Jul. 1991		3 Jan. 1994 (a)
Country/convention	CED		CERD		CRPD		CMW			
Afghanistan				6 Jul. 1983 (a)		18 Sep. 2012 (a)				
Bangladesh				11 Jun. 1979 (a)	9 May 2007	30 Nov. 2007	7 Oct. 1998	24 Aug. 2011		

(continued)

Table F.1 (continued)

Country/convention	S	R	S	R	S	R	S	R	S	R
Bhutan			26 Mar. 1973		21 Sep. 2010					
India	6 Feb. 2007		2 Mar. 1967	3 Dec. 1968	30 Mar. 2007	1 Oct. 2007				
Iran			8 Mar. 1967	29 Aug. 1968		23 Oct. 2009 (a)				
Maldives	6 Feb. 2007			24 Apr. 1984 (a)	2 Oct. 2007	5 Apr. 2010				
Nepal				30 Jan. 1971 (a)	3 Jan. 2008	7 May 2010				
Pakistan			19 Sep. 1966	21 Sep.1966	25 Sep. 2008	5 Jul. 2011				
Sri Lanka	10 Dec. 2015	25 May 2016		18 Feb. 1982 (a)	30 Mar. 2007	8 Feb. 2016		11 Mar. 1996 (a)		
Central Asia										
Kazakhstan	2 Dec. 2003	24 Jan. 2006	2 Dec. 2003	24 Jan. 2006		26 Aug. 1998 (a)	16 Feb. 1994	12 Aug. 1994		26 Aug. 1998 (a)
Kyrgyzstan		7 Oct. 1994 (a)		7 Oct. 1994 (a)		10 Feb. 1997 (a)		7 Oct. 1994 (a)		5 Sep. 1997 (a)
Tajikistan		4 Jan. 1999 (a)		4 Jan. 1999 (a)		26 Oct. 1993 (a)		26 Oct. 1993 (a)		11 Jan. 1995 (a)
Turkmenistan		1 May 1997 (a)		1 May 1997 (a)		1 May 1997 (a)		20 Sep. 1993 (a)		25 Jun. 1999 (a)
Uzbekistan		28 Sep. 1995 (a)		28 Sep. 1995 (a)		19 Jul. 1995 (a)		29 Jun. 1994 (a)		28 Sep. 1995 (a)

(continued)

Table F.1 (continued)

Country/convention	S	R	S	R	S	R	S	R	S	R
Country/convention	CED		CERD		CRPD		CMW			
Kazakhstan		27 Feb. 2009 (a)		26 Aug. 1998 (a)	11 Dec. 2008	21 Apr. 2015				
Kyrgyzstan				5 Sep. 1997 (a)	21 Sep. 2011	16 May 2019		29 Sep. 2003 (a)		
Tajikistan				11 Jan. 1995 (a)	22 Mar. 2018		7 Sep. 2000	8 Jan. 2002		
Turkmenistan				29 Sep. 1994 (a)		4 Sep. 2008 (a)				
Uzbekistan				28 Sep. 1995 (a)	27 Feb. 2009					
West Asia										
Bahrain		20 Sep. 2006 (a)		27 Sep. 2007 (a)		18 Jun. 2002 (a)		13 Feb. 1992 (a)		6 Mar. 1998 (a)
Iraq	18 Feb. 1969	25 Jan. 1971	18 Feb. 1969	25 Jan. 1971		13 Aug. 1986 (a)		15 Jun. 1994 (a)		7 Jul. 2011 (a)
Israel	19 Dec. 1966	3 Oct. 1991	19 Dec. 1966	3 Oct. 1991	17 Jul. 1980	3 Oct. 1991	3 Jul. 1990	3 Oct. 1991	22 Oct. 1986	3 Oct. 1991
Jordan	30 Jun. 1972	28 May 1975	30 Jun. 1972	28 May 1975	3 Dec. 1980	1 Jul. 1992	29 Aug. 1990	24 May 1991		13 Nov. 1991 (a)
Kuwait		21 May 1996 (a)		21 May 1996 (a)		2 Sep. 1994 (a)	7 Jun. 1990	21 Oct. 1991		8 Mar. 1996 (a)

(continued)

Table F.1 (continued)

Country/convention	S	R	S	R	S	R	S	R	S	R
Lebanon		3 Nov. 1972 (a)		3 Nov. 1972 (a)		16 Apr. 1997 (a)	26 Jan. 1990	14 May 1991		5 Oct. 2000 (a)
Oman				9 Jun. 2020 (a)		7 Feb. 2006 (a)		9 Dec. 1996 (a)		9 Jun. 2020 (a)
Palestine		2 Apr. 2014 (a)		2 Apr. 2014 (a)		2 Apr. 2014 (a)		2 Apr. 2014 (a)		2 Apr. 2014 (a)
Qatar		21 May 2018 (a)		21 May 2018 (a)		29 Apr. 2009 (a)	8 Dec. 1992	3 Apr. 1995		11 Jan. 2000 (a)
Saudi Arabia					7 Sep. 2000	7 Sep. 2000		26 Jan. 1996 (a)		23 Sep. 1997 (a)
Syria		21 Apr. 1969 (a)		21 Apr. 1969 (a)		28 Mar. 2003 (a)	18 Sep. 1990	15 Jul. 1993		19 Aug. 2004 (a)
United Arab Emirates						6 Oct. 2004 (a)		3 Jan. 1997 (a)		19 Jul. 2012 (a)
Yemen		9 Feb. 1987 (a)		9 Feb. 1987 (a)		30 May 1984 (a)	13 Feb. 1990	1 May 1991		5 Nov. 1991 (a)
Country/convention	CED		CERD		CRPD		CMW			
Bahrain				27 Mar. 1990 (a)	25 Jun. 2007	22 Sep. 2011				
Iraq		23 Nov. 2010 (a)	18 Feb. 1969	13 Feb. 1970		20 Mar. 2013 (a)				

(continued)

Table F.1 (continued)

Country/convention	S	R	S	R	S	R	S	R	S	R
Israel			7 Mar. 1966	3 Jan. 1979	30 Mar. 2007	28 Sep. 2012				
Jordan				30 May 1974 (a)	30 Mar. 2007	31 Mar. 2008				
Kuwait				15 Oct. 1968 (a)		22 Aug. 2013 (a)				
Lebanon	6 Feb. 2007			12 Nov. 1971 (a)	14 Jun. 2007					
Oman		12 Jun. 2020 (a)		2 Jan. 2003 (a)	17 Mar. 2008	6 Jan. 2009				
Palestine				2 Apr. 2014 (a)		2 Apr. 2014 (a)				
Qatar				22 Jul. 1976 (a)	9 Jul. 2007	13 May 2008				
Saudi Arabia				23 Sep. 1997 (a)		24 Jun. 2008 (a)				
Syria				21 Apr. 1969 (a)	30 Mar. 2007	10 Jul. 2009		2 Jun. 2005 (a)		

(continued)

Table F.1 (continued)

Country/convention	S	R	S	R	S	R	S	R	S	R
United Arab Emirates				20 Jun. 1974 (a)	8 Feb. 2008	19 Mar. 2010				
Yemen				18 Oct. 1972 (a)	30 Mar. 2007	26 Mar. 2009				

Note
ICCPR: International Covenant on Civil and Political Rights. New York, 16 December 1966
ICESCR International Covenant on Economic, Social, and Cultural Rights. New York, 16 December 1966
CEDAW Convention on Elimination of All Forms of Discrimination Against Women. New York, 18 December 1979
*CRC*Convention on the Rights of the Child. New York, 20 November 1989
CAT Convention Against Torture, and Other Cruel, Inhuman or Degrading Treatment or Punishment. New York, 10 December 1984
*CED*International Convention for the Protection of All Persons from Enforced Disappearance. New York, 20 December 2006
*CERD*CERD: Convention on Elimination of All Forms of Racial Discrimination. New York, 7 March 1966
CRPD Convention on the Rights of Persons with Disabilities. New York, 13 December 2006
CMW International Convention on the Protection of the Rights of All Migrants Workers and Members of Their Families. New York, 18 December 1990
S means Signature
R means Ratification
(a) means Accession
Source Table by author's team derived from https://treaties.un.org/pages/Treaties.aspx?id=4&subid=A&clang=_en, accessed 25 August 2020

Appendix G

Table G.1 Asian countries as parties to the Paris climate change agreement 2015

Country/convention	Paris agreement	
	Signature	Ratification
East Asia		
China	22 Apr. 2016	3 Sep. 2016
DPRK	22 Apr. 2016	1 Aug. 2016
Japan	22 Apr. 2016	8 Nov. 2016 (A)
Mongolia	22 Apr. 2016	21 Sep. 2016
ROK	22 Apr. 2016	3 Nov. 2016
Southeast Asia		
Brunei Darussalam	22 Apr. 2016	21 Sep. 2016
Cambodia	22 Apr. 2016	6 Feb. 2017
Indonesia	22 Apr. 2016	31 Oct. 2016
Lao PDR	22 Apr. 2016	7 Sep. 2016
Malaysia	22 Apr. 2016	16 Nov. 2016
Myanmar	22 Apr. 2016	19 Sep. 2017
Philippines	22 Apr. 2016	23 Mar. 2017
Singapore	22 Apr. 2016	21 Sep. 2016
Thailand	22 Apr. 2016	21 Sep. 2016
Timor-Leste	22 Apr. 2016	16 Aug. 2017
Viet Nam	22 Apr. 2016	3 Nov. 2016 (AA)
South Asia		
Afghanistan	22 Apr. 2016	15 Feb. 2017
Bangladesh	22 Apr. 2016	21 Sep. 2016
Bhutan	22 Apr. 2016	19 Sep. 2017

(continued)

V. Muntarbhorn, *Challenges of International Law in the Asian Region*,
https://doi.org/10.1007/978-981-16-2047-8

Table G.1 (continued)

Country/convention	Paris agreement	
	Signature	Ratification
India	22 Apr. 2016	2 Oct. 2016
Iran	22 Apr. 2016	
Maldives	22 Apr. 2016	22 Apr. 2016
Nepal	22 Apr. 2016	5 Oct. 2016
Pakistan	22 Apr. 2016	10 Nov. 2016
Sri Lanka	22 Apr. 2016	21 Sep. 2016
Central Asia		
Kazakhstan	2 Aug. 2016	6 Dec. 2016
Kyrgyzstan	21 Sep. 2016	18 Feb. 2020
Tajikistan	22 Apr. 2016	22 Mar. 2017
Turkmenistan	23 Sep. 2016	20 Oct. 2016
Uzbekistan	19 Apr. 2017	9 Nov. 2018
West Asia		
Bahrain	22 Apr. 2016	23 Dec. 2016
Iraq	8 Dec. 2016	
Israel	22 Apr. 2016	22 Nov. 2016
Jordan	22 Apr. 2016	4 Nov. 2016
Kuwait	22 Apr. 2016	23 Apr. 2018
Lebanon	22 Apr. 2016	5 Feb. 2020
Oman	22 Apr. 2016	22 May 2019
Palestine	22 Apr. 2016	22 Apr. 2016
Qatar	22 Apr. 2016	23 Jun. 2017
Saudi Arabia	3 Nov. 2016	3 Nov. 2016
Syria		13 Nov. 2017 (a)
United Arab Emirates	22 Apr. 2016	21 Sep. 2016 (A)
Yemen	23 Sep. 2016	

Note
(a) means Accession
(A) means Acceptance
(AA) means Approval
Source Table by author's team derived from https://treaties.un.org/Pages/ViewDetails.aspx?src=TREATY&mtdsg_no=XXVII-7-d&chapter=27&clang=_en, accessed 25 August 2020

Bibiliography

Books

AALCC (1997) Essays on International Law, 40th anniversary commemorative volume, AALCC Secretariat, New Delhi

https://www.aalco.int/54thsession/AALCOIEG%20Chairman's%20Statement%20and%20Special%20Rapporteur's%20Report%2020150324.pdf

AALCO (2003) Yearbook of the AALCO, vol 1

Abiad N (2008) Sharia, Muslim states and international treaty obligations. British Institute of International and Comparative Law, London

https://www.constituteproject.org/constitution/Saudi_Arabia_2013.pdf?lang=en

Agarwala PN (1983) The New International Economic Order. Pergamon, Oxford

Alexandrowicz CH (1967) An introduction to the history of the law of nations in the east Indies (16th, 17th, 18th centuries). Clarendon, Oxford

Anand RP (2004) Studies in International Law and history: an Asian perspective. Nijhoff, Leiden/Boston

Aoi C, Heng Y-K (eds) (2014) Asia Pacific nations in international peace support and stability operations. Palgrave Macmillan, New York

Baldwin R, Kawai M, Wignaraja G (eds) (2014) A WTO for the 21st century the Asian perspective, Asian Development Bank Institute, Edward Elgar Publishers, Cheltenham, Glos/Northampton

Barisitz S (2017) Central Asia and the silk road: economic rise and decline over several millennia. Springer, Cham/Switzerland

Bellamy AJ, Dunne T (eds) (2016) The Oxford handbook of the responsibility to protect, OUP, Oxford

Brownlie I (2008) Principles of Public International Law, 7th edn. OUP, Oxford

Cai P (2017) Understanding China's belt and road initiative, Lowy Institute, Sydney. https://www.lowyinstitute.org/publications/understanding-belt-and-road-initiative

Chesterman S, Owada H, Saul B (eds) (2019) The Oxford handbook on International Law in Asia and the Pacific. OUP, Oxford

Chi M (2018) Sustainable development provisions in investment treaties. UNESCAP, Bangkok

Corrales M, Fenwick M, Forgó N (eds) (2018) Robotics, AI and the future of law, Springer, Singapore

Crawford J (2012) Brownlie's principles of Public International Law revised, 8th edn. OUP, Oxford

Edmunds SE (1925) The lawless law of nations: an exposition of the prevailing arbitrary International Law system in relation to its influence upon civil liberty, disclosing it as the last Bulwark of absolutism against the political emancipation of man, J.Byrne and Company, Washington, D.C.

Fassbender B, Peters A (eds) (2012) The Oxford handbook of the history of International Law. Oxford University Press (OUP), Oxford

V. Muntarbhorn, *Challenges of International Law in the Asian Region*,
https://doi.org/10.1007/978-981-16-2047-8

Federation Internationale des Droits de l'homme (FIDH) (2015) Demystifying human rights protection in Asia, FIDH, Paris. https://www.weforum.org/agenda/2019/10/has-world-entered-asian-century-what-does-it-mean/; https://www.ft.com/content/520cb6f6-2958-11e9-a5ab-ff8ef2b976c7; https://asiancenturyinstitute.com/online-courses/20-asia-and-the-world-in-the-asian-century

FORUM ASIA (2019) A decade in review: assessing the performance of the ASEAN intergovernmental commission on human rights, vol 2. Forum Asia, Bangkok/Jakarta. https://www.forum-asia.org/uploads/wp/2019/10/AICHR10vol2FA.pdf

Global Commission on the World of Work (2019) Work for a brighter future. ILO, Geneva

Hayashi N (2017) The role and importance of the Hague conferences: a historical perspective. UN Institute for Disarmament Research (UNIDIR), Geneva

Howe B, Kondoch B (eds) (2016) Peacekeeping and the Asia-Pacific. Brill/Nijhoff, New York

ICRC (2014) Autonomous weapon systems: technical, military, legal and humanitarian aspects, 26–28 March 2014. ICRC, Expert Meeting, Geneva, Switzerland

IFRI (2014) The Asian century: what international norms and practices, IFRI, Paris

ILO (2013) Social dimensions of free trade agreements, ILO, Geneva

Information Office of the PRC (2018) China and the World Trade Organization, Information Office of the PRC, Beijing

International Commission on Intervention and State Sovereignty (2001) The responsibility to protect. International Development Research Centre, Ottawa

Jennings SR, Watts SA (eds) (1997) Oppenheim's International Law, vol 1, Peace, 9th ed. Longman, London

McCormack TLH, Tilbury MJ, Triggs GD (eds) (2001) A century of war and peace, Kluwer, Leiden

Narlikar A, Daunton M, Stern RM (eds) (2012) The Oxford handbook on the World Trade Organization. OUP, Oxford

Oberleitner G (ed) (2018) International human rights institutions, tribunals, and courts. Springer, Heidelberg

Office of the Leading Group for the Belt and Road Initiative (2017) Building the belt and road: concept, practice and China's contribution, Office of the Leading Group for the Belt and Road Initiative, Beijing. https://www.beltroad-initiative.com/documents/; https://www.pacificjournal.com.cn/EN/news/news281.shtml

Pekkanen SM, Ravenhill J, Foot R (eds) (2014) The Oxford handbook of the international relations of Asia. OUP, Oxford

Shaffer GC, Melendez-Ortiz R (eds) (2010) Dispute settlement at the WTO: the developing country experience. CUP, Cambridge

Singh K, Ilge B (eds) (2016) Rethinking bilateral investment treaties: critical issues and policy choices. Both Ends, Amsterdam

Takatoshi I, Rose AK (eds) (2005) International trade in East Asia, NBER-East Asia seminar on economics, vol 14. University of Chicago Press, Chicago and London

Taniguchi Y, Yanovich A, Bohanes J (eds) (2007) The World Trade Organization in the 21st century: dispute settlement, negotiations and regionalism in Asia, CUP, Cambridge

UNCTAD (2007) Bilateral investment treaties 1995–2006: trends in investment, UN, New York and Geneva

UNESCAP (2020) Asia and the Pacific SDG progress report 2019. ESCAP, Bangkok

van den Bossche P (2017) The law and policy of the World Trade Organization, 4th edn, Cambridge University Press, Cambridge

Vukas B, Sosic TM (eds) (2010) International Law: new actors, new concepts—continuing dilemmas: Liber Amicorum Bojisar Bakotic, Brill Nijhoff, Leiden

Williams BR (2018) Bilateral and regional trade agreements: issues for congress. Congressional Research Service, Washington

WTO (2019) Annual report 2019, WTO, Geneva, p 116

WTO (2019) WTO dispute settlement one-page case summaries 1995–2018, WTO, Geneva

Reports

AALCC (1958) Report of 2nd session, Cairo 1958, New Delhi, AALCC Secretariat
AALCC (1960) Report of 3rd session, Colombo 1960, AALCC Secretariat, New Delhi
AALCC (1965) Report of 7th session, Baghdad 1965, AALCC Secretariat, New Delhi
AALCC (1967) Report of 9th session, AALCC Secretariat, New Delhi
AALCC (1969) Report of 10th session, Karachi 1969, AALCC Secretariat, New Delhi
AALCC (1970) Report of 11th session, Accra 1970, AALCC Secretariat, New Delhi
AALCC (1971) Report of 12th session, Colombo 1971, AALCC Secretariat, New Delhi
AALCC (1972) Report of 13th session, Lagos 1972, AALCC Secretariat, New Delhi
AALCC (1988) Report of 23rd, 24th and 25th sessions held in Tokyo (1983), Kathmandu (1985) and Arusha (1986), AALCC Secretariat, New Delhi
AALCO (2015) Report by Sufian Jusoh, Chairman of AALCO's informal expert group on customary International Law
https://www.aalco.int/54thsession/AALCOIEG%20Chairman's%20Statement%20and%20Special %20Rapporteur's%20Report%2020150324.pdf
Boffa M (2018) Trade linkages between the belt and road economies. Macroeconomics, trade and investment global practice. Policy research working paper no 8423, World Bank, Washington. https://openknowledge.worldbank.org/handle/10986/29768
Chaise J, Hamanaka S (2014) The investment version of the Asian noodle bowl: the proliferation of international investment agreements. ADB working paper series on regional economic integration, No 198. ADB, Manila
Columbia Center on Sustainable Development (2018) Cost and benefits of investment treaties: practical considerations for states. Policy Paper, New York
Dhar B (2013) The future of the WTO, ADBI working paper series no. 444, ADBI, Tokyo
Drifte R (2008) Japanese-Chinese territorial disputes in the East China Sea—between military confrontation and economic cooperation, working paper 24, LSE, London
EU, Brussels, 19.2.2020 COM (2020) 65 final WHITE PAPER on artificial intelligence—a European approach to excellence and trust. https://ec.europa.eu/info/sites/info/files/commission-white-paper-artificial-intelligence-feb2020_en.pdf
EU Opinion of the European Economic and Social Committee on 'Artificial intelligence—the consequences of artificial intelligence on the (digital) single market, production, consumption, employment and society' (own-initiative opinion) (2017/C 288/01). Catelijne MULLER, Rapporteur. https://eur-lex.europa.eu/legal-content/EN/TXT/PDF/?uri=CELEX:52016IE5369&from=EN
Gowan R Navigating the storms at the UN security council, ICG (5 February 2020). https://www.crisisgroup.org/global/navigating-storms-un-security-council
Hurley J, Morris S, Portelance G (2018) Examining the debt implications of the belt and road initiative from a policy perspective, centre for global development (GDC) policy paper 121, GDC, Washington
ICG, China's growing role in UN peacekeeping, Report 166, 17 April 2009. https://www.crisisgroup.org/asia/north-east-asia/china/china-s-growing-role-un-peacekeeping
ILO (2018) Negotiating the algorithm: automation, artificial intelligence and labour protection, employment working paper no. 246, ILO, Geneva
Ip, Eric C (2010) The power of international personality in regional integration, United Nations University (UNU) comparative regional integration studies (CRIS) working papers W 2010/4, UNU, Brugge
Kawai M, Wignaraja G (2010) Asian FTAs: trends, prospects, and challenges, ADB economics working paper series no. 226, ADB, Manila
Lall SV, Lebrand M (2019) Who wins, who loses? Understanding the spatially differentiated effects of the belt and road initiative, policy research working paper. World Bank, Washington. https://siteresources.worldbank.org/INTEAPREGTOPINTECOTRA/Resources/chapter+1.pdf

Rishmawi M Proposed Arab court of human rights: rewind the process and get it right, FIDH—international federation for human rights/ICJ—International Commission of Jurists Policy Paper March 2014. https://www.fidh.org/IMG/pdf/20140320_arab_ct_pp_en.pdf

The Arab human rights system

Annex to the ABC of human rights for development cooperation, GIZ. https://www.institut-fuer-menschenrechte.de/fileadmin/user_upload/Publikationen/E-Info-Tool/e-info-tool_abc_of_hr_for_dev_coop_the_arab_hr-system.pdf

WTO (2019) Annual report 2019, WTO, Geneva

Articles

Ahl B (2009) Die Anwendung Volkerrechtlicher Vertrage in China: summary: the application of international treaties in China. Beitrage zum Auslandischen Oftenlichen Recht und Volkerrecht, Band, vol 207, pp 355–367 (Max Planck)

Ahn D (2005) WTO dispute settlements in East Asia. In: Ito T, Rose AK (eds), International trade in East Asia, NBER-East Asia seminar on economics, vol 14. University of Chicago Press, Chicago and London, pp 287–327

Albert E The Shanghai cooperation organization: a vehicle for cooperation or competition? 21 June 2019. https://thediplomat.com/2019/06/the-shanghai-cooperation-organization-a-vehicle-for-cooperation-or-competition/

Al-Qahtani M (2006) The Shanghai cooperation organization and the law of international organisations, Chinese JIL, 5(1): 129–147

Alwasil AM (2010) Saudi Arabia's engagement in, and interaction with, the UN human rights system: an analytical review. Int J Hum Rights 14(7): 1072–1091

Anand RP (2007) Development of International Law and South Asia: an historical approach. IJIL 47(4):535–593

Beckman R (2013) The UN Convention on law of the sea and the maritime disputes in the South China sea. AJIL 107(1): 142–163

Beckman R (2019) ' Law of the Sea and Asian States'. In: Chesterman S, Owada H, Saul B (eds) The Oxford handbook on International Law in Asia and the Pacific. OUP, Oxford, pp 205–236

Bellal A, Giacco G, Casey-Maslen S (2011) International Law and armed non-state actors in Afghanistan. IRRC 93(881):47–79

Bellamy A (2003) International Law and the war in Iraq. Melb J Int'l L 4(2): 497–520

Best G (1999) Peace conferences and a century of total war. The 1899 Hague conference and what came after. Int Aff 75(3): 619–634

Bijalwan A, Gupta D Justifying the unjust: an analysis of Intertemporal Law. https://ijlpp.com/justifying-the-unjust-an-analysis-of-intertemporal-law/

Boll A (2001) The Asian values debate and its relevance to international humanitarian law. IRRC 841:1–6

Bradsher K China renews its belt and road push for global sway. https://www.nytimes.com/2020/01/15/business/china-belt-and-road.html

Butkevich OV (2003) History of ancient international law: challenges and prospects. J Hist Int'l Law 189–236

Carron D (2016) When is a conflict international? Time for new control tests in IHL. RRC 98(3): 1019–1041

Cassesse A (2012) States: rise and decline of the primary subjects of the international community. In: Fassbender B, Peters A (eds) The Oxford handbook of the history of International Law, Oxford University Press (OUP), Oxford, pp 50–69

Chan PCW (2014) China's approach to International Law since the opium war. Leiden J Int Law 27: 859–892

Chang-Wee L (2013) Legal and political aspects of the Dokdo issue-interrelationship between International Law and international relations. KYIL 1:49–69
Chatsky A, McBride J China's massive belt and road initiative, 28 January 2020
Council of Foreign Relations. https://www.cfr.org/backgrounder/chinas-massive-belt-and-road-initiative
Chechi A (2016) The 2013 judgement of the ICJ in the temple of Preah Vihear case and the protection of world cultural heritage sites in wartime. Asian JIL 6(2): 353–378
Chesterman S (2016) Asia's ambivalence about International Law and institutions: past, present and future. EJIL 27(4): 945–978
Chiam M Monism and dualism in International Law. https://www.oxfordbibliographies.com/view/document/obo-9780199796953/obo-9780199796953-0168.xml. Accessed 20 Feb 2020
Cho S, Kurtz J (2018) Convergence and divergence in international economic law and politics. EJIL 29(1):169–203
Colegrove K (1932) The Japanese emperor. Am Polit Sci Rev 26(4):642–659
Coleman A, Maogoto JN (2013) " Westphalian" meets "Eastphalian" sovereignty: China in a globalised world. AJIL 3:237–269
Correa CM (2018) Flexibilities provided by the agreement on trade-related aspects of intellectual property rights. Bull World Health Organ 96(3): 148–148A
Cotler T (2012) The role of domestic courts in the implementation of WTO law. The political economy of separation of powers and checks and balances in international trade regulation. In: Narlikar A, Daunton M, Stern RM (eds) The Oxford handbook on the World Trade Organization. OUP, Oxford, pp 607–631
Danilenko GM (1999) Implementation of International Law in CIS states: theory and practice. EJIL 10:51–69
d'Aspremont J (2001) International Law in Asia: the limits to western constitutionalist and liberal doctrines Asian Year Int Law 13: 27–49
Davis MC (2015) Can International Law help resolve the conflicts over uninhabited islands in the East China Sea. Denv J Int'l l & Pol'y 43:119–163
Desierto DA (2008) Postcolonial International Law discourse on regional developments in South and Southeast Asia. Int'l J Legal Info 36(3):387–395
de Treglode B (2013) Maritime boundary delimitation and Sino-Vietnam cooperation in the Gulf of Tonkin (1994–2016). China Perspect 3: 33–41
Donaldson J, Williams A (2005) Understanding maritimes jurisdictional disputes: the East China Sea. J Int'l Aff 59(1): 135–156
Elias TO (1980) The doctrine of intertemporal law. AJIL 74(2): 285–307
Evans D, Shaffer GC (2010) 'Introduction'. In: Shaffer GC, Melendez-Ortiz R (eds) Dispute settlement at the WTO: the developing country experience. CUP, Cambridge, pp 1–10
Eyadat Z, Okasheh H (2018) Human rights mechanisms in the Arab world: politics and protection. In: Oberleitner G (ed) International human rights institutions, tribunals, and courts. Springer, Heidelberg, pp. 511–526
Faruque AA (2012) Judgement in maritime boundary dispute between Bangladesh and Myanmar: significance and implications under International Law'. 18 Asian Year Int Law, 62–84
Feener M, Cammack E (2008/2009) Islamic law in contemporary Indonesia: ideas and institutions. J L Relig 24(1): 287–292
Fern S (2005) Dokdo or Takeshima: the International Law of territorial acquisition in the Japan-Korea Island dispute. SJEAA 5(1): 78–89
Fravel MT (2014) Territorial and maritime boundary disputes in Asia. In: Pekkanen SM, Ravenhill J, Foot R (eds) The Oxford handbook of the international relations of Asia, OUP, Oxford, pp 526–546
Furtado X (1999) International Law and the dispute over the Spratly Islands: Whither UNCLOS? 21 Contemp Southeast Asia 21(3): 386–404
Gan P (2016) Shifting winds in the east: a legal analysis and case comparison of the Diaoyu/Senkaku Island dispute. South Calif Interdiscip Law J 25:685–720

Gao Z, Jia BB (2013) The nine-dash line in the south china sea: history, status and implications. AJIL 107(1): 98–124

Garg S, Tripathy IG, Roy S (2016) The India model BIT: continuity and change. In: Singh K, Ilge B (eds) Rethinking bilateral investment treaties: critical issues and policy choices, Both Ends, Amsterdam, pp 69–100

Gassama IJ (2004) International Law at a Grotian moment: the invasion of Iraq in context. 18 Emory Int'l L Rev 18(1): 1–52

Gebremariam FM (2017) New international economic order (NIEO): origin, elements and criticisms. IJMMU 4(3): 22–28

Ghazi MA (2010) Constitutional human rights: Saudi perspective. J Middle Eastern and Islamic Stud (in Asia) 4(3): 28–46

Ghobadzadeh N (2016) Electoral theocracy and hybrid sovereignty in Iran. Contemp Polit 22(4): 1–19

Girshovich M (2019) 'Central Asian States.' In: Chesterman S, Owada H, Saul B (eds) The Oxford handbook on International Law in Asia and the Pacific. OUP, Oxford, pp 703–725

Gluckman M (1949) Adat law in Indonesia. J Comp Legis Int'l Law 31(3/4): 60–65

Guo S (2009) Implementation of human rights treaties by Chinese courts: problems and prospects. Chinese JIL 8(1): 161–179

Gupta J (2016) The Paris climate change agreement: China and India. Clim Law 6(1–2): 71–81

Gupta S Don't shut down the pharmacy of the developing world. https://www.expresspharma.in/management-pharma/dont-shut-down-the-pharmacy-of-the-developing-world/382878/. Accessed 30 August 2020

Hanqin X (2007) Chinese observations on International Law. Chinese JIL 6(1): 83–93

Hanqin X, Qian J (2009) International treaties in the Chinese domestic legal system. Chinese JIL 8(2): 299–322

Higgins R (2014) The ICJ dispute settlement in the Asian Seas: an assessment. Am Soc'y Int'l Proc 107:53–56

Jailani A (2016) Indonesia's perspective on review of international investment agreement. In: Singh K, Ilge B (eds) Rethinking bilateral investment treaties: critical issues and policy choices. Both Ends, Amsterdam, pp 113–127

Jamnejad M, Wood M (2009) The principle of non-intervention. Leiden J Int Law 22(2): 345–381

Jayakumar S (1968) The Philippine claim to Sabah and International Law. Mal LR 10(2): 306–335

Jenco L (2013) Revisiting Asian values. J Hist Ideas 74(2): 237–258

Johnson M (2014) Whaling in the Antarctic—the ICJ decision and its consequences for further special permit whaling. AYBIL 32:87–96

Kathuria S, Rizwan N How South Asia can become a free trade area, 14 February 2019. https://blogs.worldbank.org/endpovertyinsouthasia/how-south-asia-can-become-free-trade-area. Accessed 6 April 2020

Kawai M, Wignaraja G (2014) Policy challenges posed by Asian FTAs: a review of the evidence. In: Baldwin R, Kawai M, Wignaraja G (eds) A WTO for the 21st century the Asian perspective, Asian development bank institute. Edward Elgar Publishers, Cheltenham:Glos/Northampton, pp 182–238

Kerwin GJ (1983) The role of United Nations general assembly resolutions in determining principles of International Law in United States courts. Duke L J 2: 876–899. https://scholarship.law.duke.edu/cgi/viewcontent.cgi?article=2852&context=dlj

Keyuan Z (2005) Implementing the UN convention on the law of the sear in East Asia: issues and trends. SYBIL 9:37–54

Keyuan Z (2010) International Law in the Chinese domestic context. Val U L Rev 44: 935–956

Keyuan Z (2012) China and the UNCLOS: recent developments and prospects. Ocean Yearb 26:161–180

Kim C (2007) East Asia in the World Trade Organisation dispute settlement mechanism. In: Taniguchi Y, Yanovich A, Bohanes J (eds) The World Trade Organization in the 21st century: dispute settlement. CUP, Negotiations and Regionalism in Asia (Cambridge), pp 261–266

Kim SY (2010) Do Asian values exist? Empirical tests of the four dimensions of Asian values. J East Asian Stud 10(2): 315–344
Koh T (2011) International Law and the peaceful resolution of disputes: Asian perspectives, contributions, and challenges. Asian JIL I(1):57–60
Koraytem T (2001) Arab Islamic developments of human rights. Arab Law Q 16(3): 255–262
Korkut E, Kang WH (2017) China's nine dash line claim in light of the ruling by the permanent court of arbitration (12 July 2018). Penn St J L Int'l Aff 5(2): 425–463
Langford P, Bryan I (2012) Hans Kelsen's theory of legal monism: a critical engagement with the emerging legal order of the 1920's. J Hist Int Law 14(1): 51–86
Lehmann J-P (2005) Asian approaches to the international trade system. In: Ito T, Re Andrew. K (eds) International trade in East Asia, University of Chicago Press, Chicago, pp 55–60
Lehmann J-P (2014) Asian approaches to the international trade system. In: IFRI, The Asian century, IFRI, Paris, pp 55–60
Leng S-C (1977) The role of law in the People's Republic of China as reflecting Mao Tse-Tung's influence. J Crim Law Criminol 68(3): 356–373
Lester S (2016) Is the Doha round over? Free Trade Bulletin 64: 1–4
Lin V, Leung G, Carter B (2019) Asia-Pacific countries moving toward universal health coverage. Health Syst Reform 2(1): 1–6
Loja MH (2017) Status quo post bellum and the legal resolution of the territorial dispute between China and Japan over the Senkaku/Diaoyu Islands. EJIL 27:979–1004
Magliveras K, Naldi G (2016) The Arab court of human rights: a study in impotence. Revue québécoise de droit international 29(2): 147–172
Malcomson S The real fight for the future of 5G. Who will patrol the borders of a new network? 14 November 2019. https://www.foreignaffairs.com/articles/2019-11-14/real-fight-future-5g
Manjiao C (2013) A note on China's legal and operational response to international piracy. Ocean Dev Int Law 44(1): 113–122
Markus KE (2012) Trade related intellectual property rights. In: Narlikar A, Daunton M, Stern RM (eds) The Oxford handbook on the World Trade Organization. OUP, Oxford, pp 394–419
Mayda J (1968) The Vietnam conflict and International Law. Nordisk Tidsskrift Int'l Ret 38(7): 7–17
Munir M (2008) Suicide attacks and Islamic law. IRRC 90(869): 71–89
Muntarbhorn V (2001) The 1899 Hague peace conference and the development of the laws of war: Asia's contribution to the quest for humanitarianism. In: Tim LH, McCormack MJ, Tilbury, Triggs GD (eds) A century of war and peace. Kluwer, Leiden, pp 111–137
Muntarbhorn V (2019) Thailand's contribution to International Law'. In: Chesterman S, Owada H, Saul B (eds) The Oxford handbook on International Law in Asia and the Pacific. OUP, Oxford, pp 363–385
Muntarbhorn V (2019) ASEAN instruments and mechanisms as pathways to human rights protection? In: A decade in review: assessing the performance of the ASEAN intergovernmental commission on human rights, vol 2. Forum Asia, Bangkok/Jakarta, pp 25–35. https://www.forum-asia.org/uploads/wp/2019/10/AICHR10vol2FA.pdf
Nagan WP, Hammer C (2004) The changing nature of sovereignty in International Law and international relations. Colum J Transnat'l l 43:141–187
Nanda VP (2001–2002) Self-determination and secession in International Law. Denv J Int'l L & Pol'y 19(4): 305–326
Nasu H, Rothwell DR (2014) ' Re-evaluating the role of International Law in territorial and maritimes disputes in east Asia'. Asian JIL 4:51–79
Ndiaye TM (2015) The judge, maritime delimitation and the grey areas. IJIL 55:493–533
Noor NM, Sundaram JK East Asian lessons for controlling covid-19. https://www.ipsnews.net/2020/03/east-asian-lessons-controlling-covid-19/. Accessed 8 April 2020
Nowrojee B It's not too late for Europe and the US to learn lessons from Asia to fight COVID-19'. https://www.euronews.com/2020/03/25/it-s-not-too-late-for-europe-and-the-us-to-learn-lessons-from-asia-to-fight-covid-19-view. Accessed 8 April 2020

Oberg MD (2005) The legal effects of resolutions of the UN security council and general assembly in the jurisprudence of the ICJ. EJIL 16(5): 879–906

Ogata S (1997) Protecting the human rights of refugees and displaced persons: the tasks ahead. In: AALCC, essays on international law, 40th anniversary commemorative volume. AALCC Secretariat, New Delhi, pp 23–42

Omar M Indonesia–Malaysia confrontation. https://eresources.nlb.gov.sg/infopedia/articles/SIP_1072_2010-03-25.html

Pangestu M Responding to the trade war: an ASEAN perspective. https://www.rieti.go.jp/en/events/18120601/summary.html

Peng S-Y (2000) The WTO legalistic approach and east Asia: from the legal culture perspective. APLPJ 1(2): 13–35

Petersen KS (1959) The uses of the uniting for peace resolution since 1950. Int. Organ. 13(2):219–232

https://www.ohchr.org/EN/HRBodies/HRC/IIMM/Pages/Index.aspx. Accessed 20 Feb 2020

Pinghua S (2016) Peng Chun Chang's contributions to the drafting of the universal declaration of human rights. JCLS 5(5): 209–217

Pitakdumrongkit K ASEAN's RCEP and sustainability challenges and achievements. East Asia Forum, 24 January 2020. file:///C:/Users/Admin/Documents/RCEP%20and%20sustainability%20challenges%20and%20achievements%20_%20East%20Asia%20Forum.html. Accessed 29 Aug 2020

Ponta A (2020) Human rights in the time of coronavirus. ASIL 24(5). https://www.asil.org/insights/volume/24/issue/5/human-rights-law-time-coronavirus. Accessed 30 Aug 2020

Radon J (2004) Sovereignty: a political emotion, not a concept? Stan J Int'l L 40(2): 195–209

Ruskola T (2011) Where is Asia—When is Asia—theorizing comparative law and International Law. U.C. Davis L'Rev 44: 879–896

Sadri A (2019) The Arab human rights system: achievements and challenges. Int J Hum Rights 23(7): 1166–1182

Seyadi RM (2017) Understanding the jurisprudence of the Arab Gulf states national courts on the implementation of the 1958 New York convention on the recognition and enforcement of foreign arbitral awards. Int Rev Law 3:1–14

Shafaeddin SM (2002) Some implications of accession to WTO for China's economy. Int J Dev Issues 1(2): 93–128

Shaw M (1996) The heritage of states: the principle of uti possidetis Juris today. BYIL 67:75–154

Sidhu WPS What drives South Asians to peacekeeping? 11 January 2016. https://peaceoperationsreview.org/article/what-drives-south-asians-to-peacekeeping/; https://www.unv.org/Success-stories/Volunteering-forefront-peace-operations; https://www.babseacle.org/articles/collaborative-pro-bono-asia/; https://www.volunteerworld.com/en/volunteer-abroad/asia. Accessed 30 Aug 2020

Singh AN, Singh P (2009) What can International Law learn from Indian mythology. Hinduism and history. J East Asia Int Law (Spring), 239–271

Singh P (2015) India before and after the right of passage case. Asian JIL 5:176–208

Sinha MK (2005) Hinduism and International Law. IRRC 87(858): 285–294. https://www.itu.int/en/history/Pages/ITUBorn1865.aspx. Accessed 19 Aug 2020

Skrk M (2010) International Law and internal law in the case-law of the slovene constitutional court. In: Vukas B, Sosic TM (eds) International Law: new actors, new concepts—continuing dilemmas: liber Amicorum Bojisar Bakotic. Brill Nijhoff, Leiden, pp 41–74

Smith SW (2016) ASEAN, China and the South China Sea: between a rock and a low-tide elevation. U.S.F. Mar L J 29: 29–40

Sumner BT (2004) Territorial disputes at the ICJ. Duke L J 53(6): 1779–1812

Takahashi T What Beijing really wants from South China Sea code of conduct, 12 Aug 2019

https://asia.nikkei.com/Spotlight/Comment/What-Beijing-really-wants-from-South-China-Sea-code-of-conduct

Thakur R (2001) Global norms and international humanitarian law: an Asian perspective. IRRC 841:1–12

The Nation, 'Which Asian country provides the most troops for the UN peacekeeping mission?', December 2017.https://www.nationthailand.com/asean-plus/30333379. Accessed 30 Aug 2020

The World Policy Forum, 'The Future of Multilateralism'. https://www.global-solutions-initiative.org/press-news/the-future-of-multilateralism/

Tkatova R (2010) Central Asian states and International Law: between post-soviet culture and Eurasian civilization. Chinese JIL 9(1):201–220

Tomuschat C (2011) Asia and International Law—common ground and regional diversity. Asian JIL I:217–231

Tonneson S (2015) The South China sea: law trumps power. Asian Surv. 55(3): 455–477

Traviss AC (2012) Temple of Preah Vihear: lessons on provisional measures. Chic J Int Law 13(1): 317–344

Turner, Jacob, 'Towards a Synthesis between Islamic and Western Ius in Bello', *J.Transnat'l. L.& Pol'y.*, 21(2011)3, pp. 165–204.

Valencia Mark J (1997) Asia, the law of the sea and international relations. Int Aff (Royal Institute of International Affairs) 73(2): 263–282

Vermulst E, Ikenson D (2007) Zeroing under the WTO anti-dumping agreement: where do we stand? Glob Trade Cust J 2(6): 231–242

von Einsiedel S, Yazaki A East Asian perceptions of the UN and its role in peace and security', UN University, 1 June 2016. https://cpr.unu.edu/east-asian-perceptions-of-the-un-and-its-role-in-peace-and-security.html

Wallace DE (2014) An analysis of chinese maritime claims in the south China Sea. Nav Law Rev 63:128–159

Wang Z (2015) Chinese discourse on the nine dashed line. Asian Surv 55(3): 502–524

Watanabe Y (2005) Trans Pacific partnership versus regional comprehensive economic partnership : what future norms for free trade in the Asia Pacific? In: Ito T, Re AK (eds) International trade in east Asia. University of Chicago Press, Chicago, pp 61–68

Weatherford J Genghis Khan: hero of religious freedom? https://www.ozy.com/opinion/genghis-khan-hero-of-religious-freedom/72553

Weissman M (2015) The South China sea: still no war on the horizon. Asian Surv 55(3): 596–617

Wetter JG (1971) The Rann of Kutch arbitration. AJIL 65(2): 346–357

https://www.britannica.com/event/Hague-Conventions. Accessed 13 July 2020

Whomersley C (2017) The award on the merit in the case brought by the Philippines against China relating to the South China Sea: a critique. Chinese JIL 16(3): 387–423

Xinmin M (2012) China's mechanism and practice of treaty dispute settlement. Chinese JIL, 11(3): 387–392

Yee S (2015) Report on the international law commission (ILC) project on identification of customary International Law. Chinese JIL 14(2): 375–398

Yixing Z (2012) A Deconstruction of the notion of acquisitive prescription and its implications for the Diaoyu Islands dispute. AJIL 2:323–338

Zhan J (2016) Trends, challenges and way forward. In: Singh K, Ilge B (eds) Rethinking bilateral investment treaties: critical issues and policy choices. Both Ends, Amsterdam, pp 17–28

Zhaojie L (1995) The effect of treaties in municipal law of People's Republic of China: practice and problems. Asian yearb Int Law 5: 185–223

Zoli C, Schneider E, Schuster C (2014) Armed conflict and compliance in muslim state, 1947–2014: does conflict look different under international humanitarian law?', N.C.J. Int'l L Com Reg 40(3): 679–738

Zuercher C China's peacekeepers—new resources, new values; Democratic nations should resist Beijing's attempts to downgrade human rights', *Nikkei Asian Review*, 12 February 2019. https://asia.nikkei.com/Opinion/China-s-peacekeepers-new-resources-new-values. Accessed 8 April 2020

Select List of International Judicial and Arbitral Cases

ICJ, Case concerning Right of Passage over Indian Territory (Portugal v India): (Merits) Judgment of 12 April 1960, ICJ Reports 1960. https://www.icj-cij.org/files/case-related/32/032-19600412-JUD-01-00-EN.pdf

ICJ, Case concerning Preah Vihear (Cambodia v Thailand), Merits, Judgment of 15 June 1962, ICJ Reports 1962. https://www.icj-cij.org/en/case/45/judgments

ICJ, Request for interpretation of the judgment of 15 June 1962 in the case concerning the temple of Preah Vihear (Cambodia v. Thailand) Request for the Indication of Provisional Measures Order of 18 July 2011, ICJ Reports 2011. https://www.icj-cij.org/files/case-related/151/151-20110718-ORD-01-00-EN.pdf

ICJ, Request for Interpretation of the Judgment of 15 June 1962 in the Case concerning the Temple of Preah Vihear (Cambodia v Thailand) Judgment of 11 November 2013, ICJ Reports 2013. https://www.icj-cij.org/files/case-related/151/151-20131111-JUD-01-00-EN.pdf

ICJ, Case concerning Maritime Delimitation and Territorial Questions between Qatar and Bahrain (Qatar v. Bahrain), Merits Judgment of 16 March 2001, ICJ Reports 2001. https://www.icj-cij.org/files/case-related/87/087-20010316-JUD-01-00-EN.pdf

ICJ, Case concerning Sovereignty over Pulau Ligitan and Pulau Sipadan (Indonesia v Malaysia), Judgment of 17 December 2002, ICJ Reports 2002. https://www.icj-cij.org/files/case-related/102/102-20021217-JUD-01-00-EN.pdf

ICJ, Legal Consequences of the Construction of a Wall in the Occupied Palestinian Territory, Advisory Opinion of 9 July 2004. ICJ Reports 2004. https://www.icj-cij.org/en/case/131

ICJ, Case concerning Sovereignty over Pedra Branca/Pulau Batu Puteh, Middle Rocks and South Ledge (Malaysia/Singapore) Judgment of 23 May 2008. ICJ Reports 2008. https://www.icj-cij.org/files/case-related/130/130-20080523-JUD-01-00-EN.pdf

ICJ, Case concerning Whaling in the Antarctic (Australia v Japan: New Zealand intervening) Judgment of 31 March 2014, ICJ Reports 2014. https://www.icj-cij.org/files/case-related/148/148-20140331-JUD-01-00-EN.pdf

ICJ, Application of the International Convention on the Elimination of All Forms of Racial Discrimination (Qatar v. United Arab Emirates) Request for the Indication of Provisional Measures Order of 23 July 2018, ICJ Reports 2018. https://www.icj-cij.org/files/case-related/172/172-20180723-ORD-01-00-EN.pdf

ICJ, Application of the International Convention on the Elimination of All Forms of Racial Discrimination (Qatar v. United Arab Emirates) Request for the Indication of Provisional Measures Order of 14 June 2019, ICJ Reports 2019. https://www.icj-cij.org/files/case-related/172/172-20190614-ORD-01-00-EN.pdf

ICJ, Application of the Convention on the Prevention and Punishment of the Crime of Genocide (The Gambia v. Myanmar) Order of 23 January 2020. ICJ Reports 2020. https://www.icj-cij.org/files/case-related/178/178-20200123-ORD-01-00-EN.pdf

ITLOS, Case concerning Land Reclamation by Singapore in and around the Straits of Johor (Malaysia v Singapore) Provisional Measures Order of 8 October 2003. https://www.itlos.org/fileadmin/itlos/documents/cases/case_no_12/Order.08.10.03.E.pdf

ITLOS, Dispute concerning Delimitation of the Maritimes Boundary between Bangladesh and Myanmar in the Bay of Bengal (Bangladesh/Myanmar) Judgment of 14 March 2012. https://www.itlos.org/fileadmin/itlos/documents/cases/case_no_16/C16_Judgment_14_03_2012_rev.pdf

PCA, Island of Palmas (or Miangas) (The Netherlands/The United States of America) Final Award of 04 April 1928. https://pca-cpa.org/en/cases/94/

PCA, in the Matter of the Bay of Bengal Maritimes Boundary Arbitration between—The People's Republic of Bangladesh and the Republic of India—Award of 7 July 2014. https://pcacases.com/web/sendAttach/383

PCA, Case No 2013–19 in the Matter of the South China Sea Arbitration—before an Arbitral tribunal constituted under annex VII to the 1982 convention on the law of the sea—between the Republic of the Philippines and the People's Republic of China—award of 12 July 2016. https://www.pcacases.com/pcadocs/PH-CN%20-%2020160712%20-%20Award.pdf

The Indo-Pakistan Western Boundary (Rann of Kutch) between India and Pakistan (India, Pakistan) 19 February 1968, Reports of International Arbitral Awards, vol XVII, UN (2006), pp 1–576. https://legal.un.org/riaa/cases/vol_XVII/1-576.pdf

Texaco Overseas Petroleum Co. v. Libyan Arab Republic, ILM (1978), p 1 et seq. https://www.trans-lex.org/261700/_/texaco-overseas-petroleum-company-v-the-government-of-the-libyan-arab-republic-yca-1979-at-177-et-seq

Index

V. Muntarbhorn, *Challenges of International Law in the Asian Region*,
https://doi.org/10.1007/978-981-16-2047-8

B

J

K

L

Q

R

S

T

U